Haegue Yang

In the Cone of Uncertainty

HATJE CANTZ

THE BASS

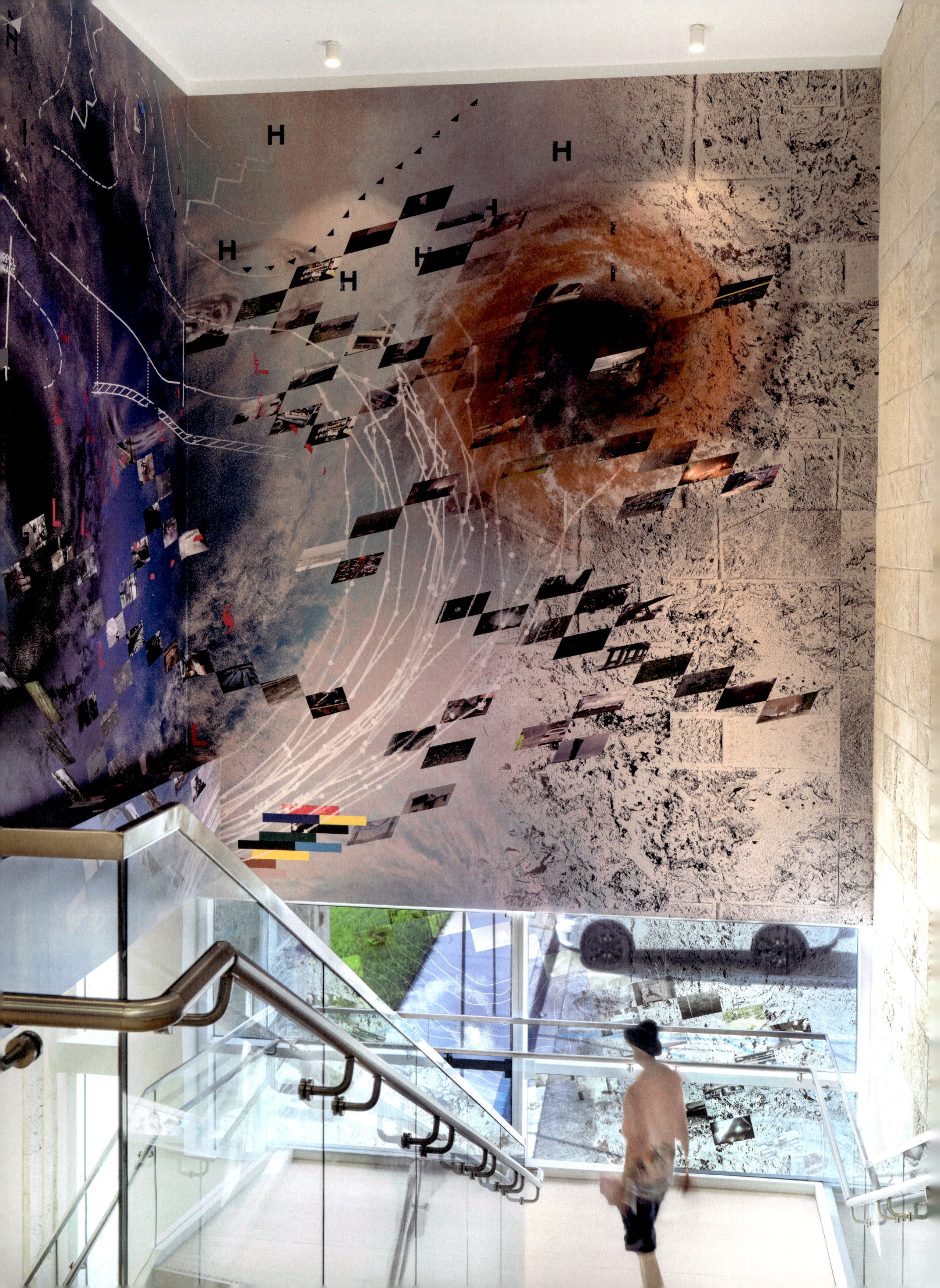

Contents

Foreword

IN THE CONE OF UNCERTAINTY: AN EXHIBITION BY HAEGUE YANG

by Silvia Karman Cubiñá

Haegue Yang's work explores the complexities of negotiating cultural identity through time and place. Visually abstract and nuanced, the artist's sculptures, installations, wallpapers, elements of sound, and objects dissect historical narratives, aspects of acculturation and memory. Oftentimes, her works are multisensorial and participatory, engaging the viewer with the immediacy of touch, sound, and smell. Yang's exhibition, *In the Cone of Uncertainty*, brings these ongoing investigations to The Bass with an air of urgency.

Two years ago in Paris, in an early conversation about the exhibition, Haegue Yang posited one very important question: What is the one thing that unifies people in Miami? What trait or experience does everyone in Miami have in common? How do you answer this question in a city where 54.1 percent of residents come from somewhere else? How do you answer this question when 75.4 percent speak a language other than English at home? Lively conversations like this one, in which the artist sought to understand the context of her exhibition, resulted in the eventual and timely discussion of climate, nature, and environment in their many definitions. This exhibition, *Haegue Yang: In the Cone of Uncertainty*, takes its title from the scientific model that measures and outlines degrees of variability in the trajectory of a hurricane; and a motif that is borrowed and appears in Yang's site-specific wallpaper titled *Coordinates of Speculative Solidarity* (2019). The digitally rendered work sweeps through the first and second floors of the exhibition, serving as a backdrop element for her sculptures and alluding to a widened concept of precariousness and instability inherent in issues as varied as the environment, immigration, and cultural assimilation.

Yang often recruits narratives from historical or artistic figures and intertwines them in her works. A sound element in the exhibition is a combination of open-sourced recordings of birds singing and a recording taken from the recent historical encounter between the two leaders of North and South Korea. The simple yet specific gesture creates further conjecture around the subject and result of the meeting. While "uncertainty" is a word borrowed from hurricanes, in this case it can simultaneously refer to the cultural space where languages, ethnicities, and histories collide, and are negotiated.

TRAJECTORY AND TRANSLATION

by Leilani Lynch

To paraphrase curator Doryun Chong, Haegue Yang's work is not the sort of work that can be fully known or understood.[1] It is like trying to comprehend what is in your peripheral vision in order to form a complete understanding of the environment and world around you. There are shapes and movement, just out of view, which can be sensed or hypothesized about. The task is nearly impossible, yet it pushes you to new limits of perception and awareness. Haegue Yang's art beckons us into this speculative arena unfolding rhizomatically around you. Her work supersedes place, space, and time, unifying disconnected, parallel histories, reconciling disparate cultures, and digesting the diasporic experience through an abstract visual language. Over the course of her career, Yang has maintained a process of translating cultural and visual struggles with profound alienation and otherness, through an inner, irresolvable contradiction between the form and content of her work,[2] aided by movement and trajectory.

Perhaps this is why the title of Yang's exhibition at The Bass—*In the Cone of Uncertainty*—resonates on many levels. The term refers to a state of being within an atmosphere of instability, as well as a journey along a continually defining course. It implies the possibility of gradual resolution, or a (re)gained stability through the passing of time. It not only contextualizes the exhibition within the site of Miami Beach, Florida, within a region that is increasingly rife with climate disasters, but also locates the exhibition in the Global South in 2019, a setting at the epicenter of conversations and actions around the legal and illegal (im)migration of peoples and postcolonial communities in the midst of political crisis and chaos. While Yang's exhibition does not directly interrogate or posit solutions to those complex issues, this gathering of work is indelibly tethered to the network of histories, presents, and futures woven together throughout her practice. Rather like a community, the works in the exhibition *In the Cone of Uncertainty* are gathered perhaps to commiserate with us, propose answers to underlying questions, or to simply bear witness. Like the meteorological models, which elucidate the "cone of uncertainty," Yang's storytelling, both personal and historical, places value on specific figures, whose lives and work warrant closer consideration.

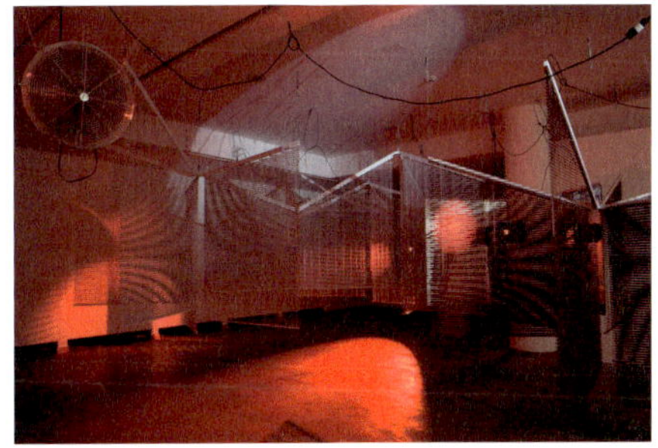

Yearning Melancholy Red, 2008, *Asymmetric Equality*, REDCAT, Los Angeles, CA, USA, 2008

A champion of untold or lesser-known histories and historical figures, many works in Yang's oeuvre and The Bass exhibition are tied to elucidating these stories in varying forms. Two of Yang's early blind works, *Yearning Melancholy Red* (2008) and *Red Broken Mountainous Labyrinth* (2008) anchor the "atmosphere of tropical melancholy"[3] felt throughout the show. Installed together in the museum's loftiest gallery, *Yearning Melancholy Red* takes the life story of French writer and filmmaker Marguerite Duras as its subject, while *Red Broken Mountainous Labyrinth* focuses on the numerous, daring encounters between Korean Communist resistance fighter Kim San and journalist Nym Wales. Though Kim San and Nym Wales never met Duras, Yang's installation stages an imaginary encounter between these historic figures, who would have shared personal experiences living in colonial/postcolonial contexts through their memoirs and writing, as well as commitment to political resistance.

The works have formal differences: *Yearning Melancholy Red* is made up of white blinds and faux wood in a flower-like arrangement, while *Red Broken Mountainous Labyrinth* is composed of red blinds in a tighter, broken geometric

1 Doryun Chong, "Haegue Yang: Integrity of the Insider," *Walker Reader: Sightlines*, August 21, 2009, https://walkerart.org/magazine/haegue-yang-integrity-of-the-insider (all URLs accessed in August 2019).

2 T. J. Demos, "Accommodating the Epic Dispersion: Haegue Yang in Conversation with T. J. Demos," in *Haegue Yang: Accommodating the Epic Dispersion – On Non-Cathartic Volume of Dispersion*, part of the series *DER ÖFFENTLICHKEIT: Von den Freunden Haus der Kunst*, exh. cat. Haus der Kunst, Munich (Cologne: Verlag der Buchhandlung Walther König, 2013), p. 78.

3 "Interview with Haegue Yang by Clara Kim," exhibition brochure, *Haegue Yang: Asymmetric Equality*, REDCAT, Los Angeles, CA, USA.

pattern, yet their abstract language unifies them. The former is augmented by elements that can, or do, manipulate their environment: a heat lamp and fan, which face each other; theatrical lights that rove the walls and filter through the blinds; and a drum kit, which disrupts the lighting's choreography when played by visitors. In navigating through and around these works, we're forced to suspend our inclination toward narrative or objective information, and subjectively absorb the created environment via a perceptive exchange—through the restless, searching glow of the oscillating red and white lights, the tight passages of blinds, the windy-warm standoff between the opposing fan and heat lamp, and the staccato of the drum strike.

4 Yang's series of mural and wallpaper works derives from her interest in the concept of "flatness." For a detailed chronology of this series from 2011 to 2019, see pp. 64–107 in this volume.

Further utilizing non-visual, particularly aural space as a means to encompass the gallery environment, Yang has included two sound elements. Like the exhibition's additionally constructed shaped walls, these components craft one's experience of the exhibition. The melodic, if frenetic, sound of chirping birds emits from two clusters of speakers. One sonic element takes the April 27, 2018, meeting between South and North Korean leaders Moon Jae-in and Kim Jong-un as its historical reference point. During this historic summit, a private thirty-minute meeting between the leaders took place on a footbridge, while international press observed from a distance. Long range photography and sound documentation were permitted, however the only sounds captured were ambient noises, notably the birdsong emanating from the surrounding trees. Yang combines the recording of birds from this historic meeting with bird sounds taken from an open-source digital database—together they are indistinguishable—fueling an atmosphere of speculation and highlighting the increasingly hard to differentiate border between truth and fabrication present evermore in our digital age. The avian sound element coupled with the density of anthropomorphic sculptures in the adjacent room imbues an energy that gives those entering the space an uncanny feeling of happening upon a meeting or gathering of sentient beings.

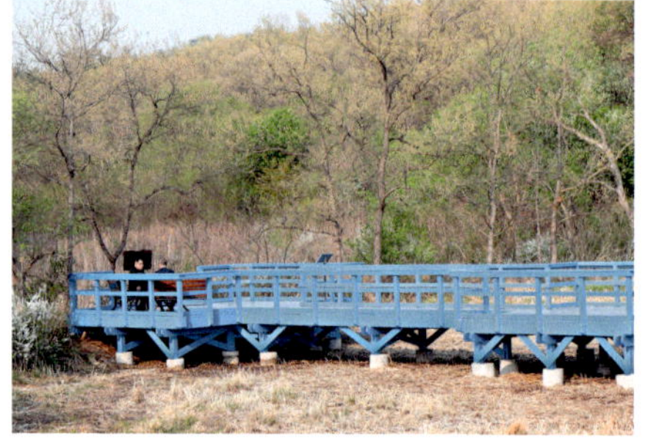

South Korean President Moon Jae-in in conversation with North Korean leader Kim Jong-un on the historical footbridge in the Demilitarized Zone (DMZ) on April 27, 2018

Yang's work not only occupies the traditional white-cube galleries of The Bass. A new work, *Coordinates of Speculative Solidarity* (2019), part of her evolving group of wallpaper murals, inhabits the interstitial space within the stairway from the first to the second floor. The wallpaper murals (which are more deeply explored elsewhere[4] in the exhibition catalogue) are often tied to the exhibition site and context exploring three-dimensional space by digitally collaging color, graphics, and objects from related research, as well as truncated images of her own work within a flattened, condensed form. The Bass work delves into the climate-focused reference of the "cone of uncertainty," using imagery of hurricane thermo-mapping, bird's-eye view images of homes and palm trees, and visual echoes of the museum's oolitic façade. The myriad elements appear swirling amidst wind speed symbols and distorted by whirlpools. Transforming the intermediary space into a portal that communes the titular uncertainty with emotive movement, this work tugs and pulls you up the museum stairs, each step, as with the shaped walls below, shifting and altering your field of vision and horizon line.

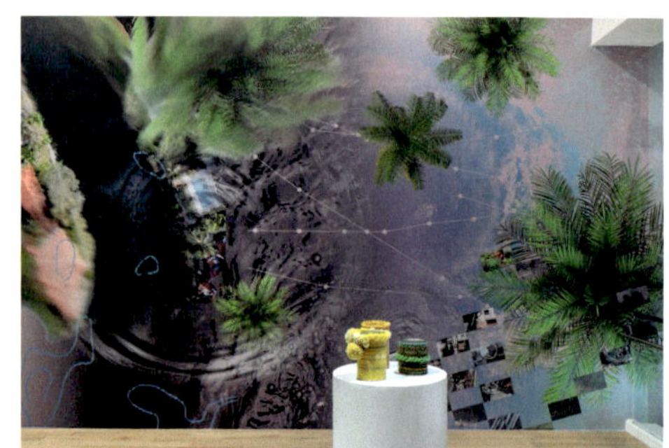

Coordinates of Speculative Solidarity, 2019 (detail)

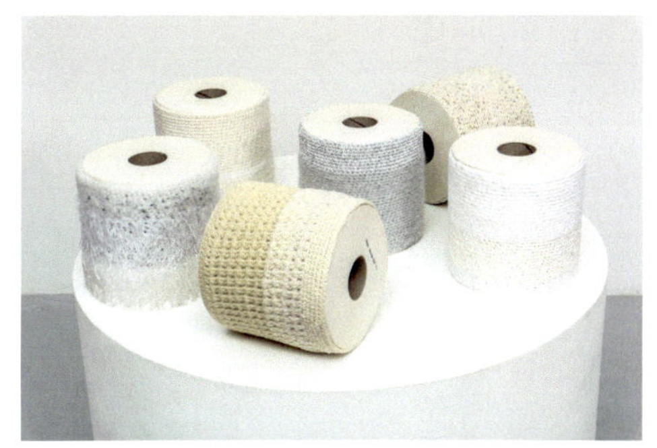

Roll Cosies – Toilet Tissue Jumbo Rolls, 2011

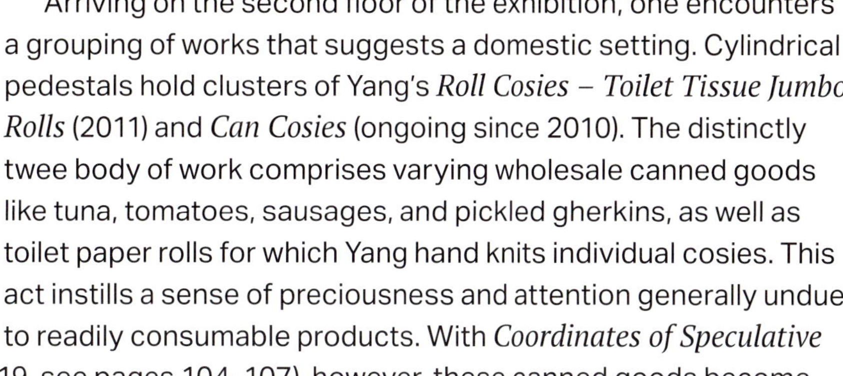

Arriving on the second floor of the exhibition, one encounters a grouping of works that suggests a domestic setting. Cylindrical pedestals hold clusters of Yang's *Roll Cosies – Toilet Tissue Jumbo Rolls* (2011) and *Can Cosies* (ongoing since 2010). The distinctly twee body of work comprises varying wholesale canned goods like tuna, tomatoes, sausages, and pickled gherkins, as well as toilet paper rolls for which Yang hand knits individual cosies. This act instills a sense of preciousness and attention generally undue to readily consumable products. With *Coordinates of Speculative Solidarity* (2019, see pages 104–107), however, these canned goods become as precious as the tea kettle for which a cosy might normally be fashioned, because they contain valuable nourishment in the face of impending disaster. Here, a strange sense of community materializes with this grouping of foods and supplies, calling to mind communities of "doomsday preppers" who hoard non-perishables and essential supplies in the wake of (un)predicted world end. In the same room, two works—*Jahnstraße 5* (2017) and *Dircksenstraße 37* (2019)—are installed on the walls. With materials including light bulbs, power cords, and colored venetian blinds, these recent works hybridize Yang's Light Sculptures and her larger blind works. The merged and tethered histories of Marguerite Duras, Kim San, and Nym Wales found in *Red Broken Mountainous Labyrinth* and *Yearning Melancholy Red*, and of Duras and Isang Yun in *A Chronology of Conflated Dispersion – Duras and Yun* (2018), find kinship with the references made in *Jahnstraße 5* and *Dircksenstraße 37* to the artist's current and former addresses in Berlin. Each to-scale representation of heating implements (boilers and radiators) from these homes includes a tangle of lights obscured by partly drawn blinds. As with many works in Yang's oeuvre, their forms echo the familiar but remain firmly alien. While not generating heat, these hybrid appliance-like works document Yang's own history of movement, recreating a quasi-domestic atmosphere in the exhibition space.

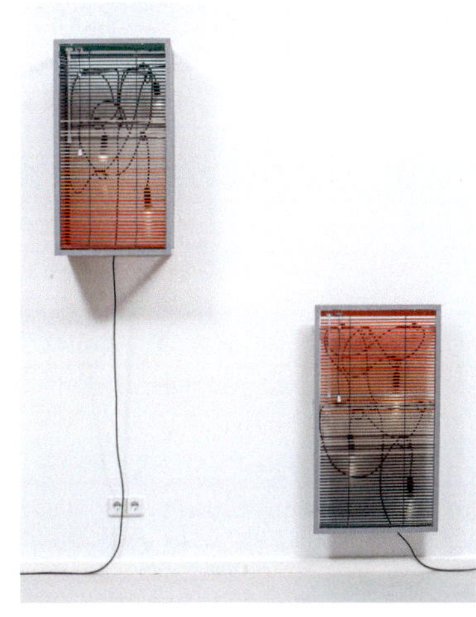

Jahnstraße 5, 2017 (detail)

Haegue Yang's focus and interest in movement, in all senses of the term, are foregrounded in the exhibition at The Bass. Yang's overarching visual studies of migration, exploration into non-physical movements, political, historical, and artistic, as well as the conditions that bring about the formation and reformation of community are mediated by her movable two- and three-dimensional work, exhibition elements and work materials like shaped walls and venetian blinds, which structure visitors' participation as they journey through the exhibition spaces. Through varying material and metaphorical vehicles and devices, Yang's works translate these complex explorations, with seemingly unrelated narratives, into visually abstract installations that hold a transportive potential. They guide and shepherd viewers into, through, and around the institution's spaces, through other sensorial elements, like heat, sound, and wind. Her works transport us to historical events (recorded and unrecorded) in South Korea in 2018, French Indochina in the 1920s, and to the mountains of China's Yan'an province in the 1930s. More intimately, her works-cum-records of movement, *Carsick Drawing – Toward Huu Nghi and Youyiguan #1* and *#2* (2016), *Jahnstraße 5*, and *Dircksenstraße 37*, trace the artist's own movements across landscapes, borders, regions, and from residence to residence.

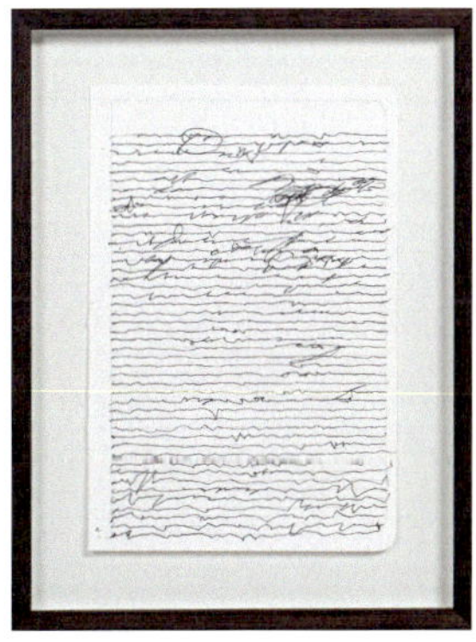

Carsick Drawing – Toward Huu Nghi and Youyiguan #2, 2016

In the Cone of Uncertainty begins with Yang's *Rotating Notes – Dispersed Episodes* (2013), a set of five irregularly shaped metal discs with printed quotes, chronologies, and ongoing research by Yang on important postcolonial writers, diasporic figures, and theorists: Primo Levi, Suh Kyungsik, Isang Yun, Edward Said, George Orwell, and Ghassan Kanafani magnetized to each face. While the biographical text is able to be read by the viewer, the discs (as suggested by the work's title) can be rotated and spun, unleashing a latent energy[5] within the work and transforming the text into unintelligible blurs. This potentiality of these forms to commute between static and dynamic is a trait found amongst Yang's numerous bodies of work, and elsewhere throughout the exhibition. The work is also a poignant starting point for the show as it relates to Yang's fascination with learning and unlearning as a means to (re)process history. Here, the dislocation of history via the movement of the text forces tangible, written, and recorded history to become abstract and illegible. However, the potential for new meanings is presented, and as with many of Yang's works, a certain amount of lingual and cultural translation occurs as a byproduct of her abstract making.

5 Yang's interest in the concealed potential of latent energy can be found in many of her works. See p. 63 in this volume.

In the next room, a gathering of Yang's light and anthropomorphic sculptural groups—*The Intermediates* (2015–ongoing) and *Strange Fruit* (2012–13) are staged among triangularly shaped walls (a trademark exhibition element for Yang). We first encounter the six Light Sculptures comprising *Strange Fruit*. Visually and conceptually nuanced, *Strange Fruit* takes its title from Jewish-American Abel Meeropol's poem famously vocalized by Billie Holiday in 1939. Each sculpture is made up of an amalgam of materials that resonate with the poem's subject matter: cable ties, colorfully painted papier-mâché bowls, and Styrofoam hands holding artificial plants, nylon cord, light bulbs, and cable, draped and hung from wheeled, metal clothing racks. The work reflects a recurring interest within Yang's practice, illuminating unlikely, lesser-known connections throughout history and elucidating asymmetrical relationships among figures of the past. In the story of *Strange Fruit*, the point of interest is in a poem about the horrors and tragedy of lynching of African-Americans in the American South born from the empathies of a Jewish man and member of the Communist party. Yang's interests are filtered through different geopolitical spheres with a keen concentration in collapsing time and place, unlike today's compartmentalized diasporic studies.

Strange Fruit, 2012–13, Anna Schwartz Gallery, Sydney, Australia, 2013

The trajectory through *Strange Fruit* and the triangularly shaped walls through the linear gallery filters—hiding and revealing—the view of *The Intermediate – Monsoon Mourning Saekdong Cone* (2017) and *The Intermediate – Monsoon Mourning Spheres and Disks* (2017). Intricate weavings of materials with folk connotations, like Indian bells, straw, colorful Korean Saekdong fabric with artificial plants and metal turbine vents, and casters, again blend the seemingly organic with inorganic into a hybrid, human-scaled object. Art historian Chus Martínez characterizes *The Intermediates* as a series that "actively addresses the significance of making our senses oscillate wildly between these real objects and all the imaginations they provoke in us, this movement between them as identical

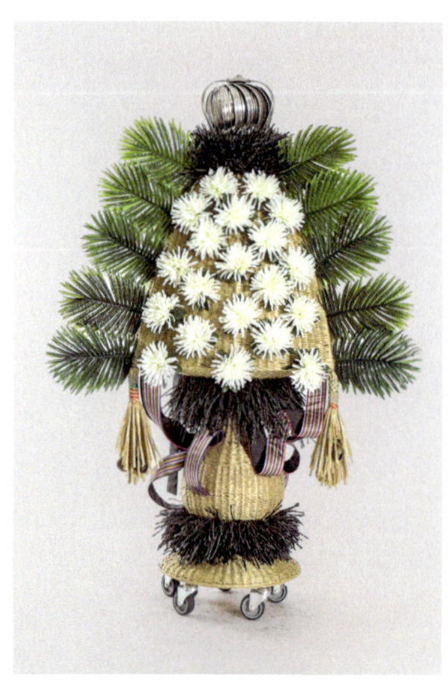

The Intermediate – Monsoon Mourning Saekdong Cone, 2017

replications of themselves—artifices full of fetishistic character—and them as doors, entrances, and passageways."[6] Yang's *Intermediates* incorporate elements of traditional craft into her art-making. They mediate, as their name would suggest, between cultural distinctions and pejorative valuations of "tradition," synthesizing within singular sculptures negotiations of identity and material commonality. The proximity of *The Intermediate* sculptures to *Strange Fruit*, though from different sculptural groups in Yang's extensive and meticulous categorization and subcategorization of her works, highlights the formal similarities of their exposed metal armatures and casters. As with the previous gallery's *Rotating Notes – Dispersed Episodes*, the potentiality of their movement is laid bare to the viewer.

The prospect of catharsis and knowledge acquisition vis-à-vis movement plays a central role elsewhere in the exhibition *In the Cone of Uncertainty*. The room-sized installation *Boxing Ballet* (2013–15), for example, charts Yang's personal reconciliation with her Eastern origins and her encounters with the canon of the Western avant-gardes triggered by her relocation to Germany.[7] With particular reference to the Bauhaus legacies, Yang's tête-à-tête response to Oskar Schlemmer's *Triadic Ballet* (1922) comprises a seventeen-part troupe of individually titled works, which directly reference the details of Schlemmer's production: anthropomorphic sculpture danseuses, yellow, black, and pink painted walls, and a configuration of her two-dimensional *Trustworthies*. The Sonic Sculptures are adorned with bells, and either suspended or on casters and equipped with handles, which unlike their distant cousins in the exhibition, *The Intermediates* and *Strange Fruit*, invite movement. The sculptures can be pushed and pulled in a choreographed manner along the swirling vinyl lines on the floor. As with the Bauhaus principles of educating mind, body, and spirit in a holistic manner to equip students to create the *Gesamtkunstwerk*,[8] *Boxing Ballet* offers Yang's struggle to find holistic alignment through cultural digestion and translation. Here, Yang's tongue-in-cheek "combative" reckoning with the new cultural and art historical frameworks imposed around her are processed through the capabilities of, and with reference to, improvised and choreographed movement.

The ongoing transmutation of ideas, experiences, and history that takes place within Yang's work requires calculated motility, continual deconstruction, and translation. Yang's elucidation of these actions—from subject matter around the ebb and flow of migration, refugeeism, and distortion, to the suggested mobility of her forms—generates new understandings of our environment. These acts unite the artist's inclination to "lose the power of and didactic control over content, reality, and history, in order to regain them in a new manner, in a materialized language,"[9] with the writing of cultural theorist Rey Chow on the verbalization of the postcolonial experience. Chow describes the role of translation as "something (ap)proximate to an arbiter of value." The translator is someone who "underscores the fact that storytelling, too, is a form of exchange," and makes "newly legible problems of unevenness that are inherent to postcolonial cross-cultural encounters."[10] Yang's unique material language aids in the renewed legibility of situations of "unevenness" espoused by Chow, digesting and alchemizing the ongoing issues of metaphorical homelessness and placelessness, kinship and community, history and the future.

6 Chus Martínez, "Nature Loves to Hide: On Haegue Yang," in *Haegue Yang: ETA 1994–2018*, ed. Yilmaz Dziewior (Cologne: Verlag der Buchhandlung Walther König, 2018), p. 8.

7 For a complete and thorough (as of 2018) biography of the artist, please reference: Leonie Radine, "About Haegue Yang," in Dziewior 2018 (see note 6), pp. 378–401.

8 Johannes Itten, *Mein Vorkurs am Bauhaus* (Ravensburg: Otto Maier Verlag, 1963), p. 11.

9 Demos 2013 (see note 2), p. 79.

10 Rey Chow, *Not Like a Native Speaker: On Languaging as a Postcolonial Experience* (New York: Columbia University Press, 2014), pp. 65–67.

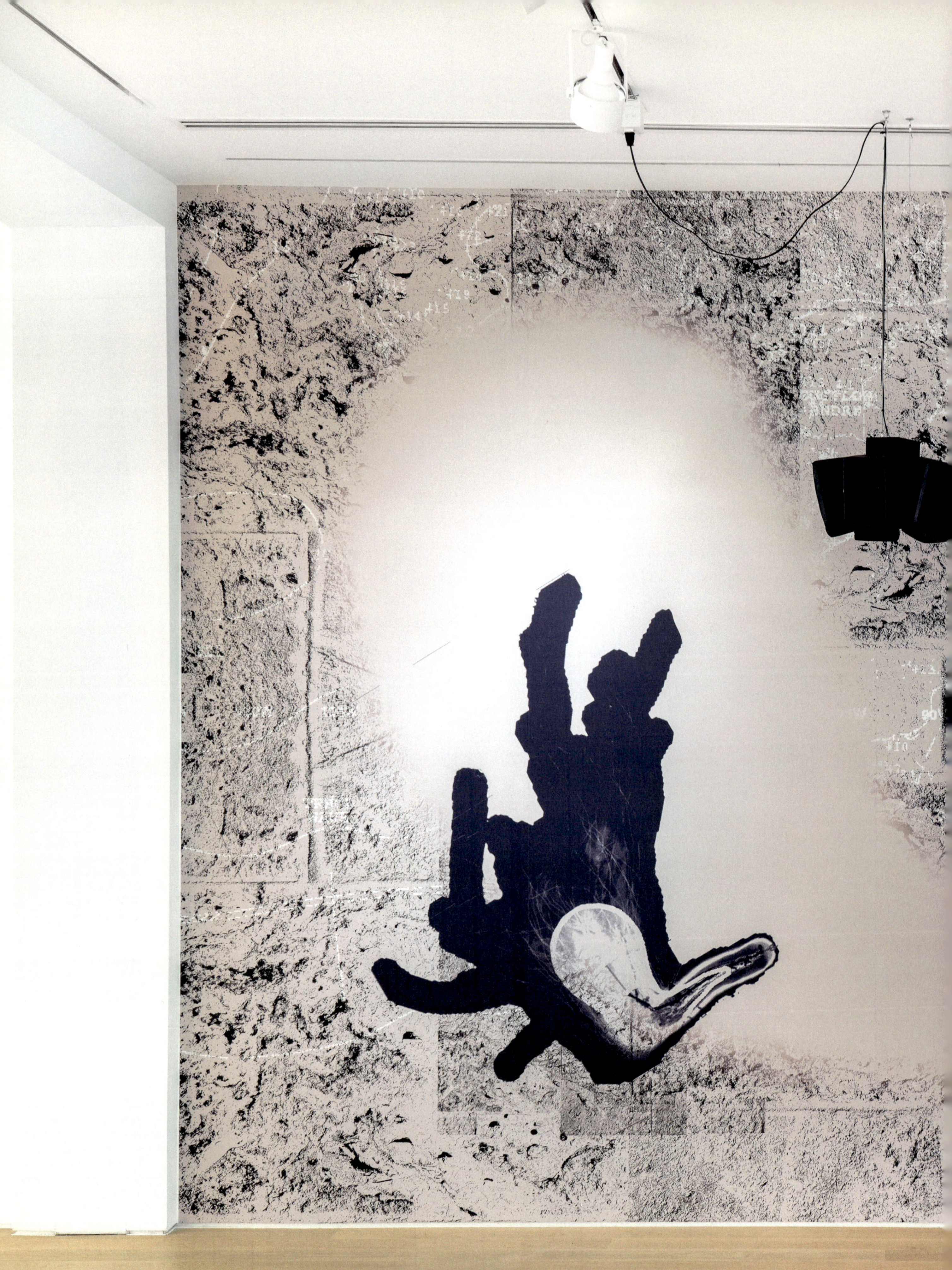

Coordinates of Speculative Solidarity, 2019

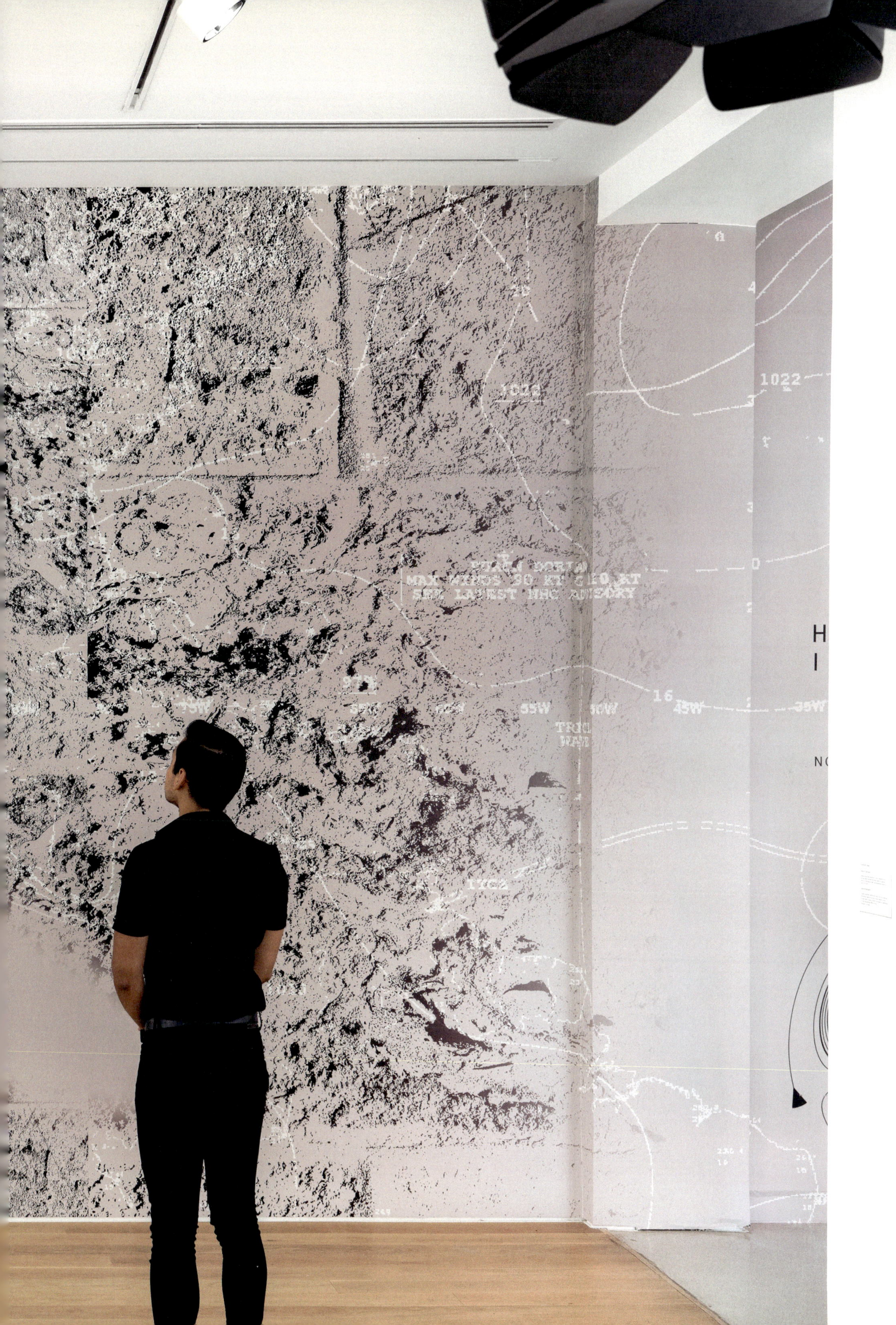

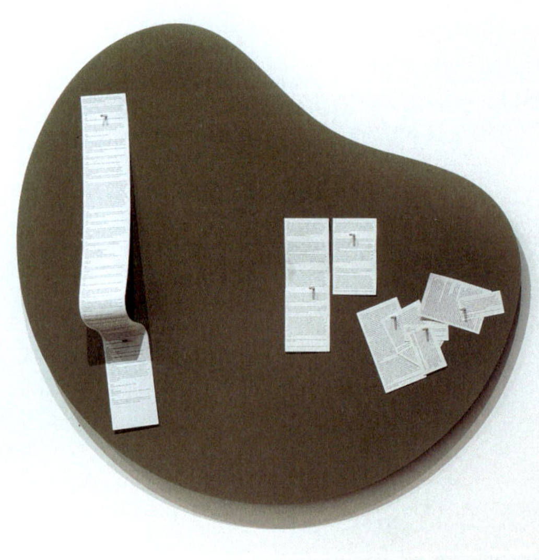

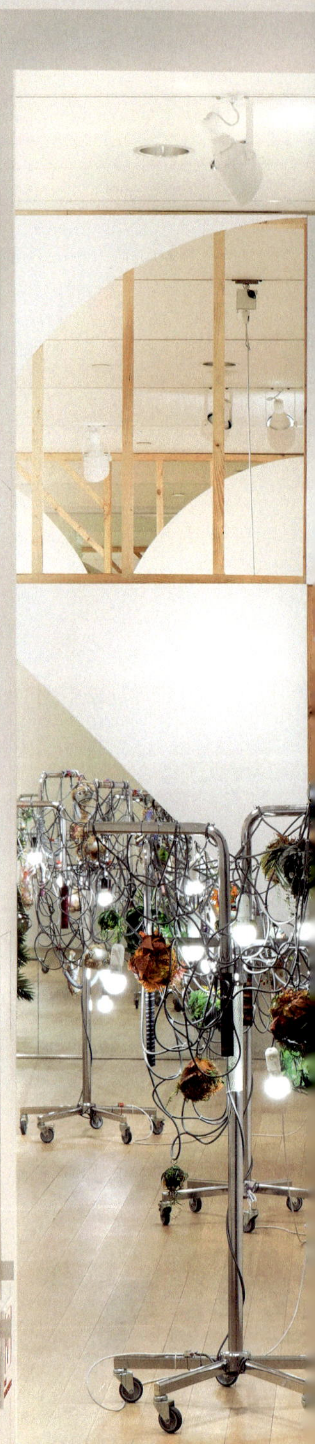

Rotating Notes – Dispersed Episodes, 2013

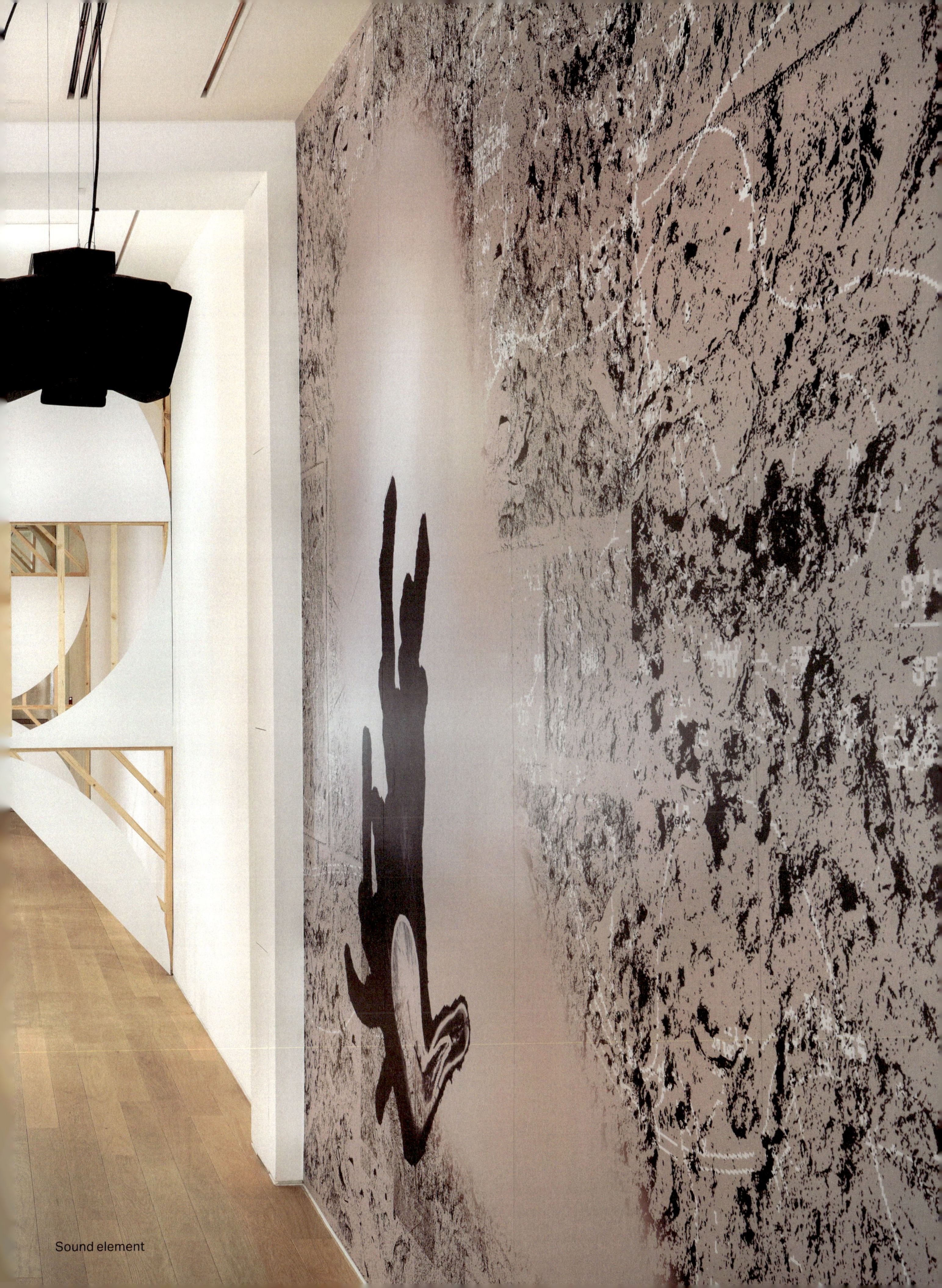

Sound element

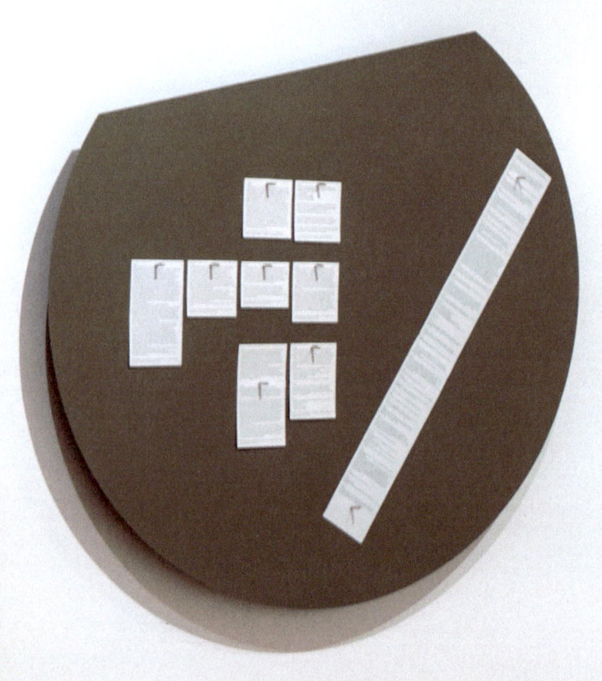

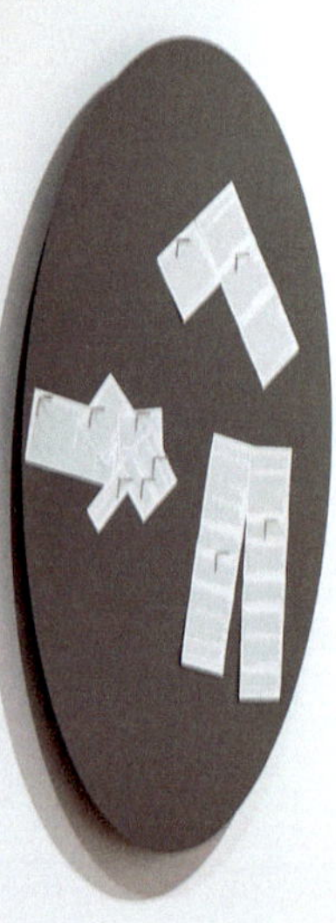

Rotating Notes – Dispersed Episodes, 2013

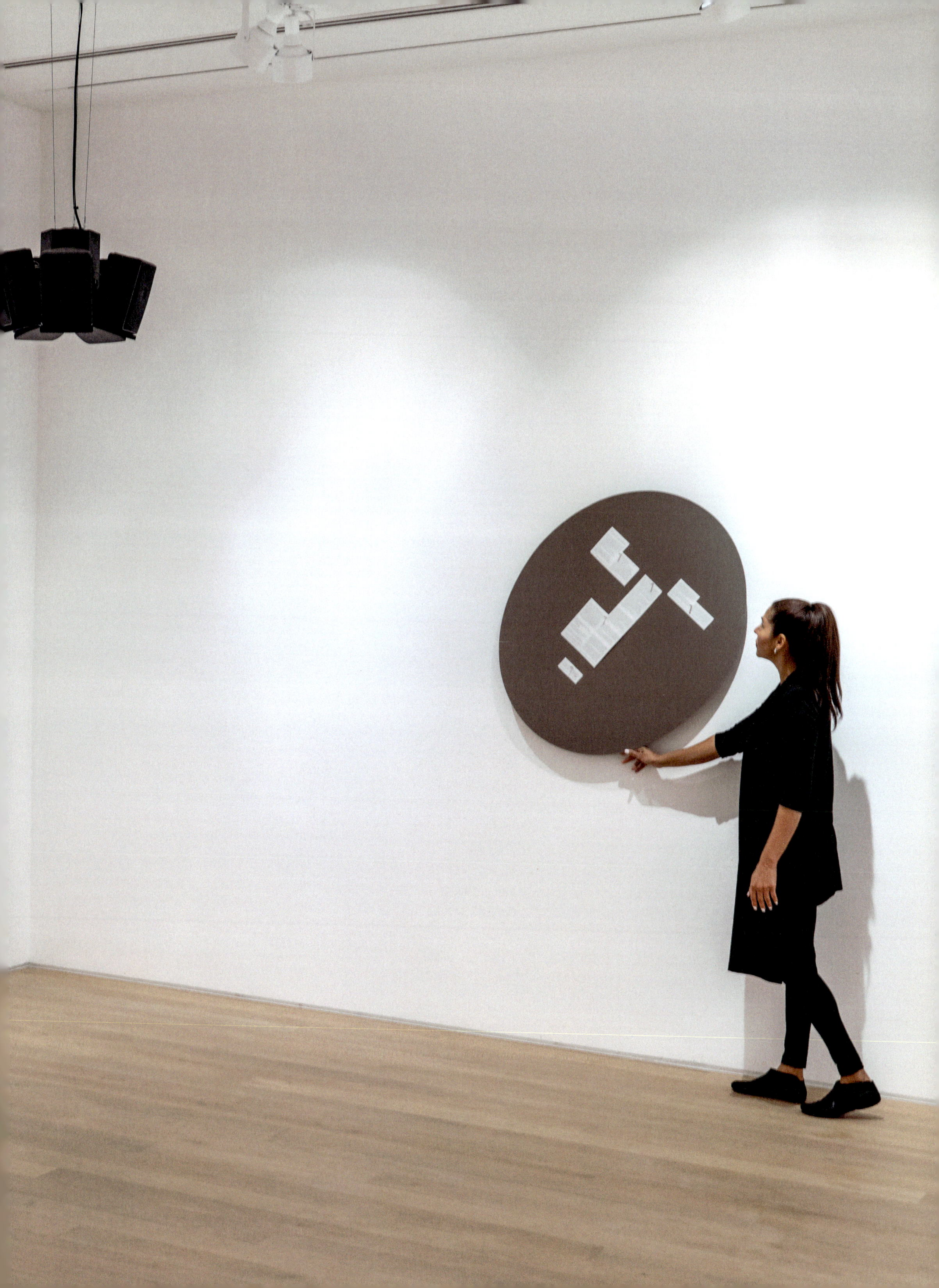

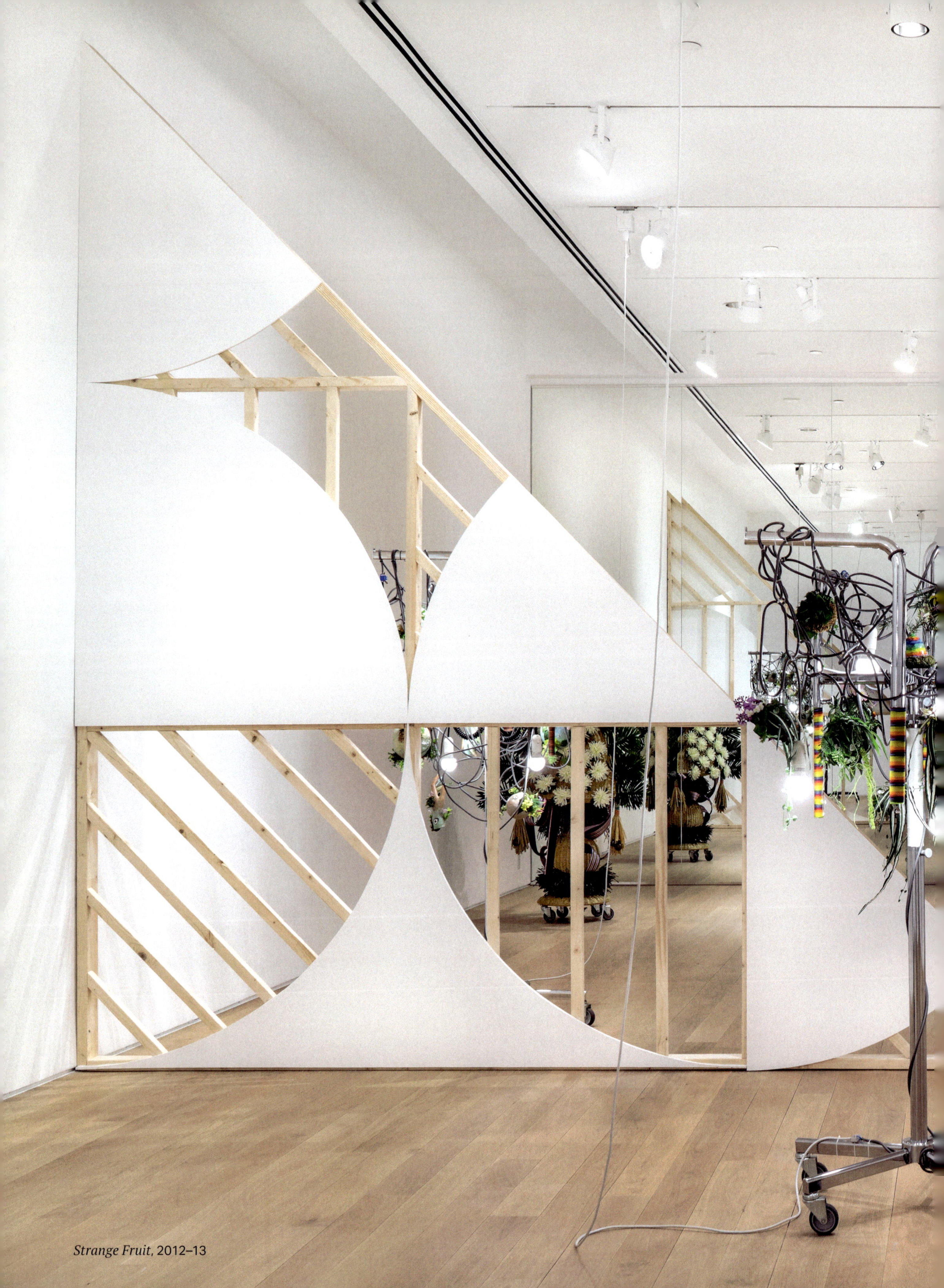

Strange Fruit, 2012–13

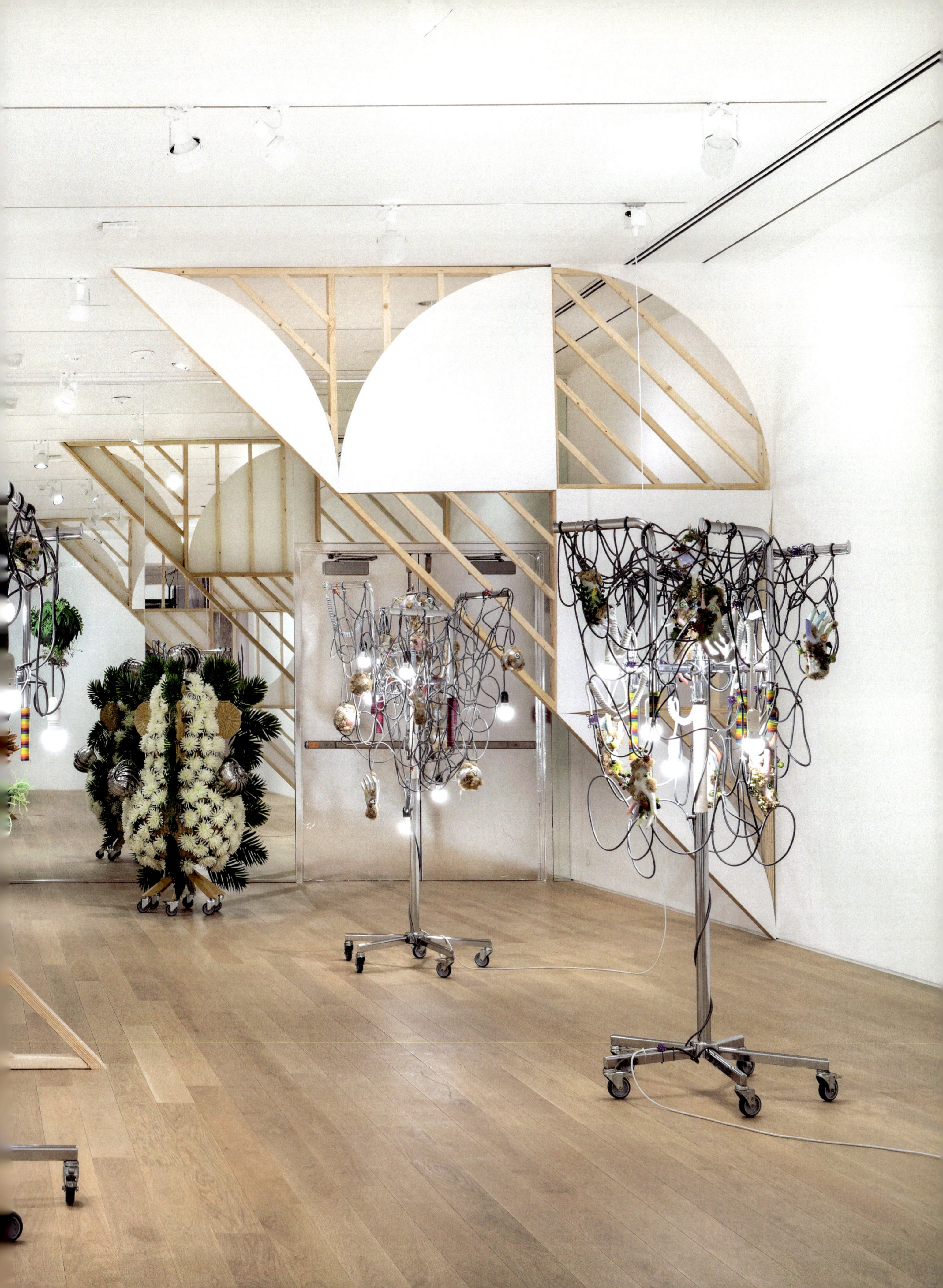

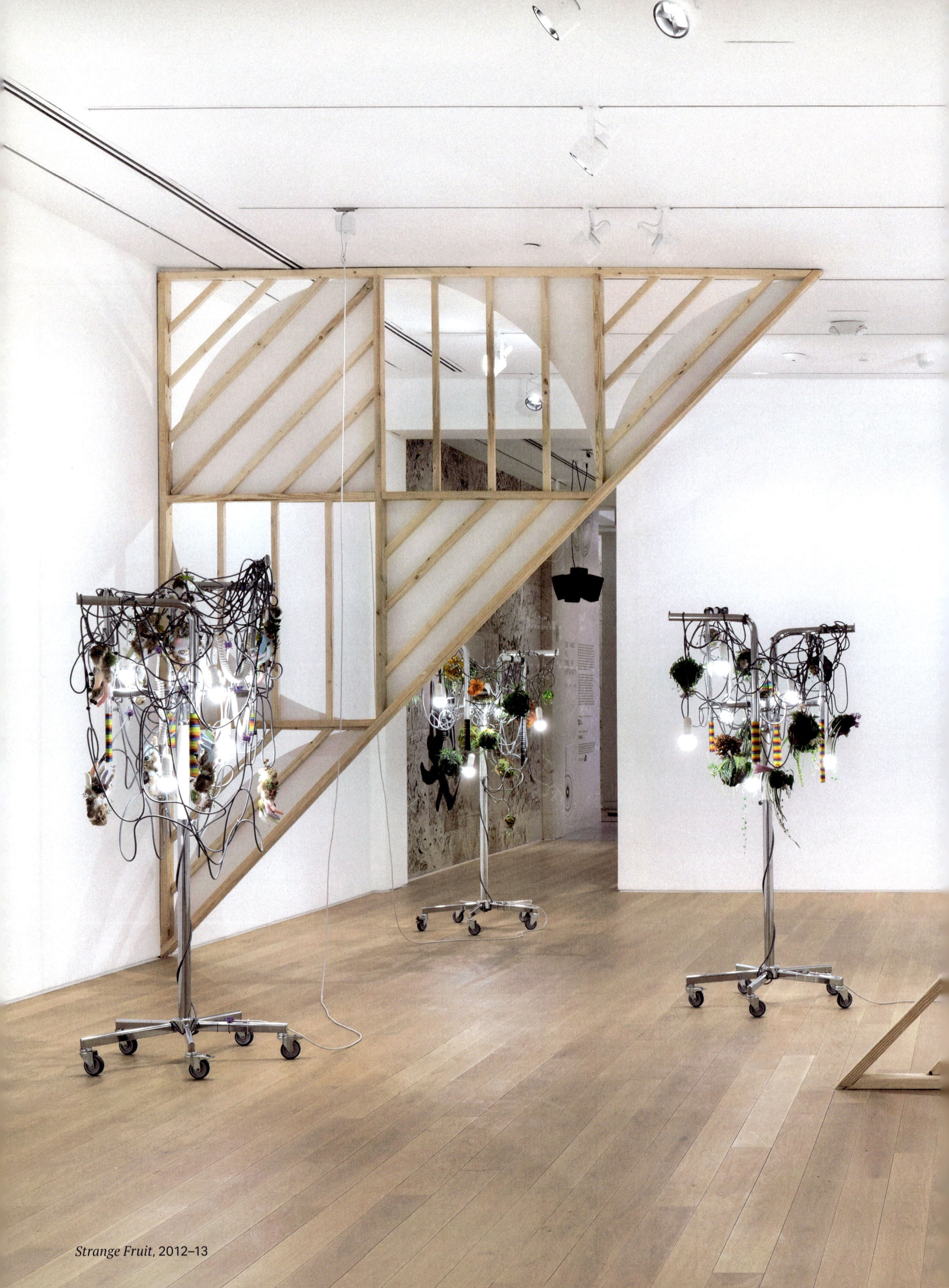

Strange Fruit, 2012–13

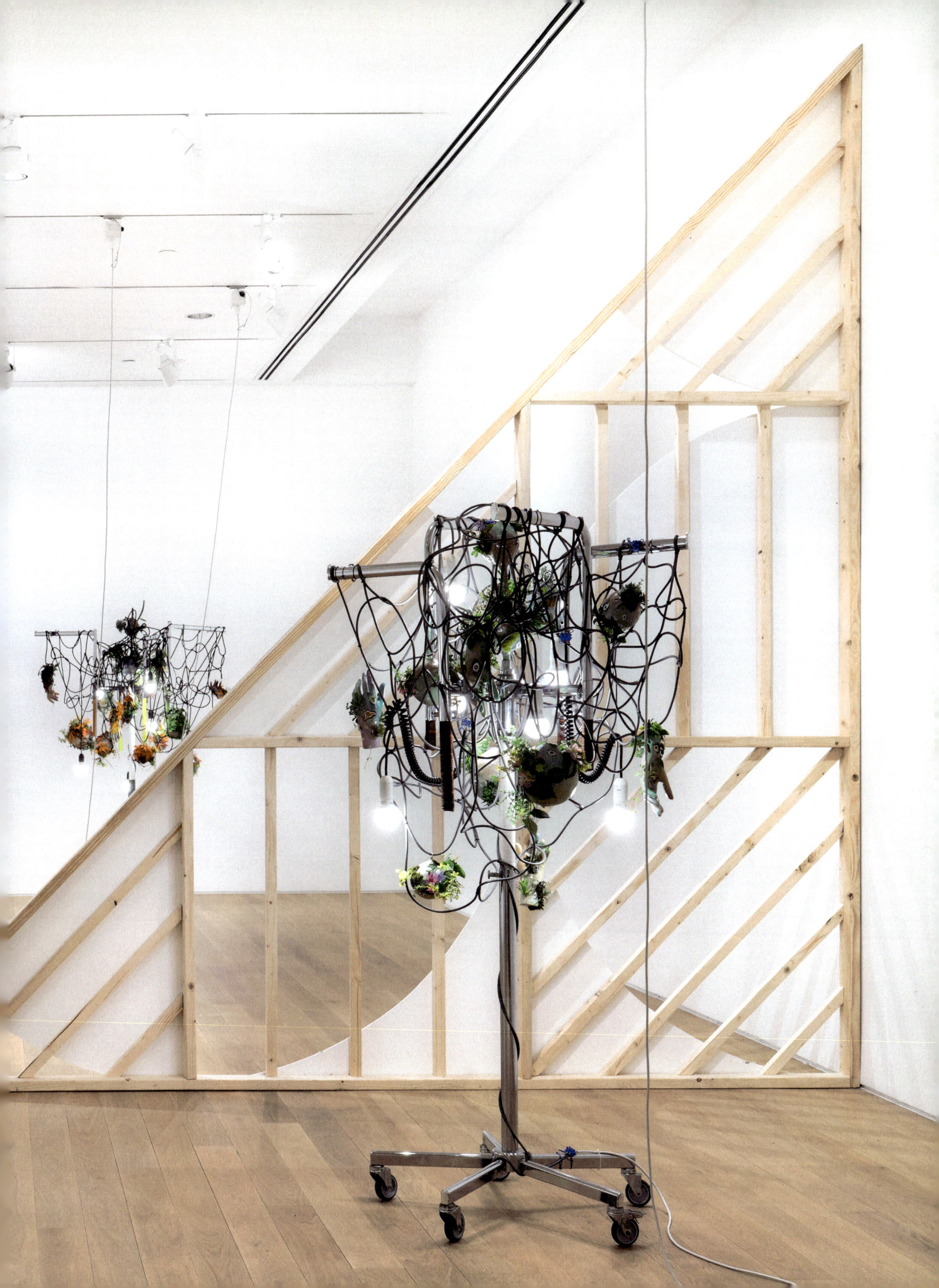

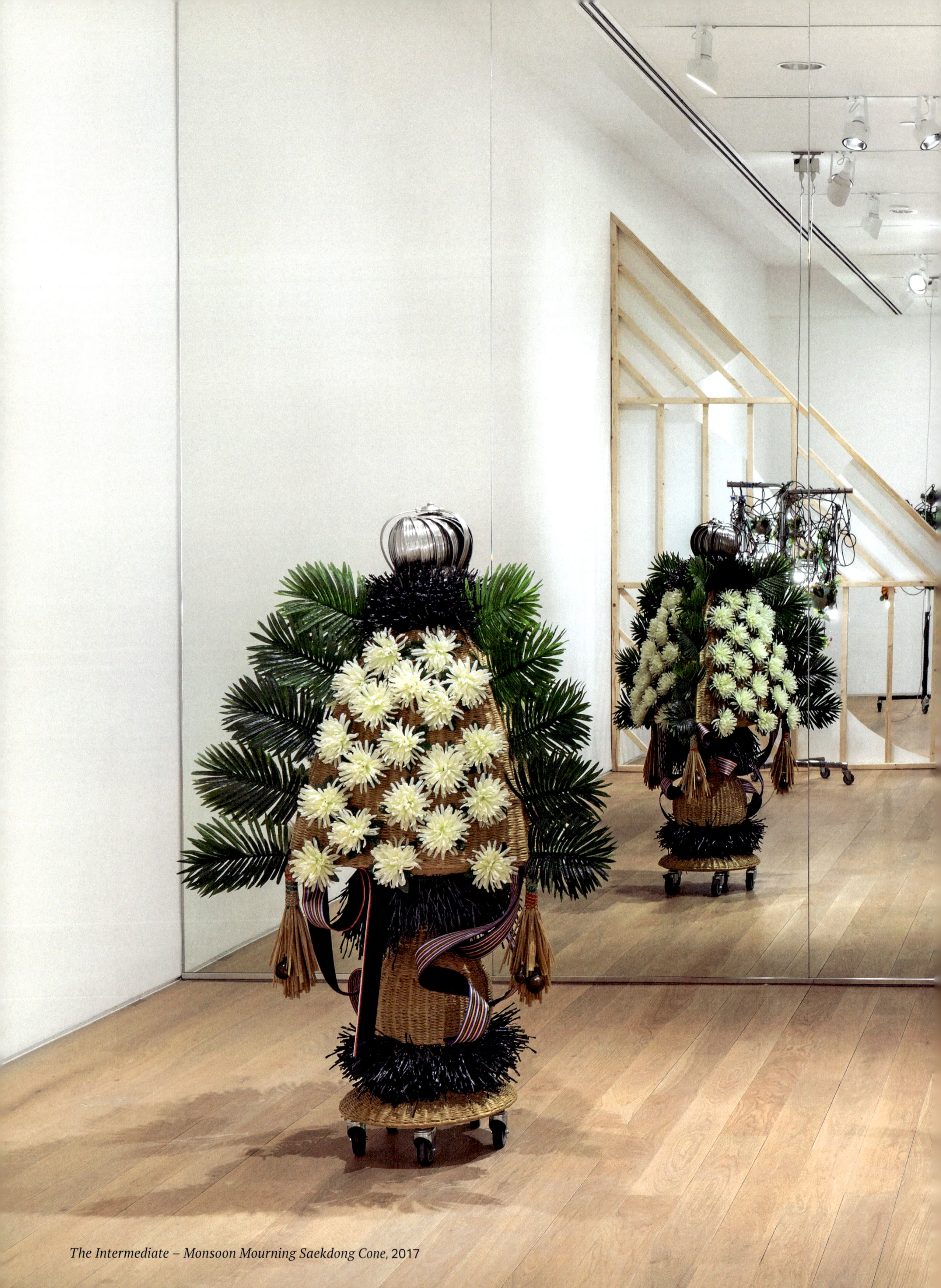

The Intermediate – Monsoon Mourning Saekdong Cone, 2017

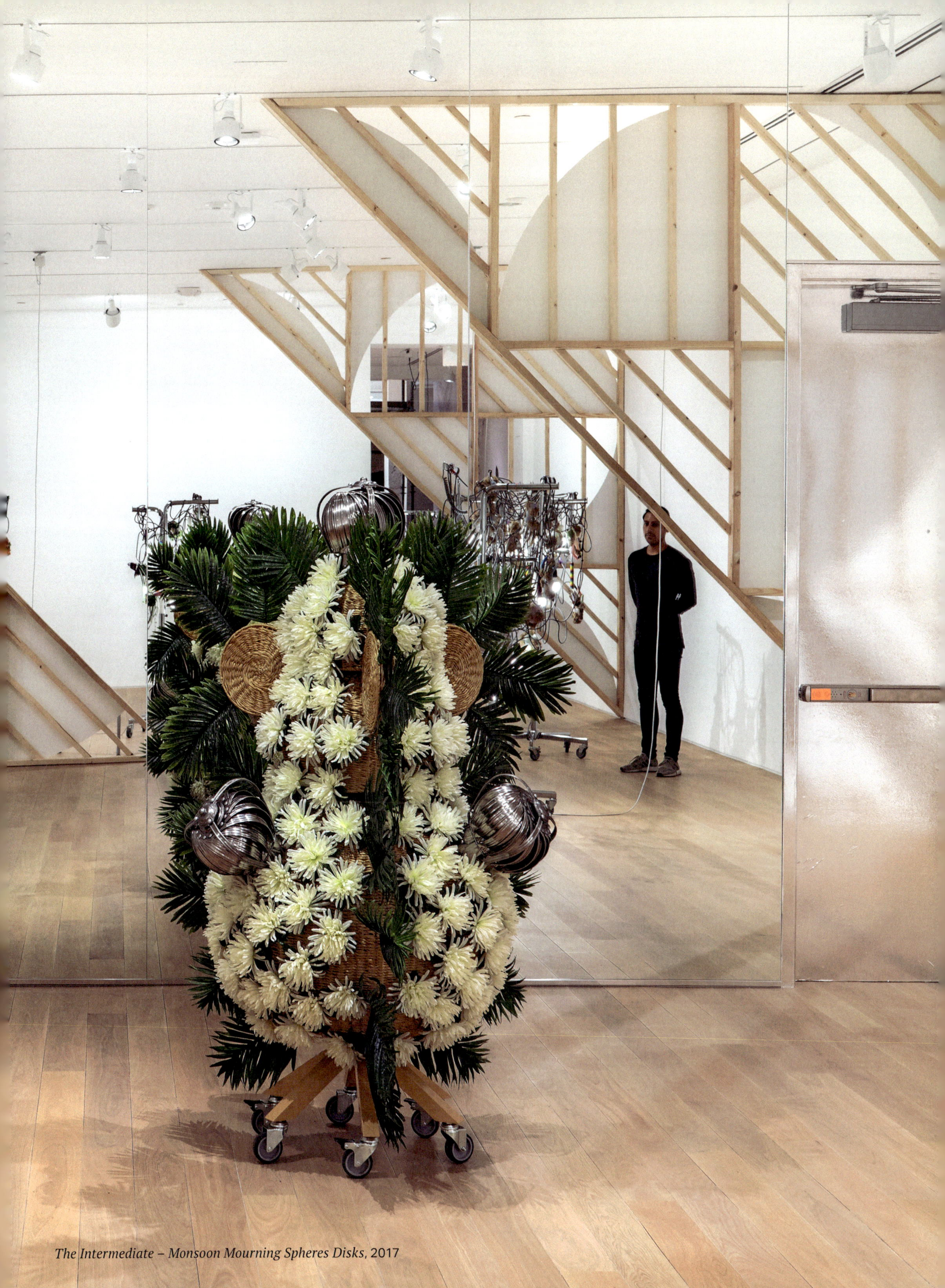

The Intermediate – Monsoon Mourning Spheres Disks, 2017

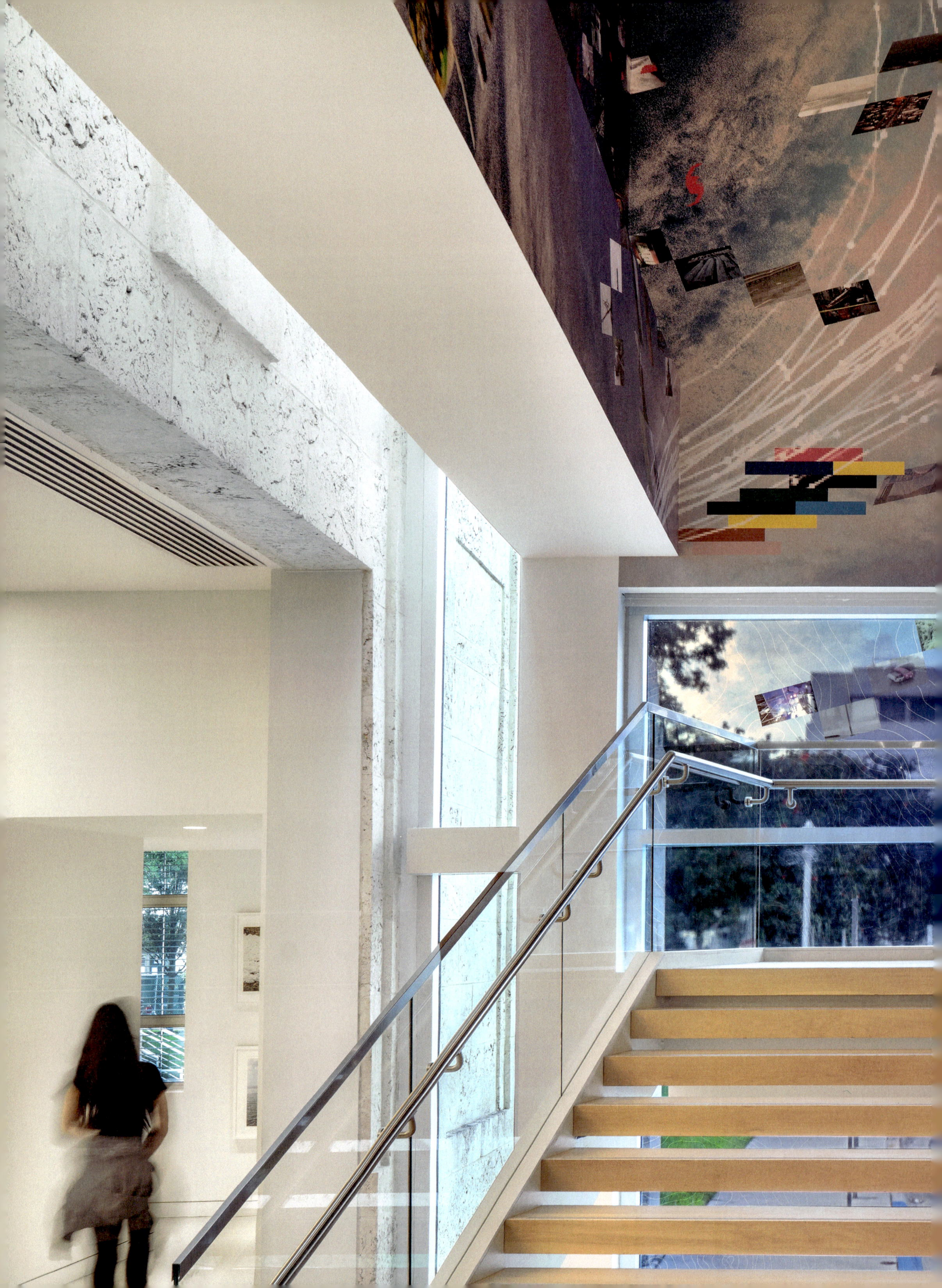

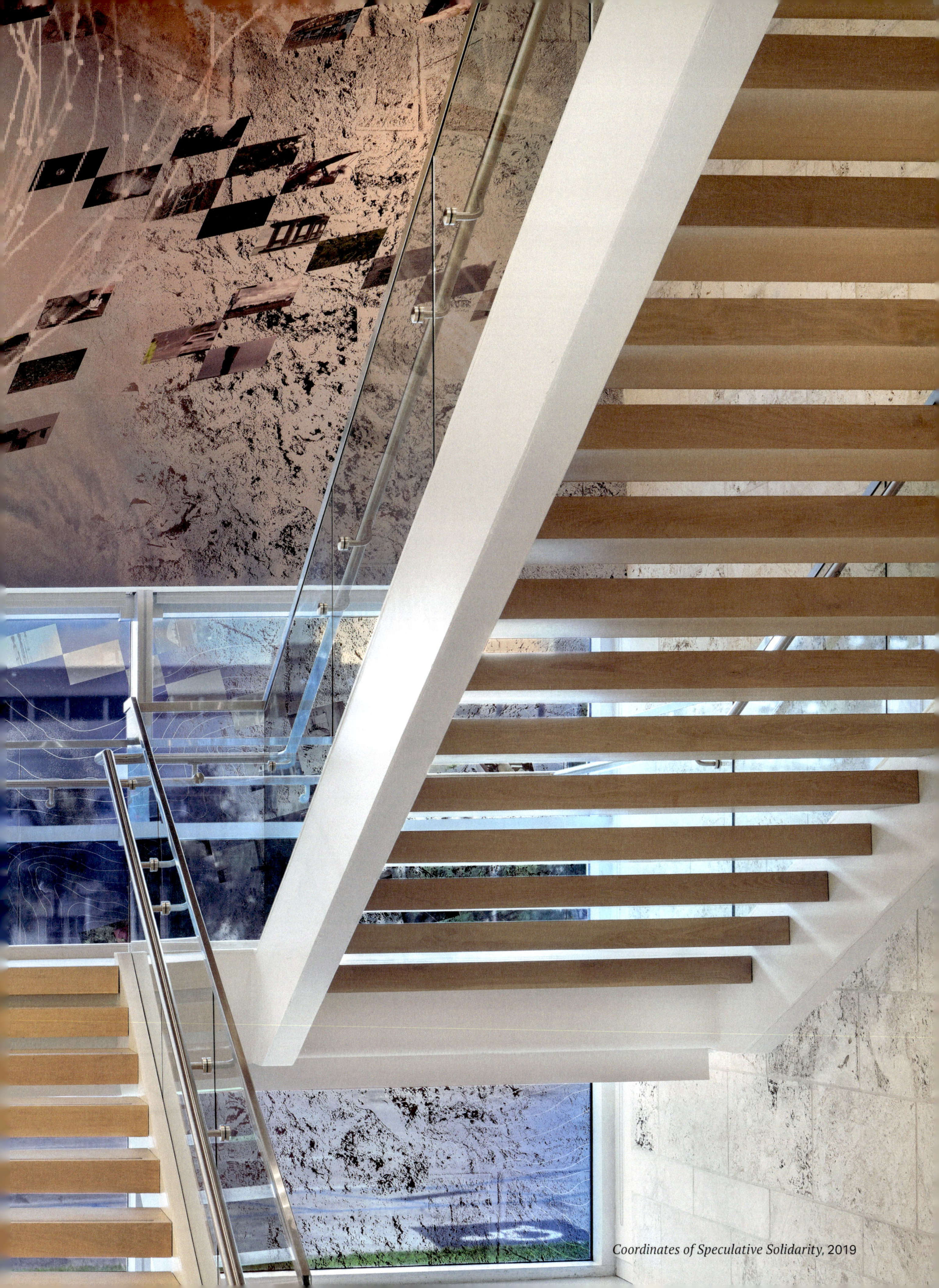

Coordinates of Speculative Solidarity, 2019

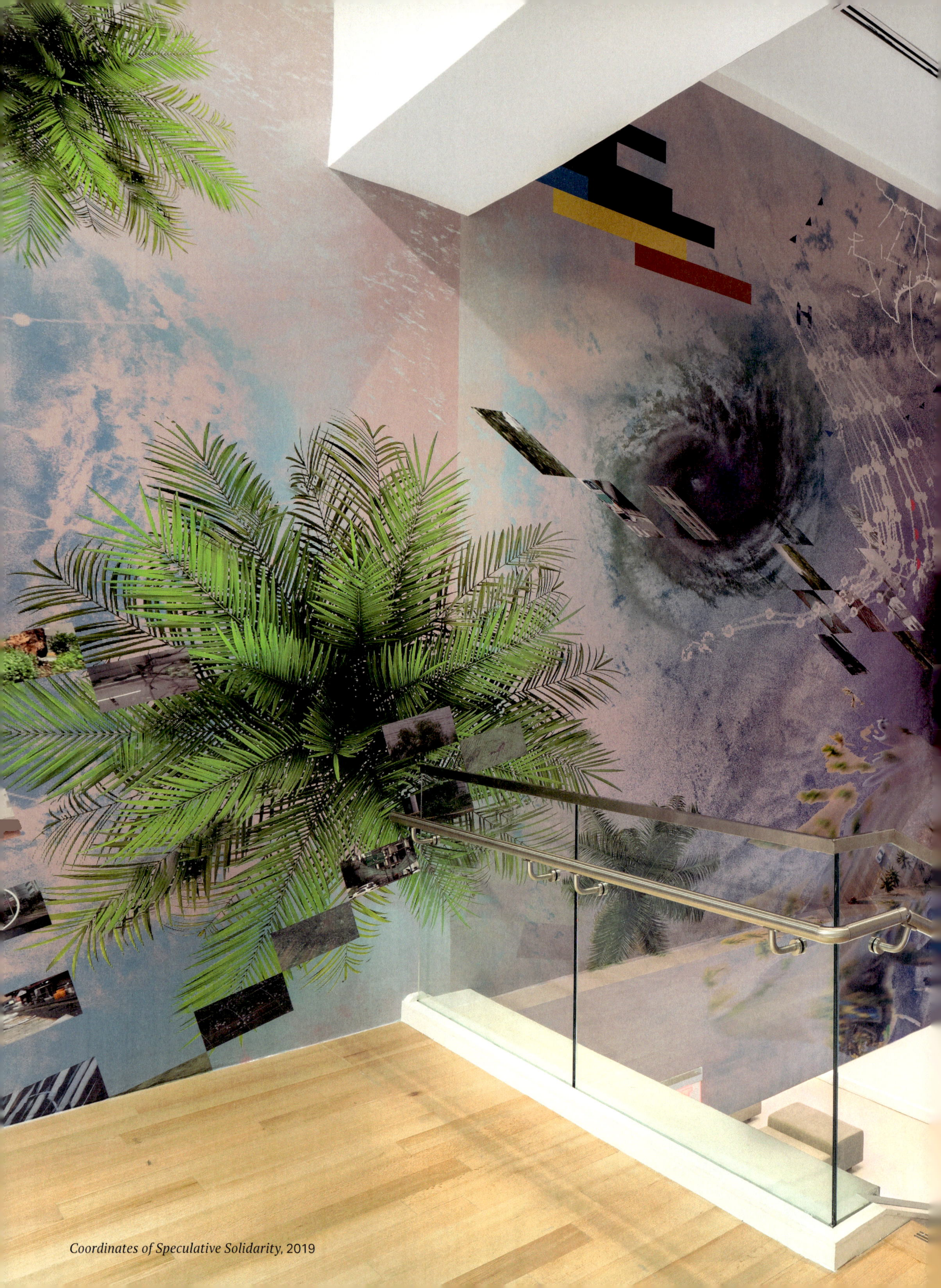

Coordinates of Speculative Solidarity, 2019

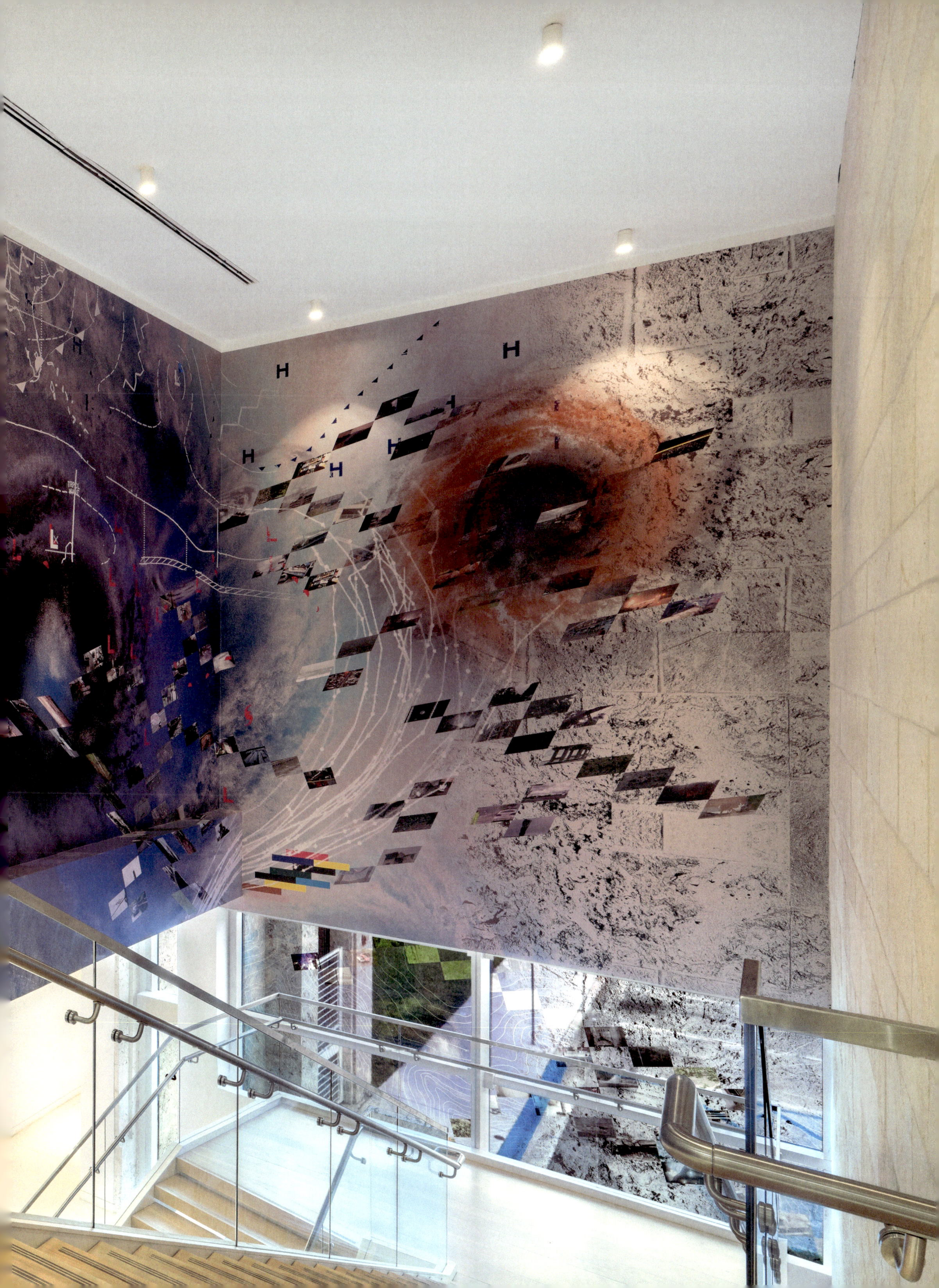

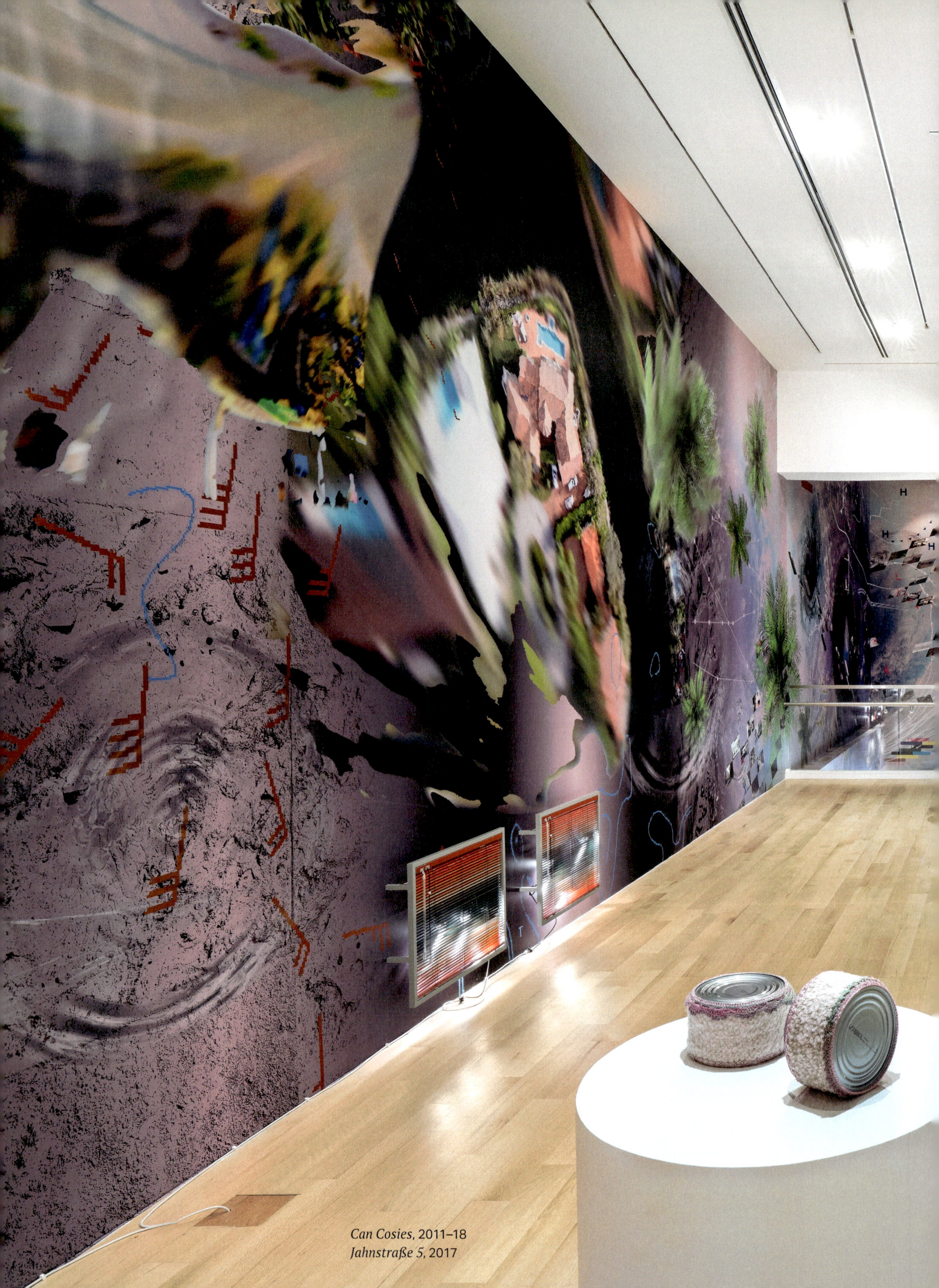

Can Cosies, 2011–18
Jahnstraße 5, 2017

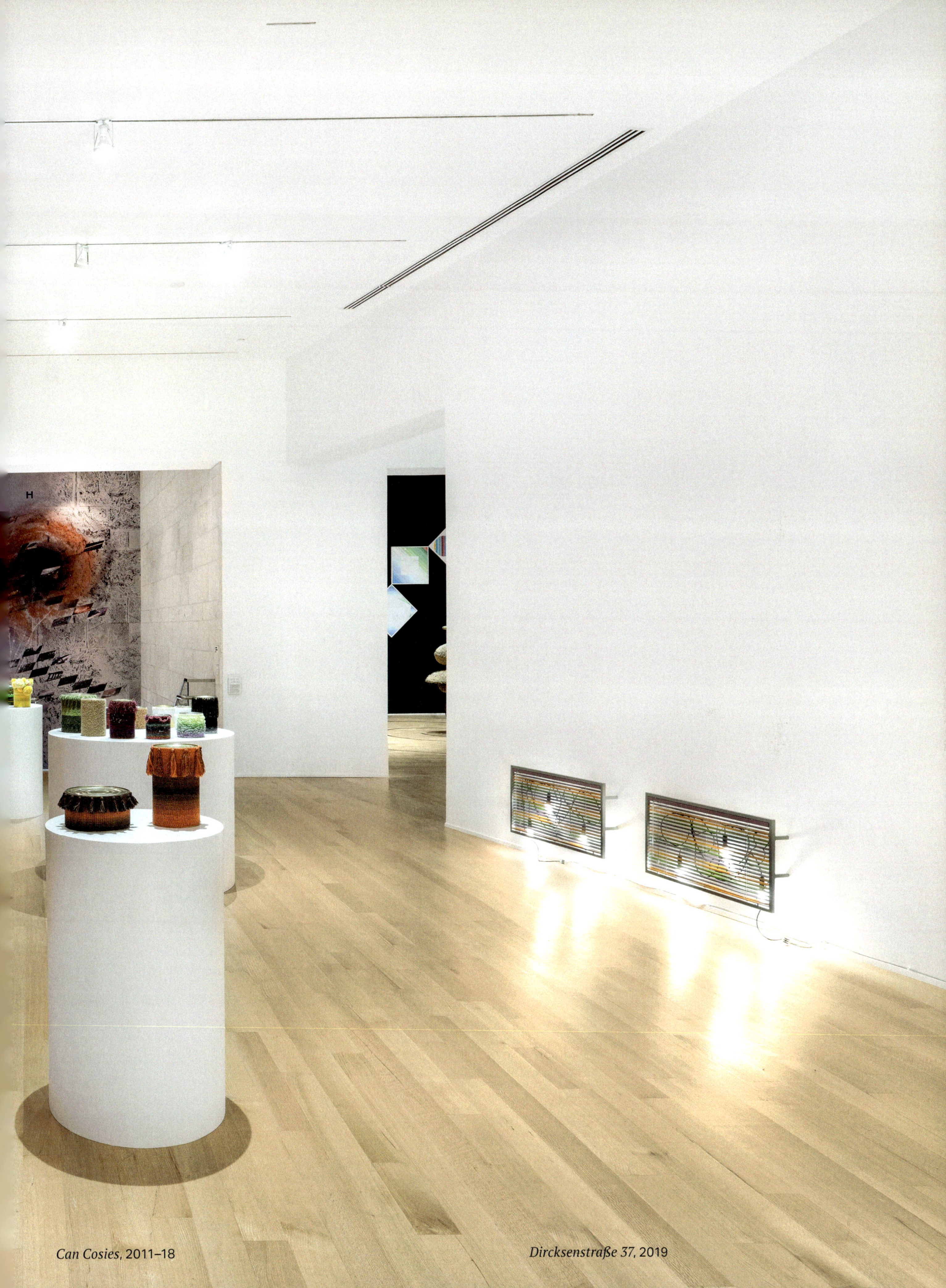

Can Cosies, 2011–18

Dircksenstraße 37, 2019

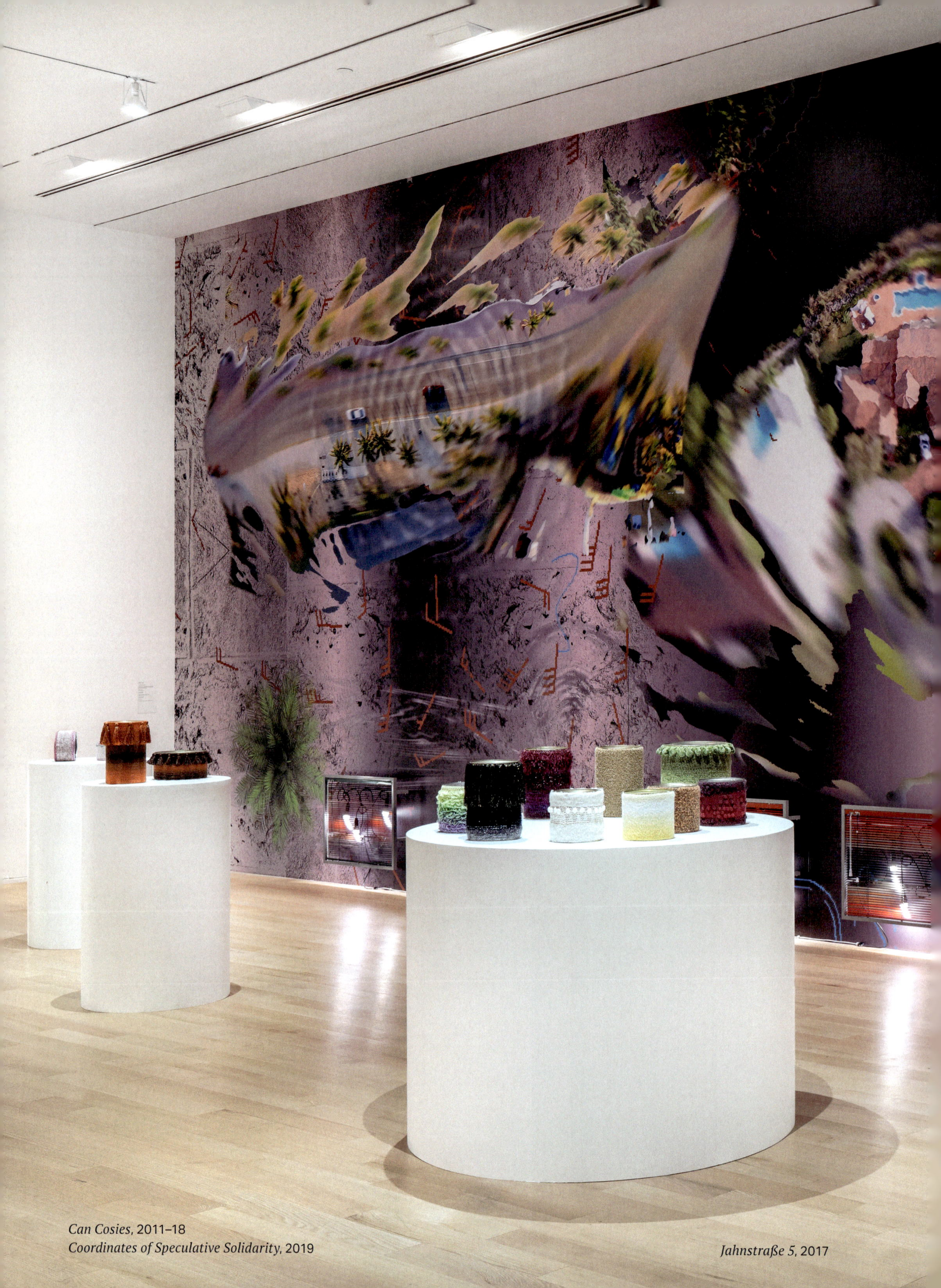

Can Cosies, 2011–18
Coordinates of Speculative Solidarity, 2019

Jahnstraße 5, 2017

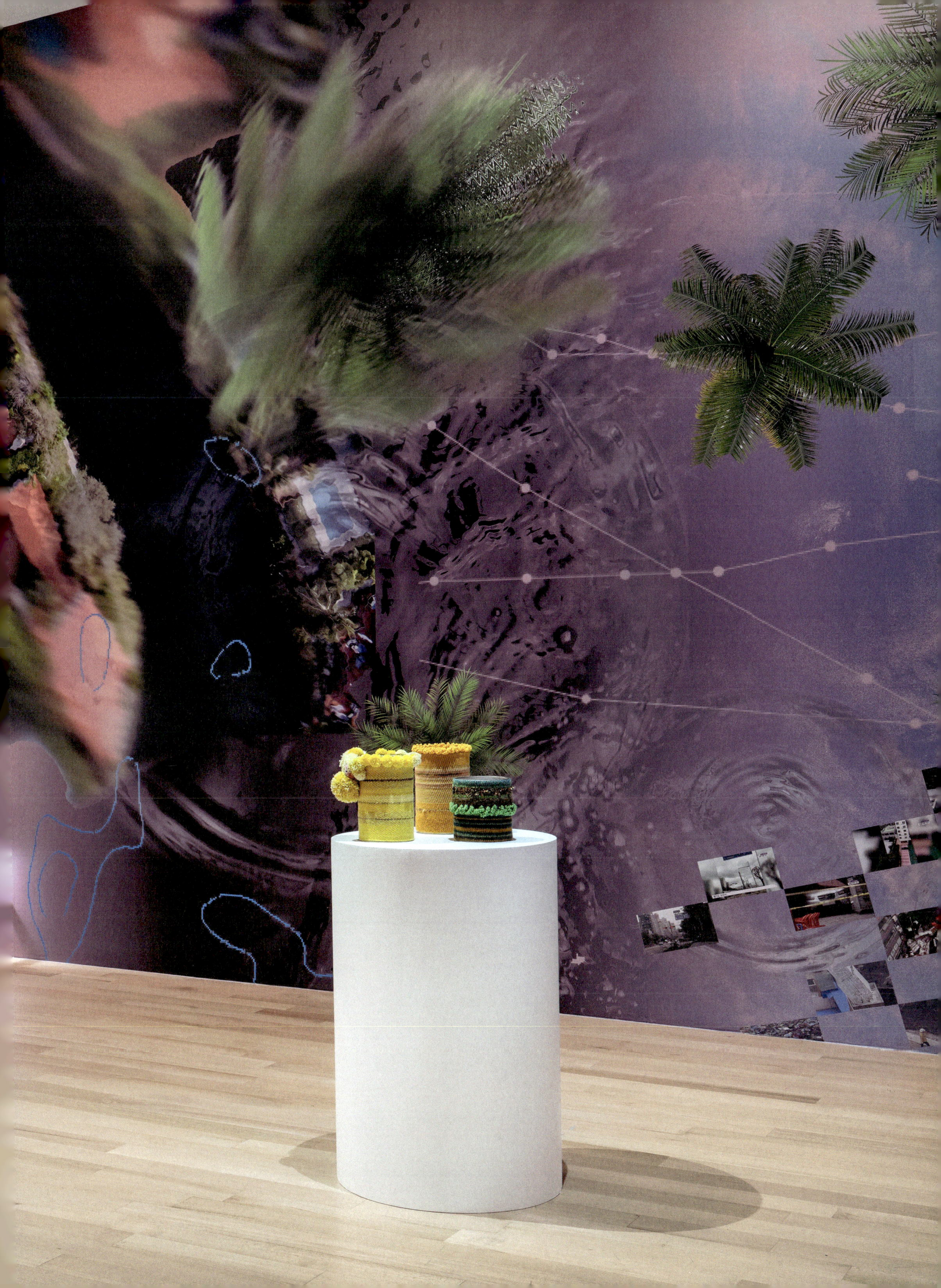

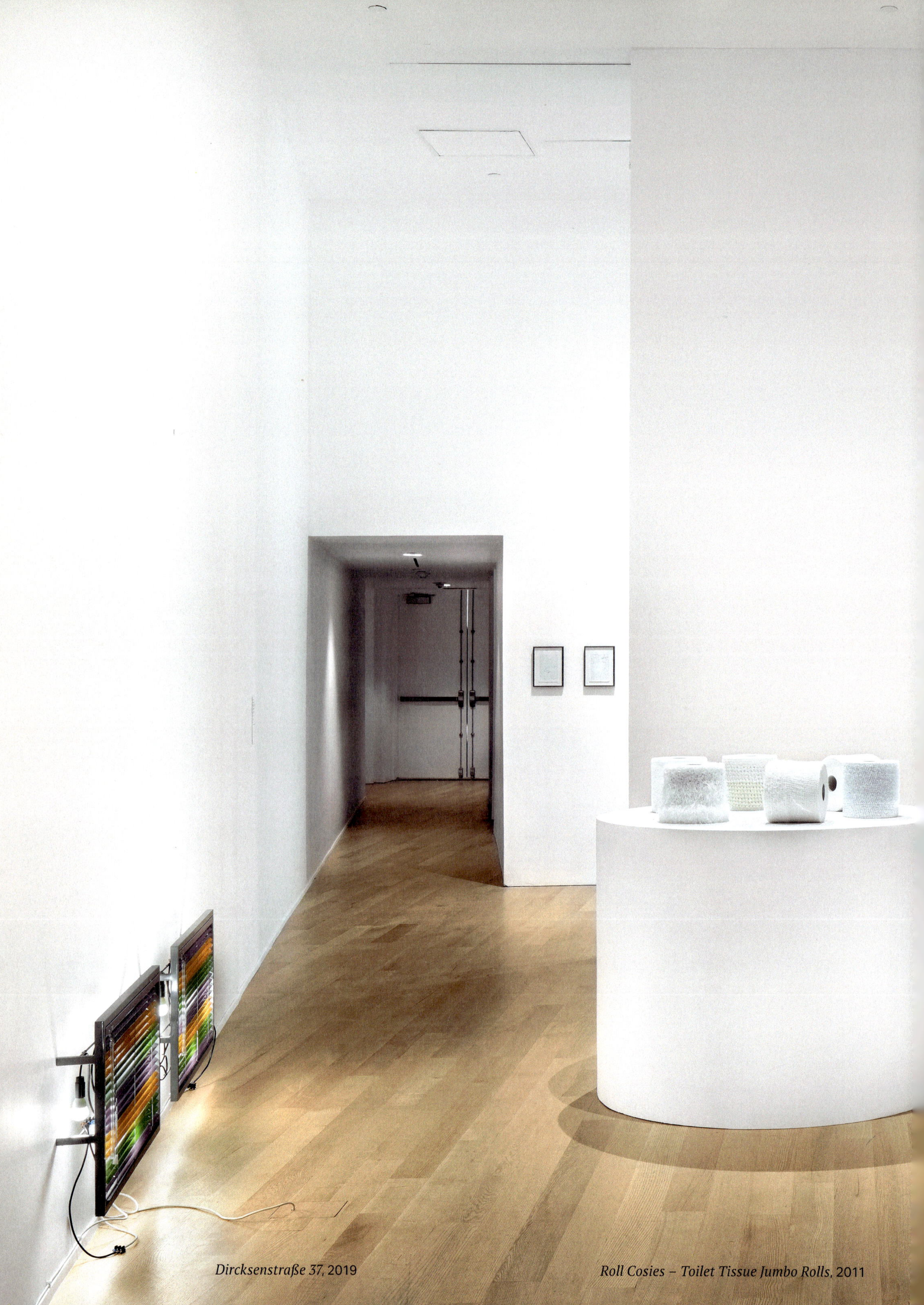

Dircksenstraße 37, 2019

Roll Cosies – Toilet Tissue Jumbo Rolls, 2011

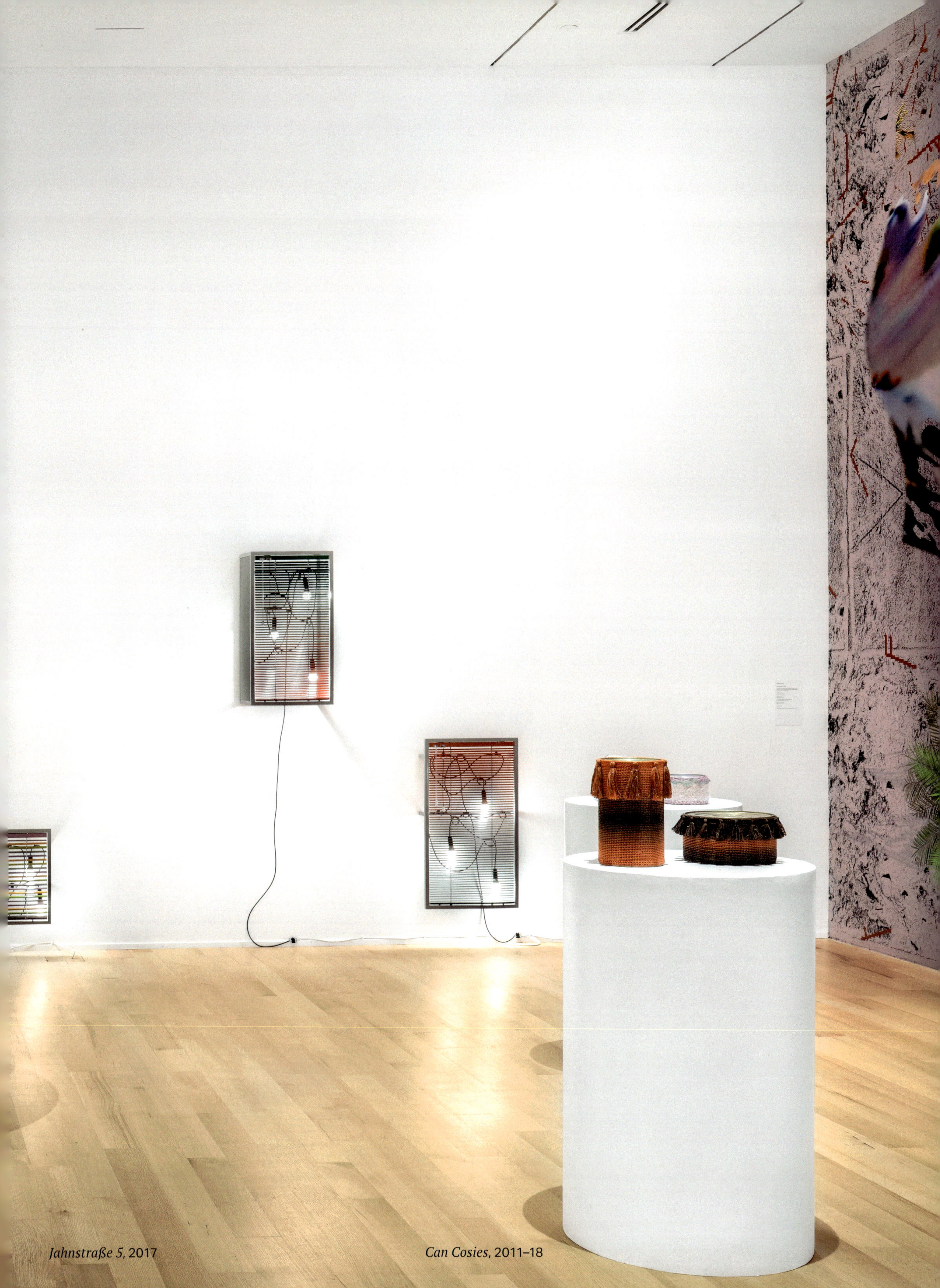

Jahnstraße 5, 2017

Can Cosies, 2011–18

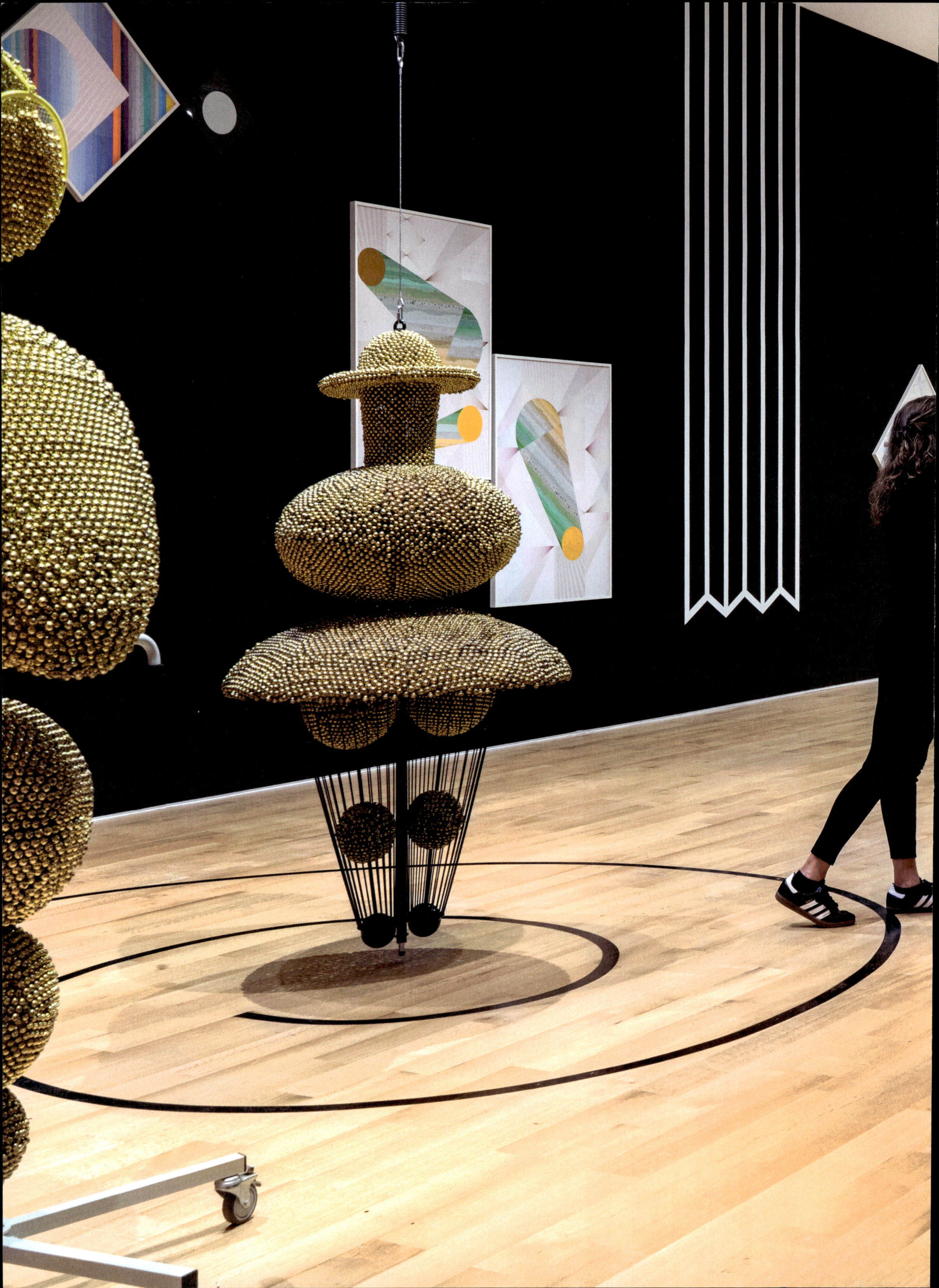

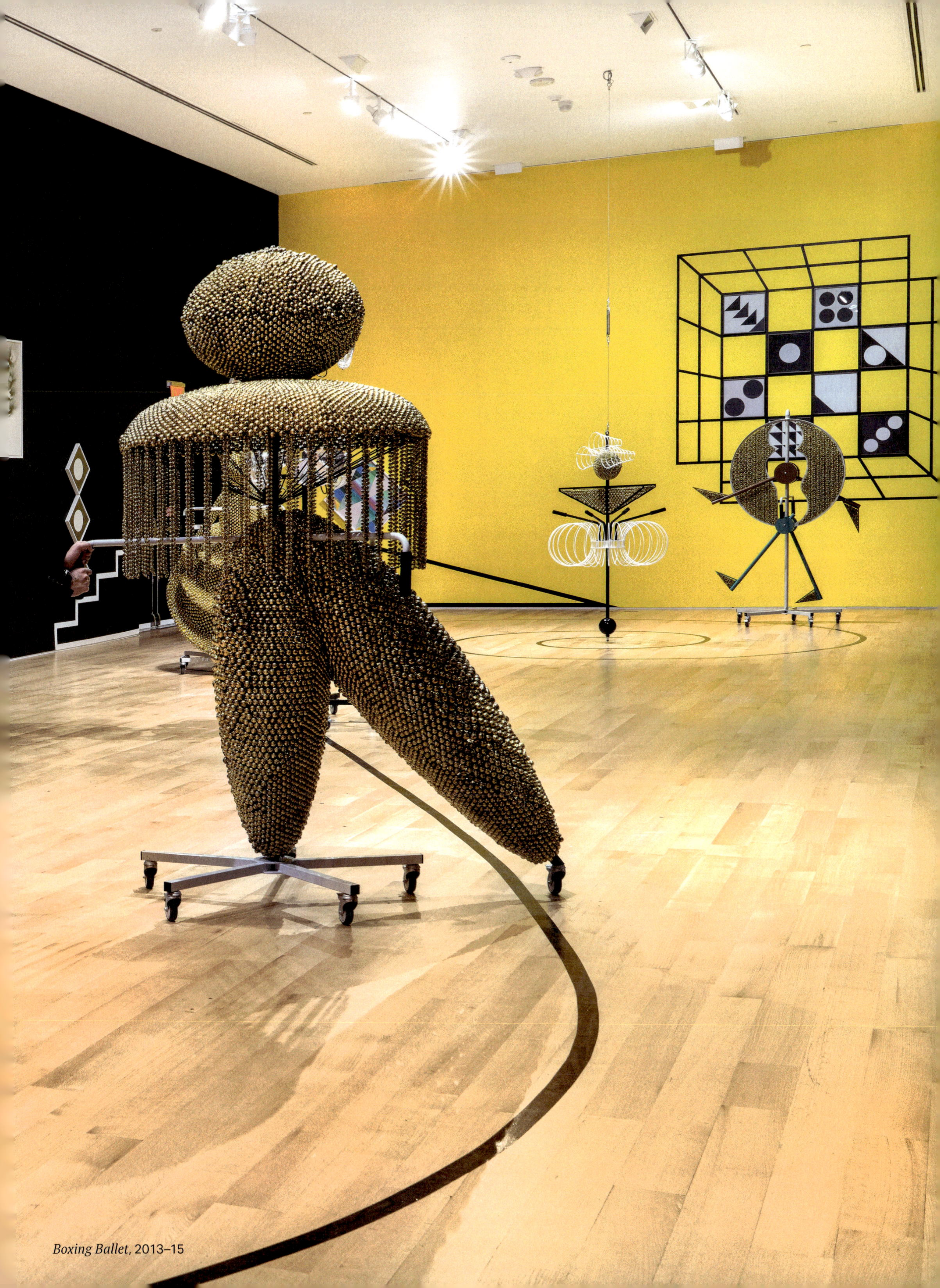

Boxing Ballet, 2013–15

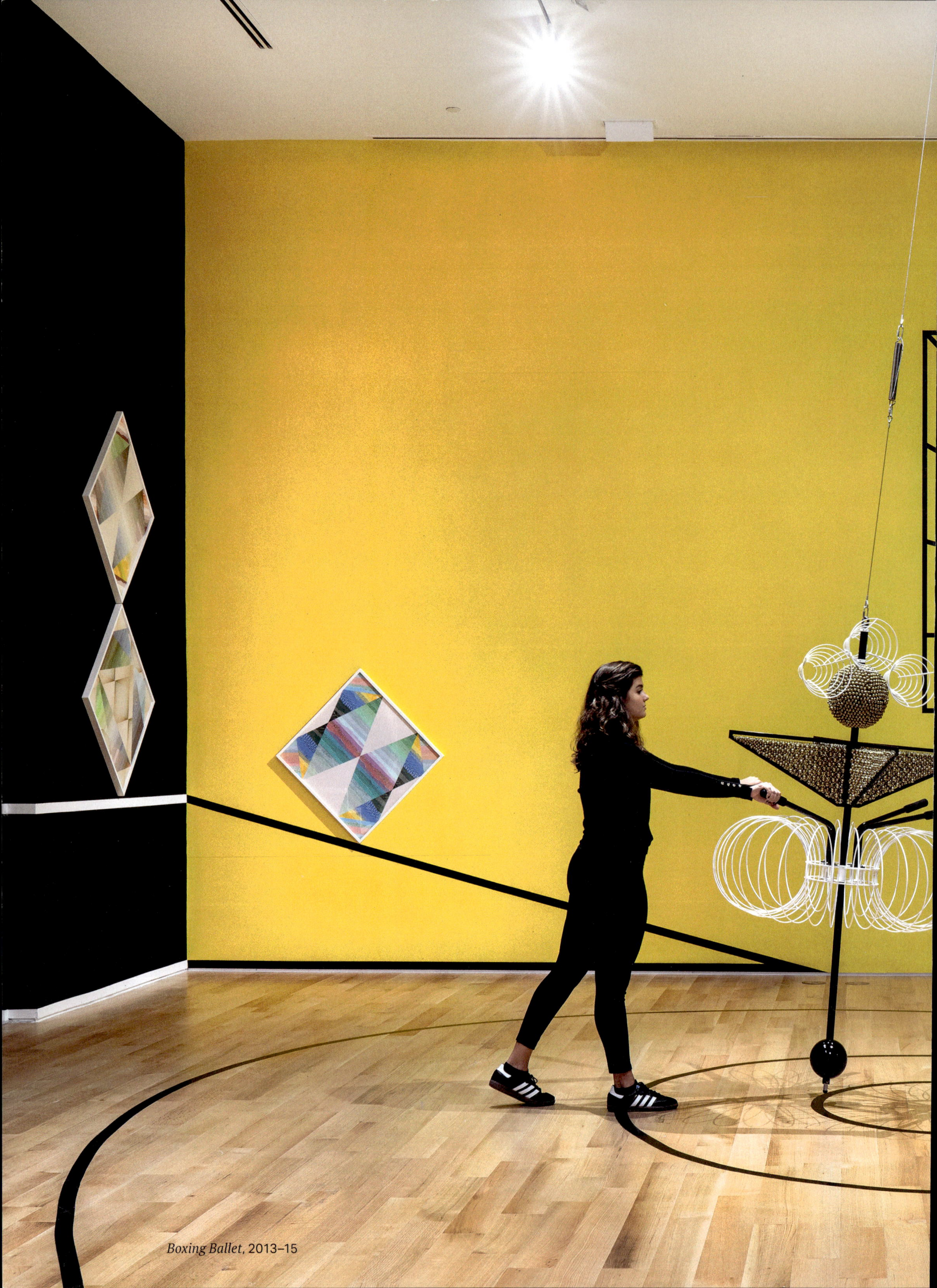

Boxing Ballet, 2013–15

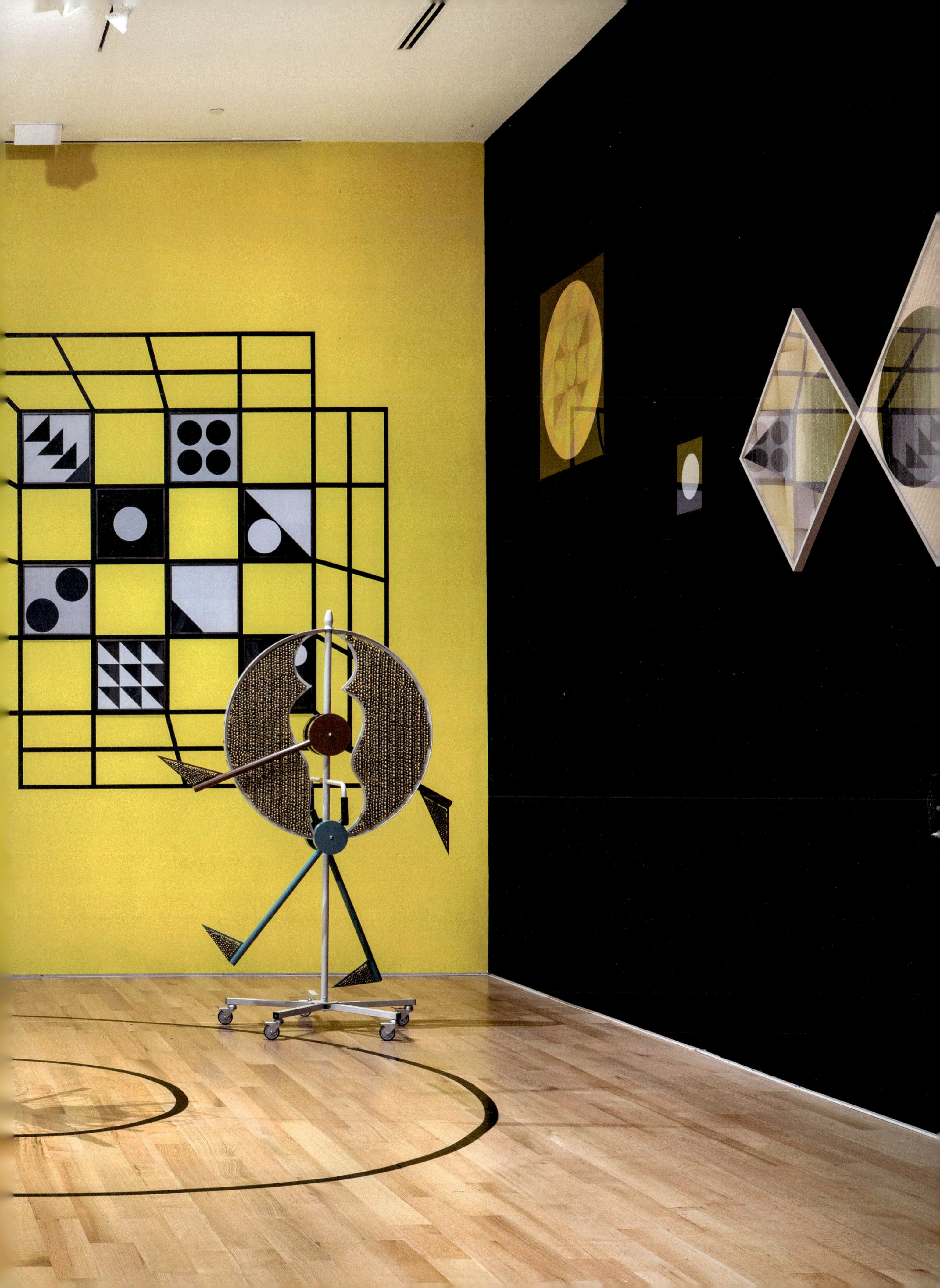

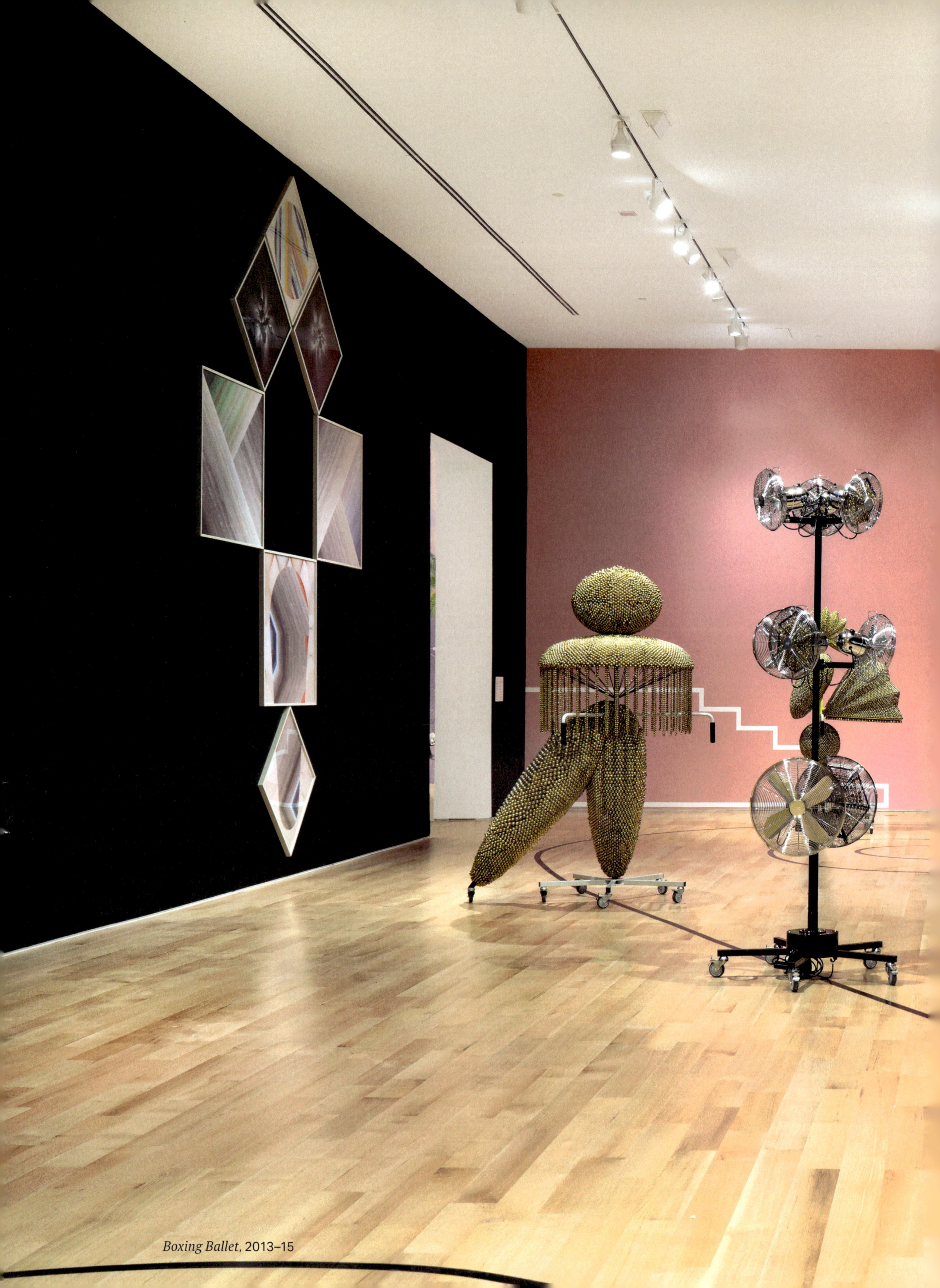

Boxing Ballet, 2013–15

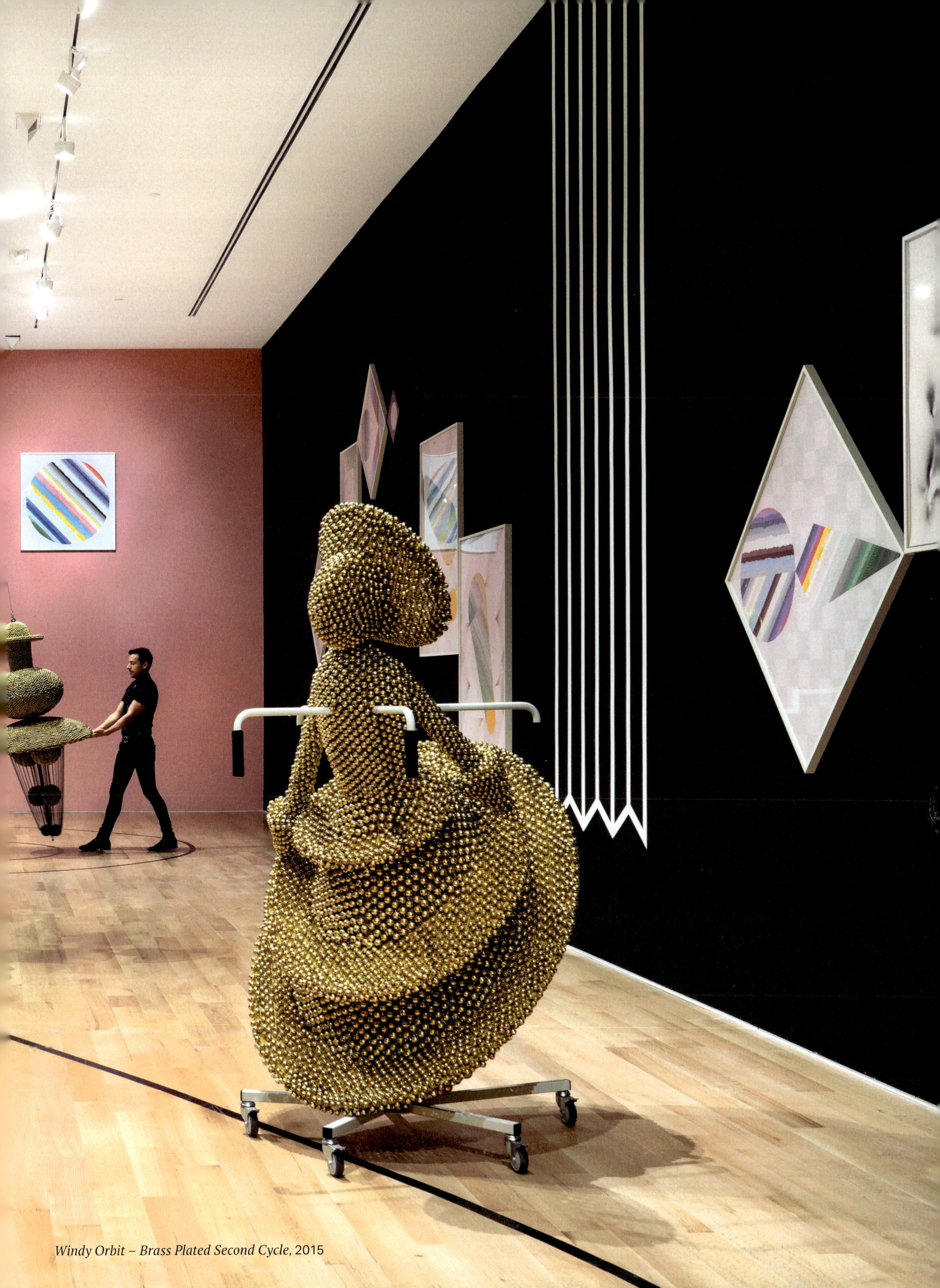

Windy Orbit – Brass Plated Second Cycle, 2015

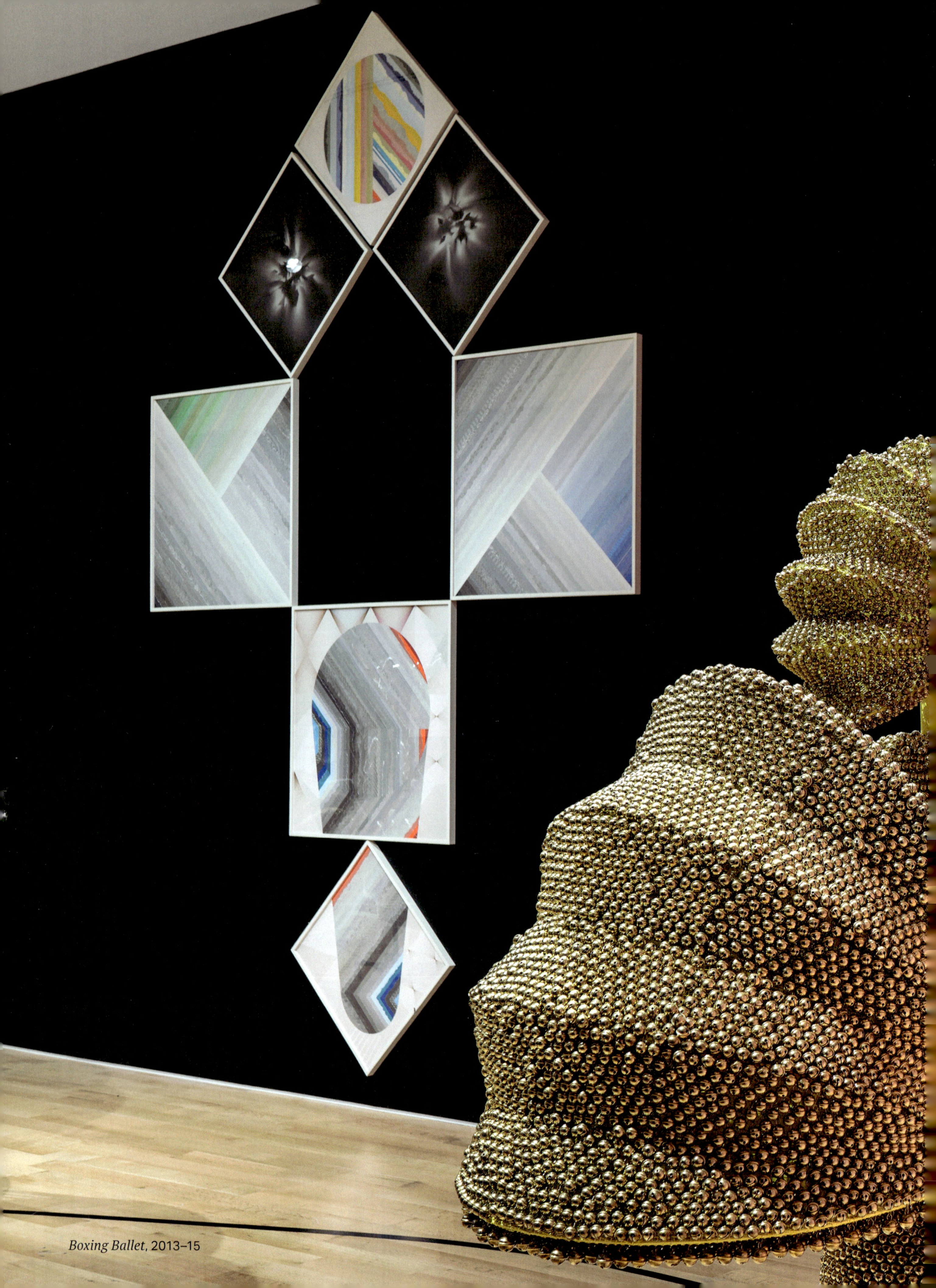

Boxing Ballet, 2013–15

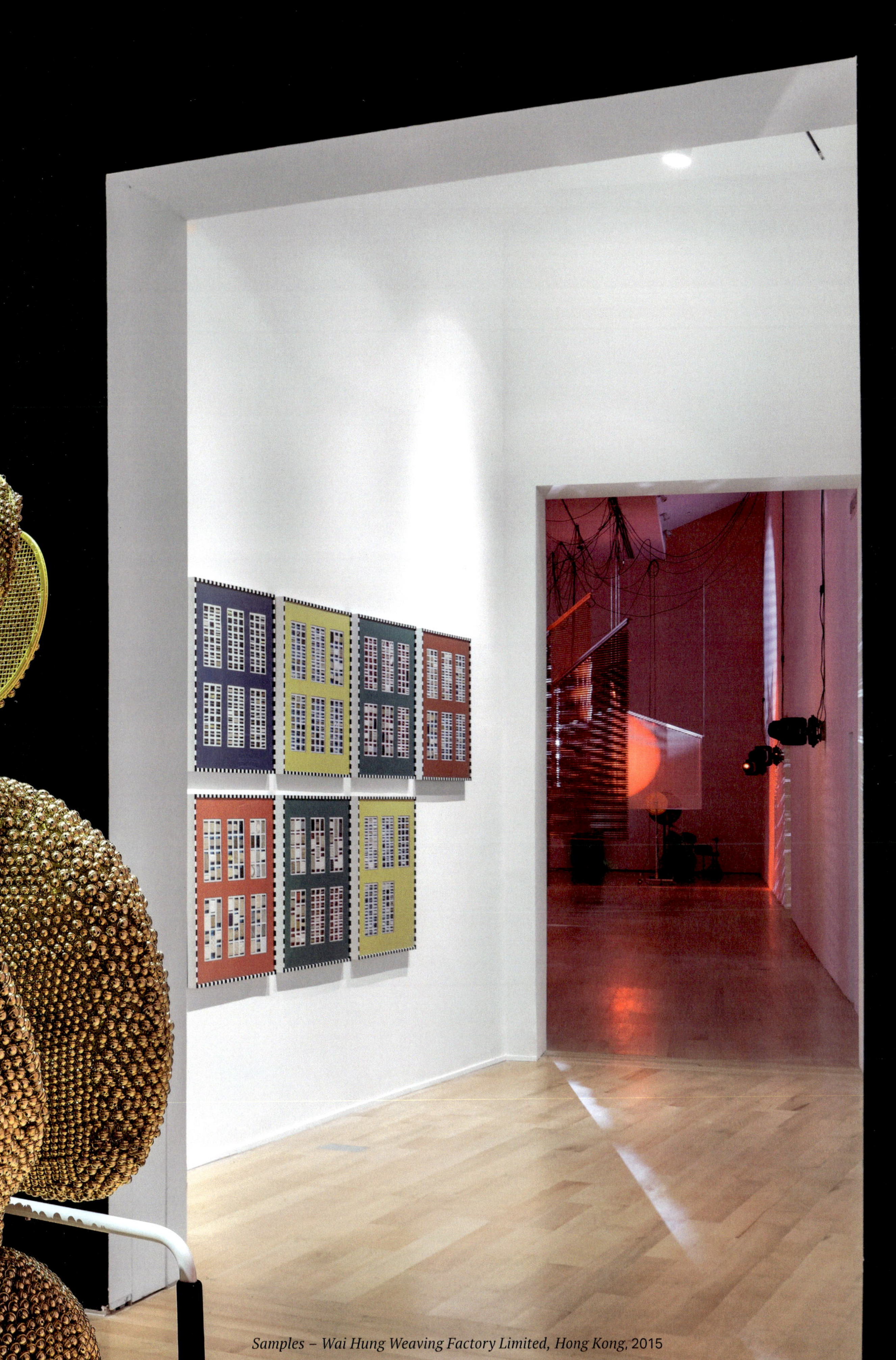

Samples – Wai Hung Weaving Factory Limited, Hong Kong, 2015

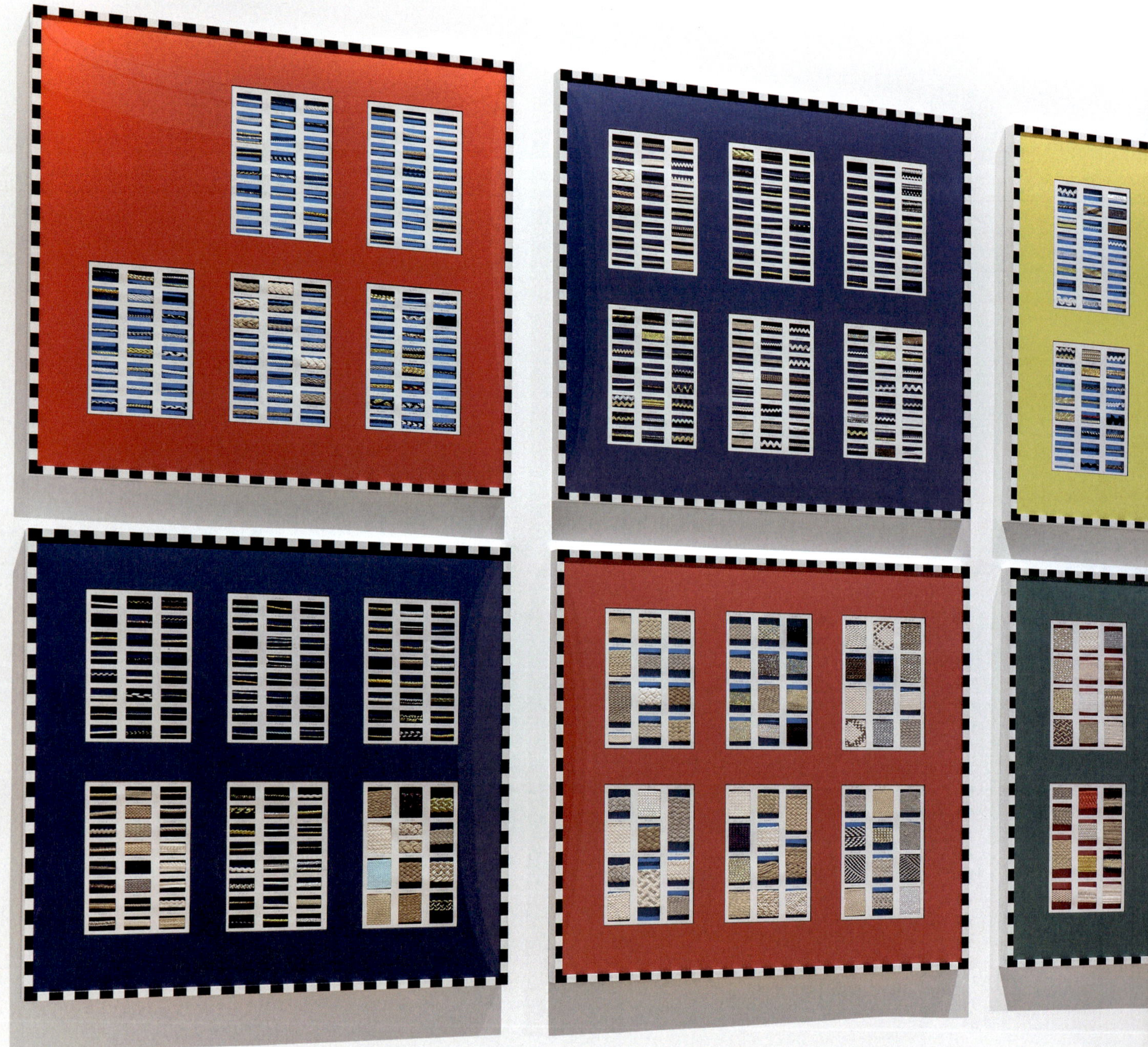

Samples – Wai Hung Weaving Factory Limited, Hong Kong, 2015

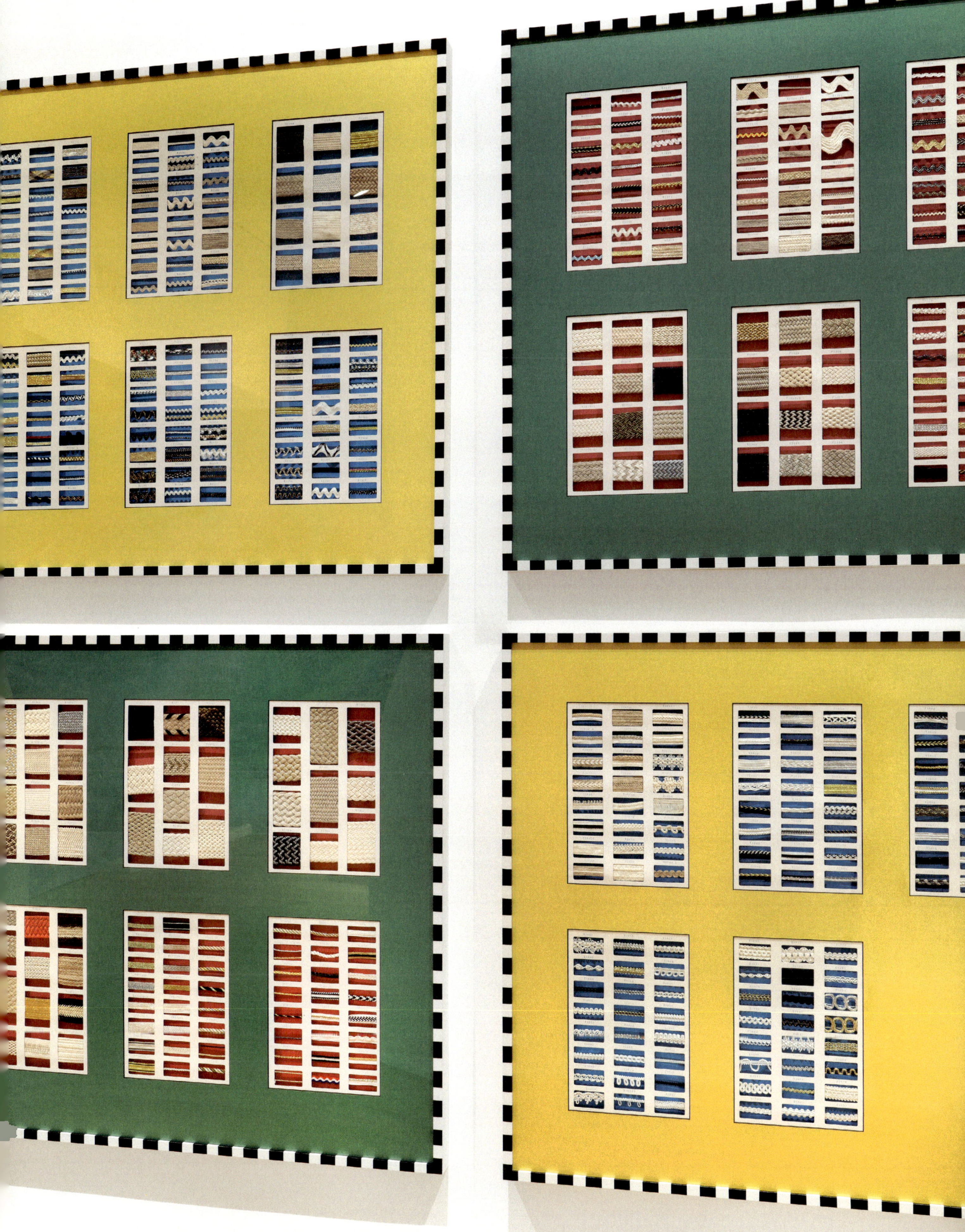

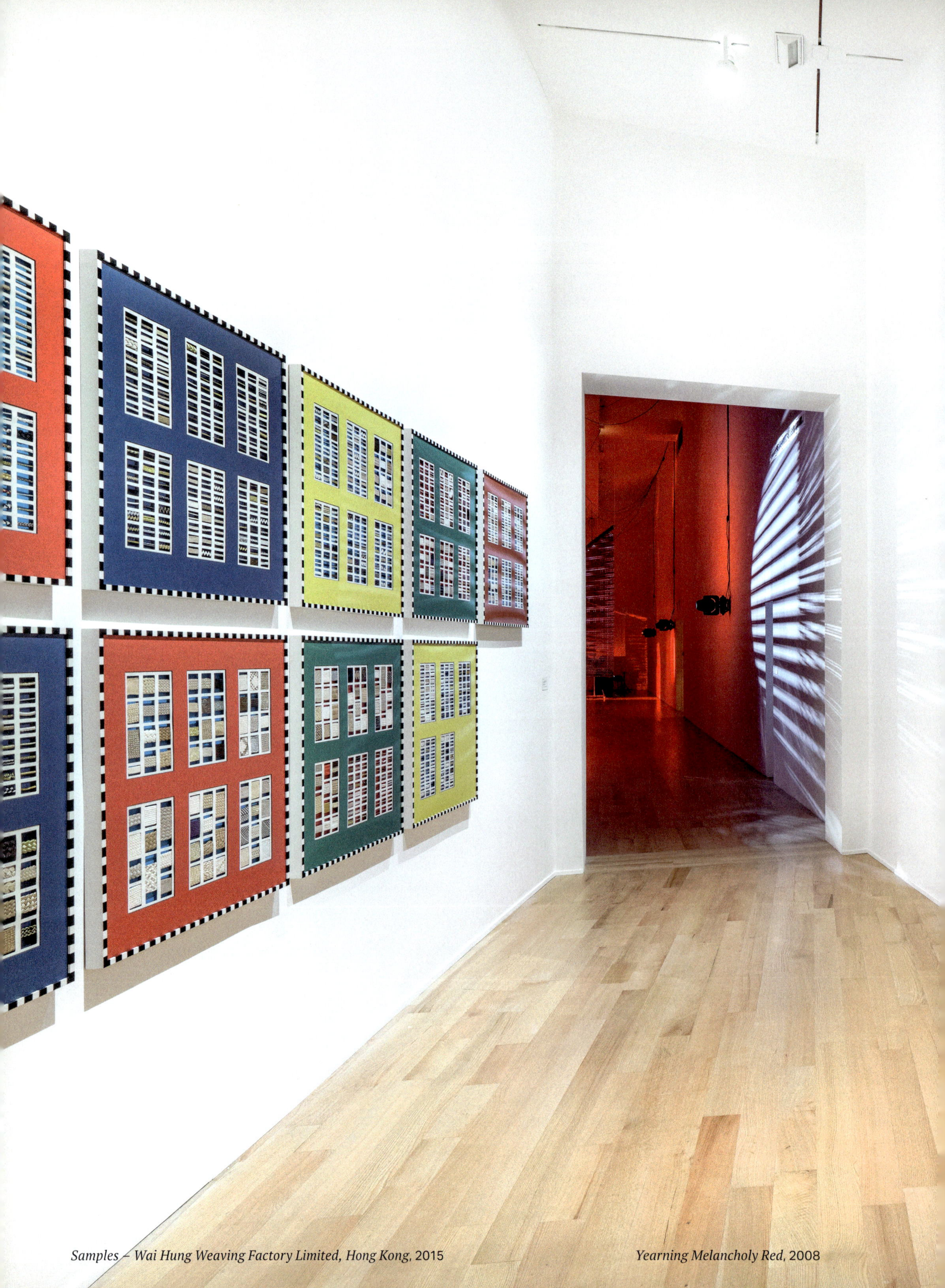

Samples – Wai Hung Weaving Factory Limited, Hong Kong, 2015

Yearning Melancholy Red, 2008

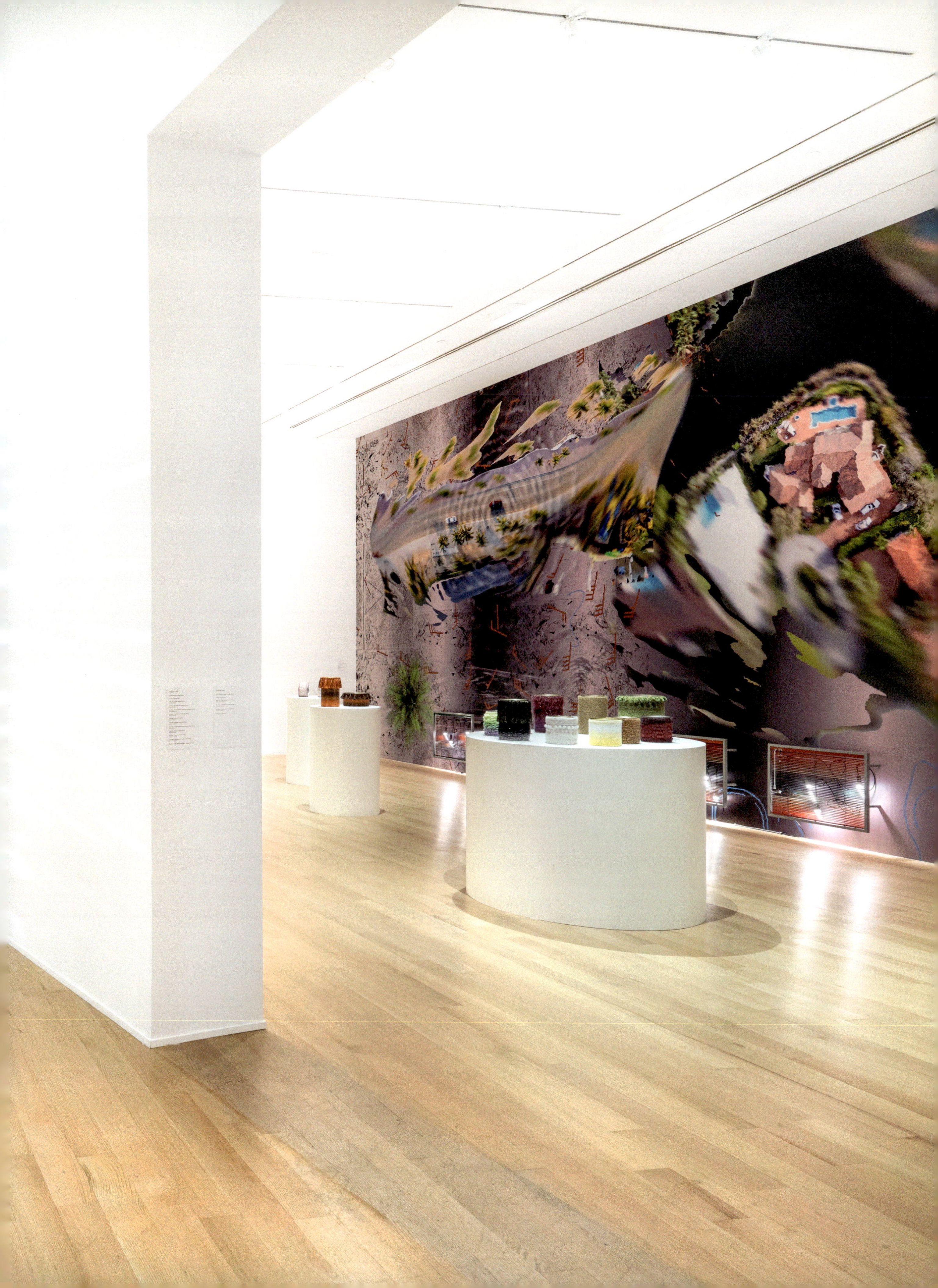

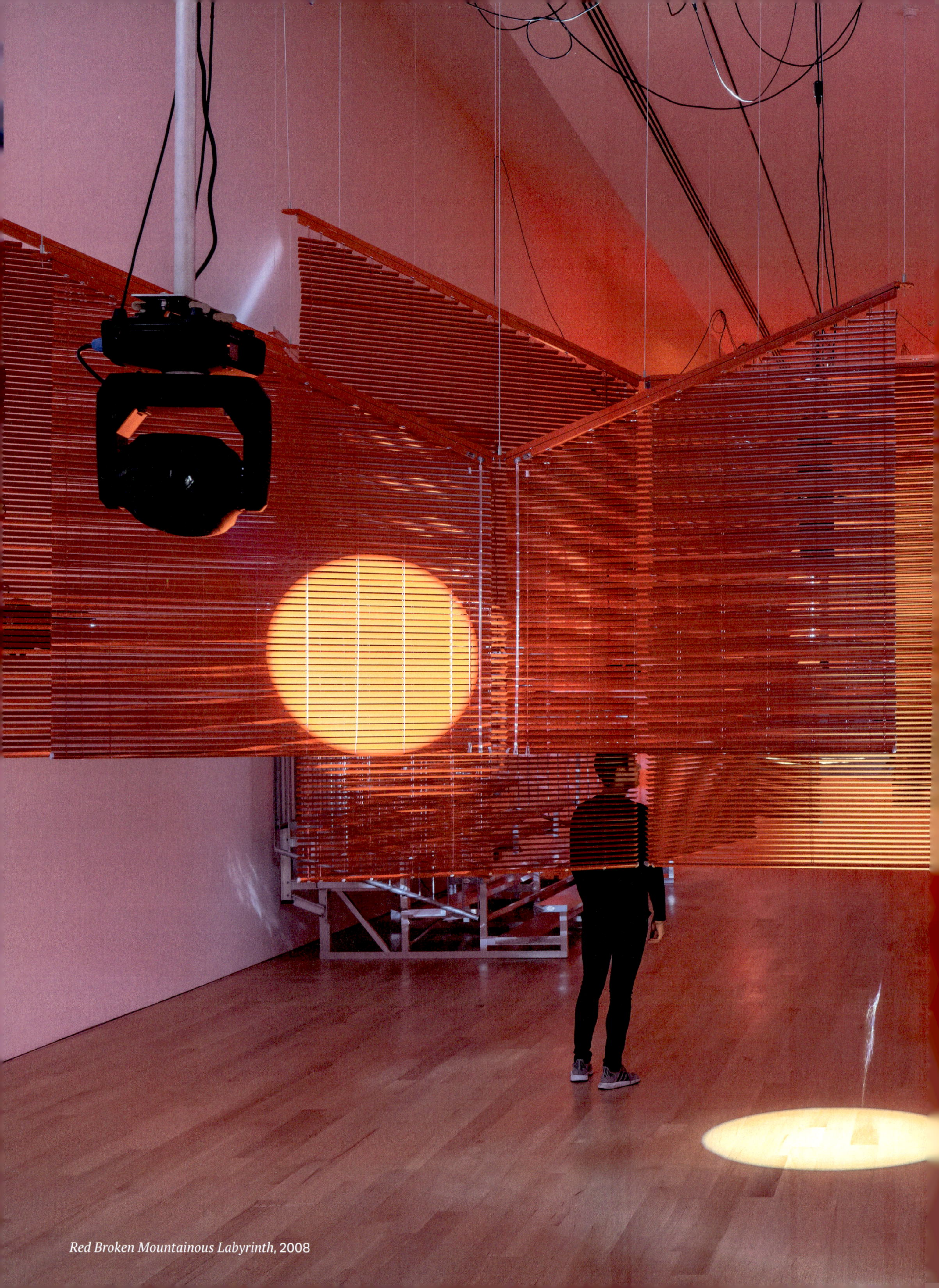

Red Broken Mountainous Labyrinth, 2008

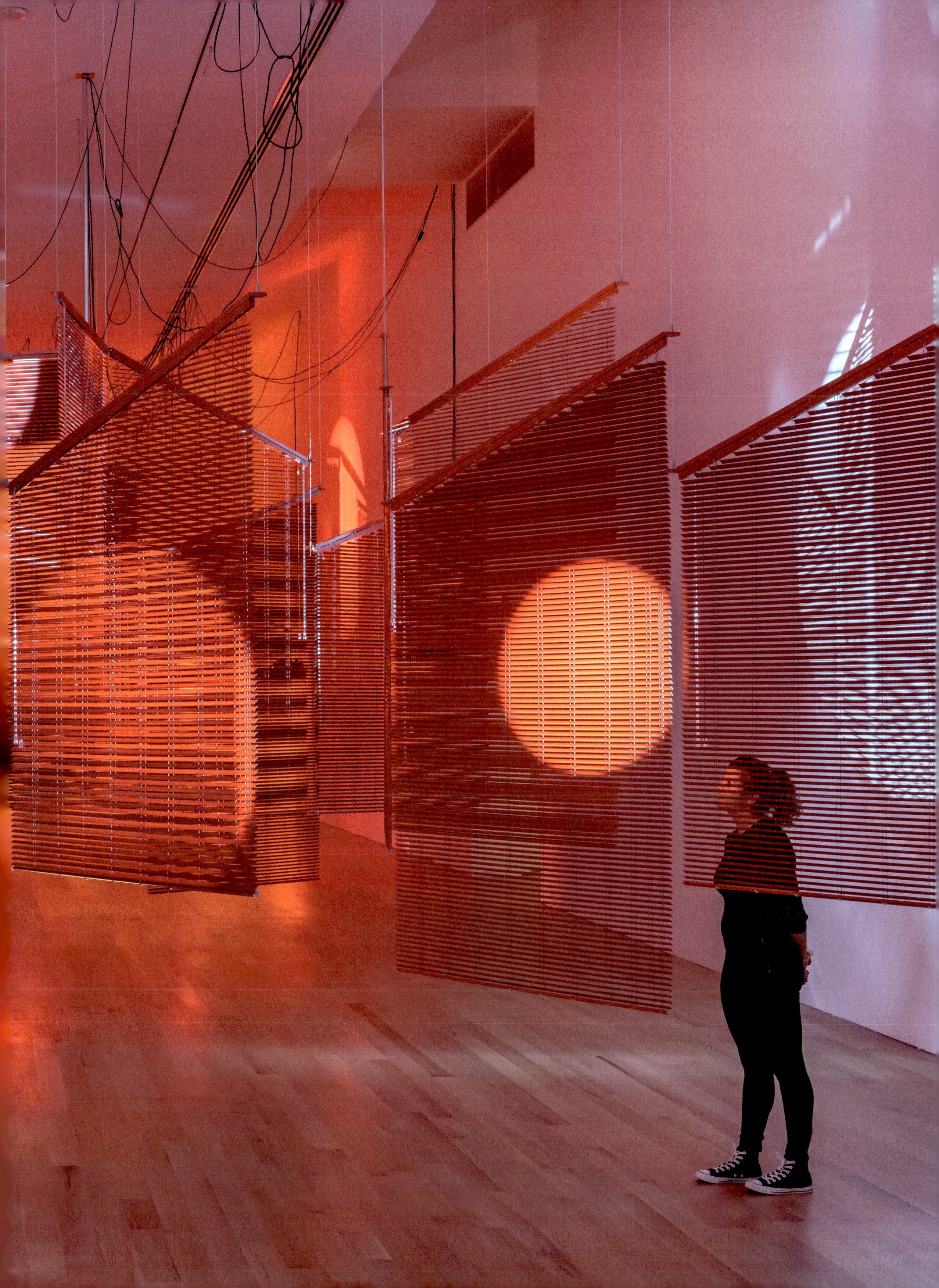

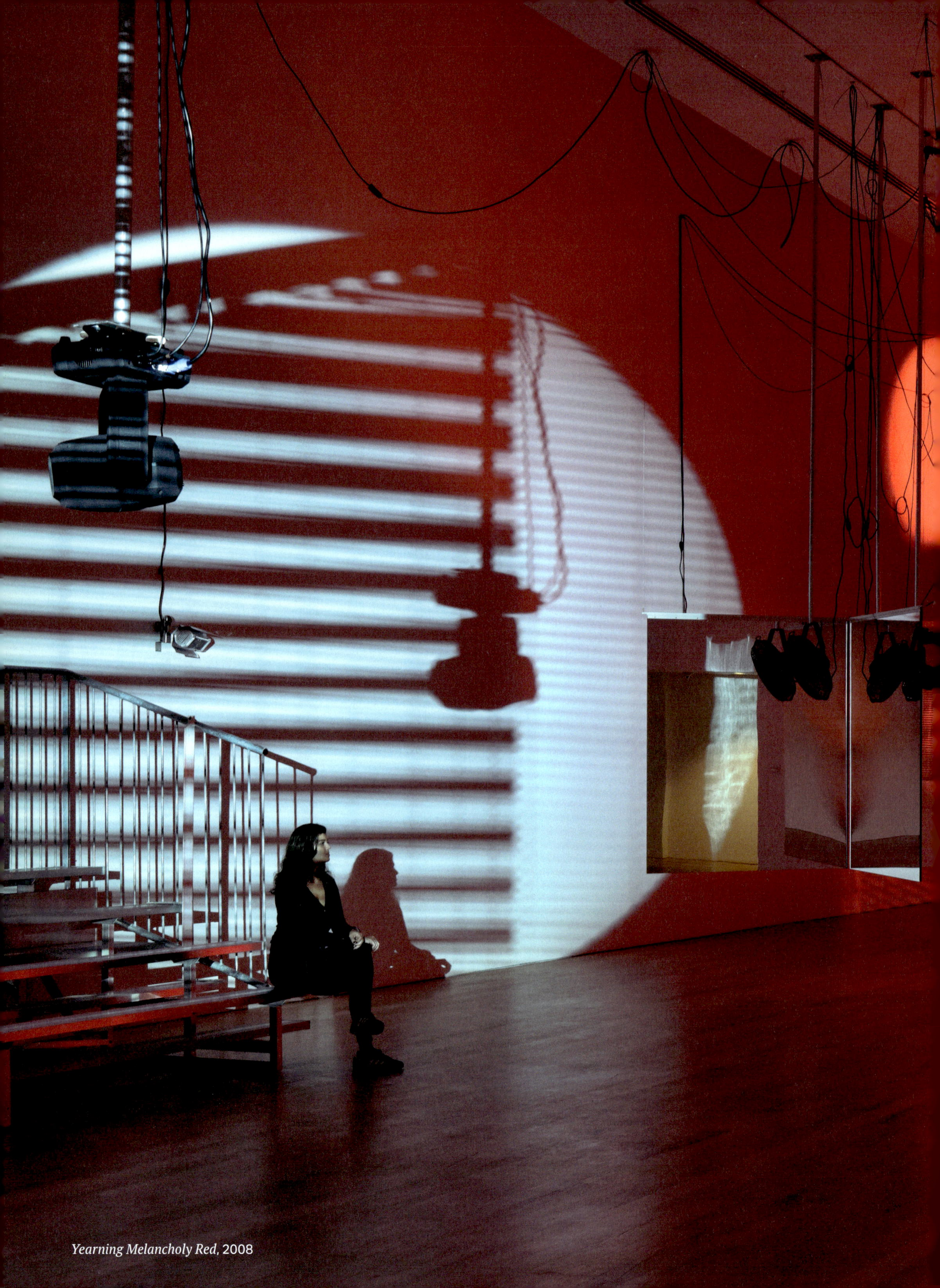

Yearning Melancholy Red, 2008

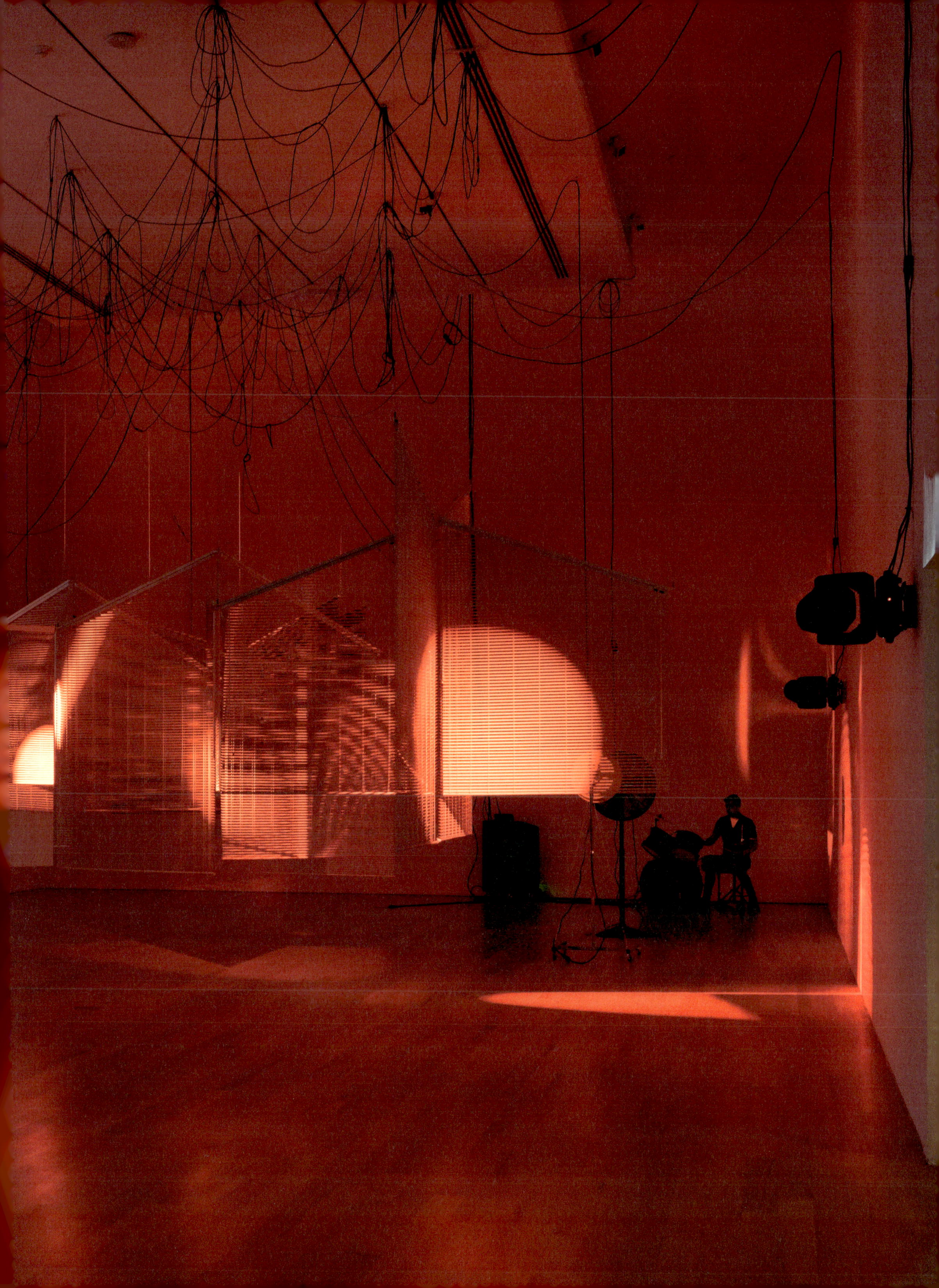

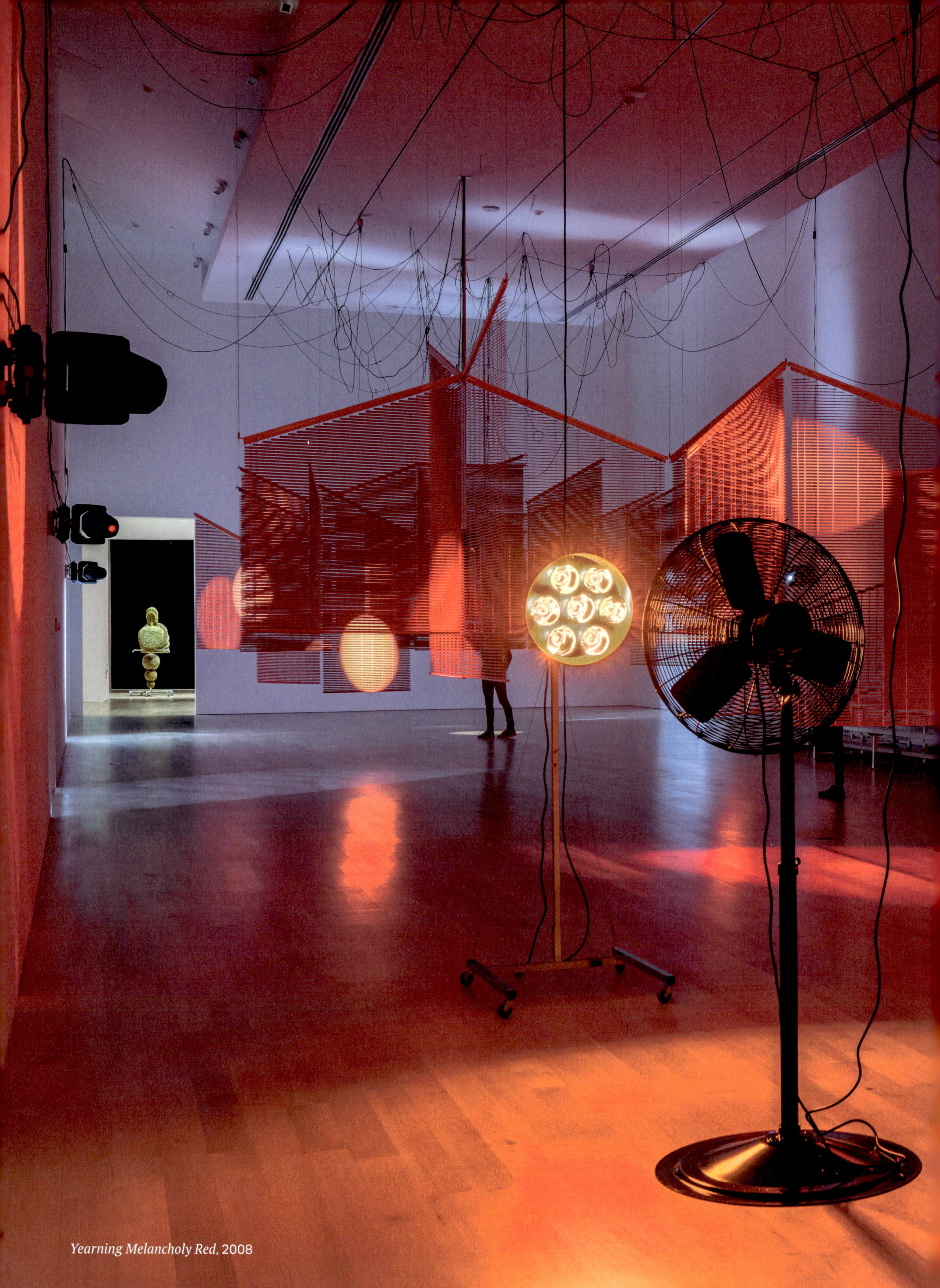

Yearning Melancholy Red, 2008

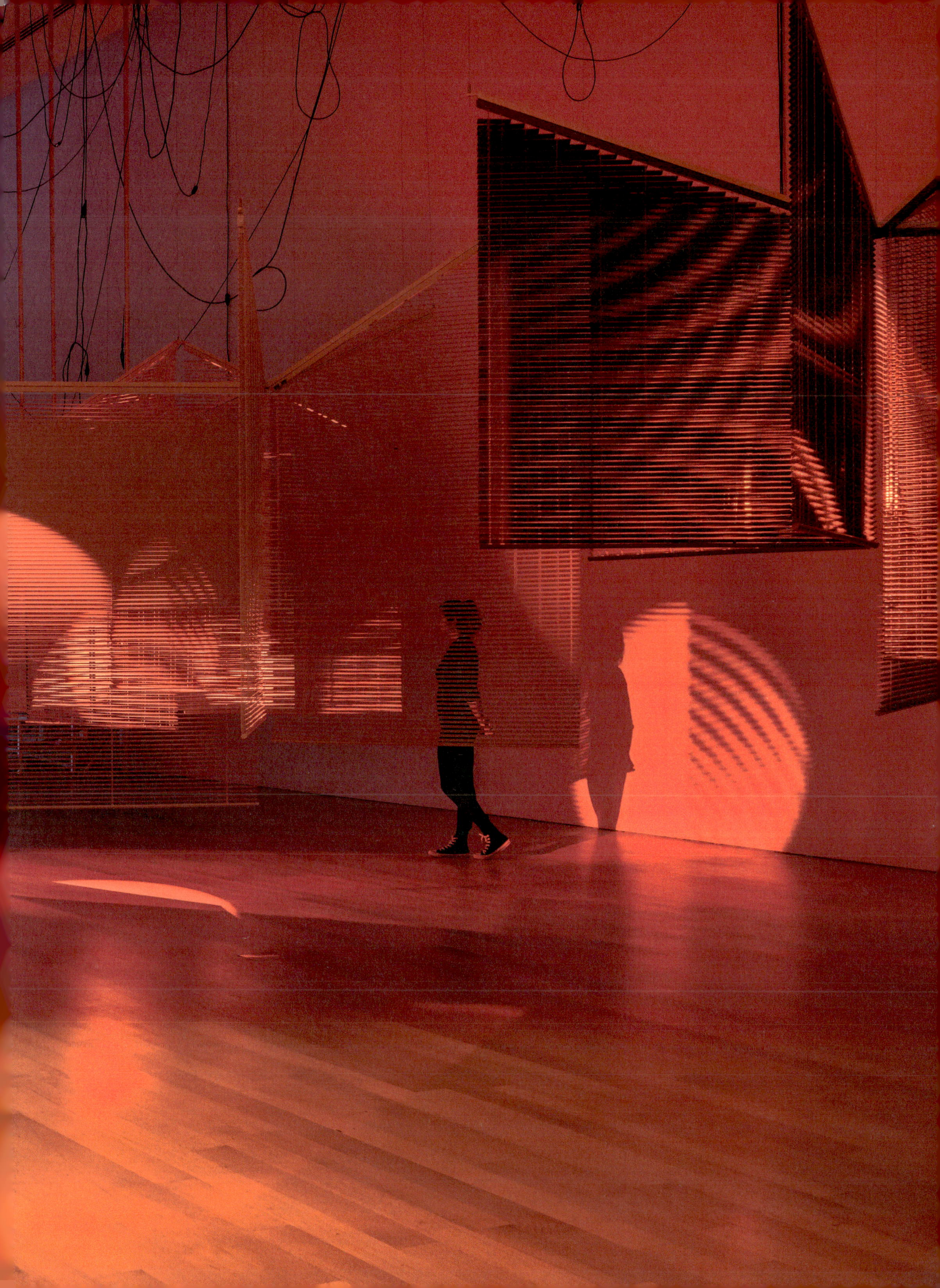

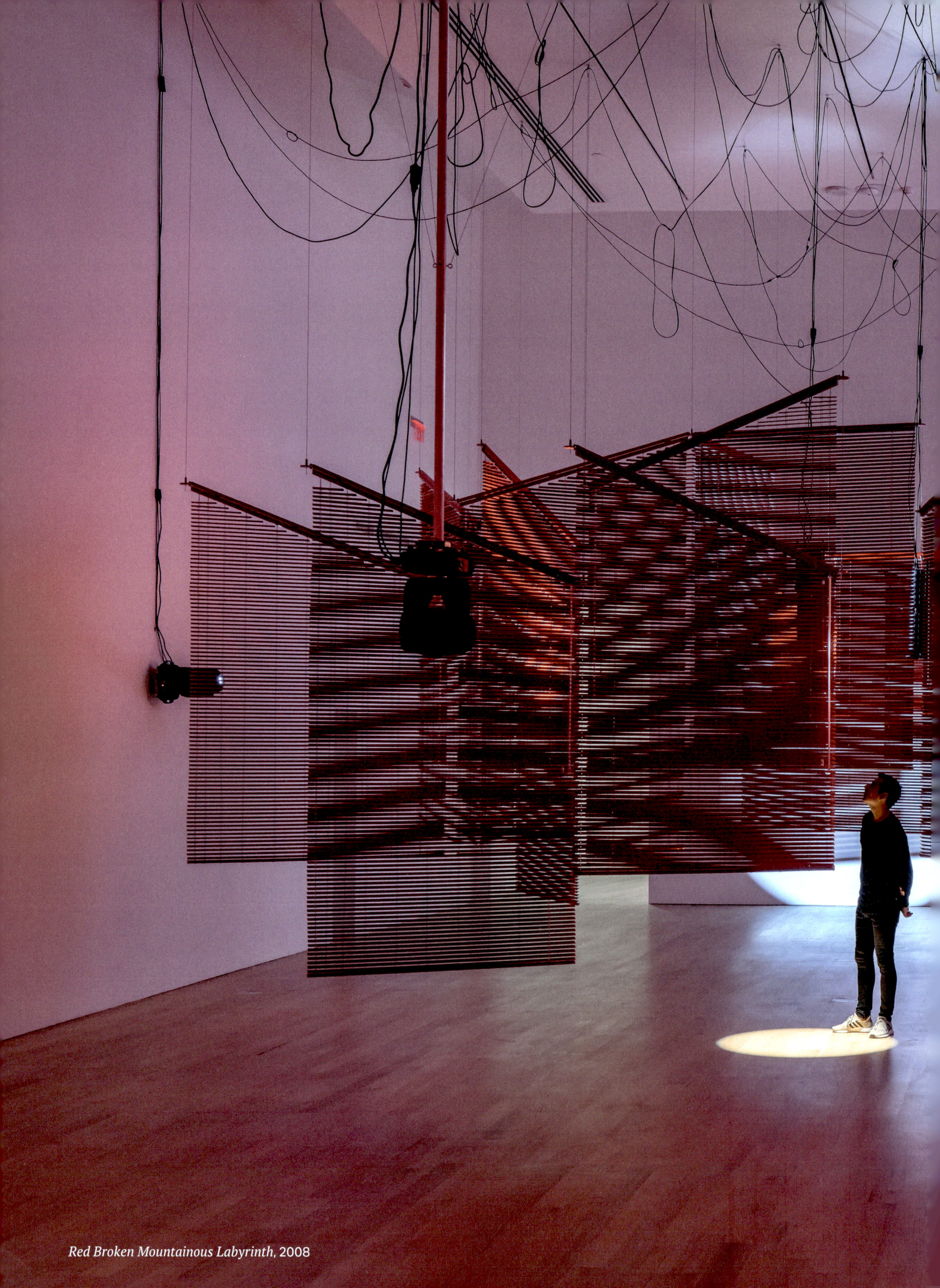

Red Broken Mountainous Labyrinth, 2008

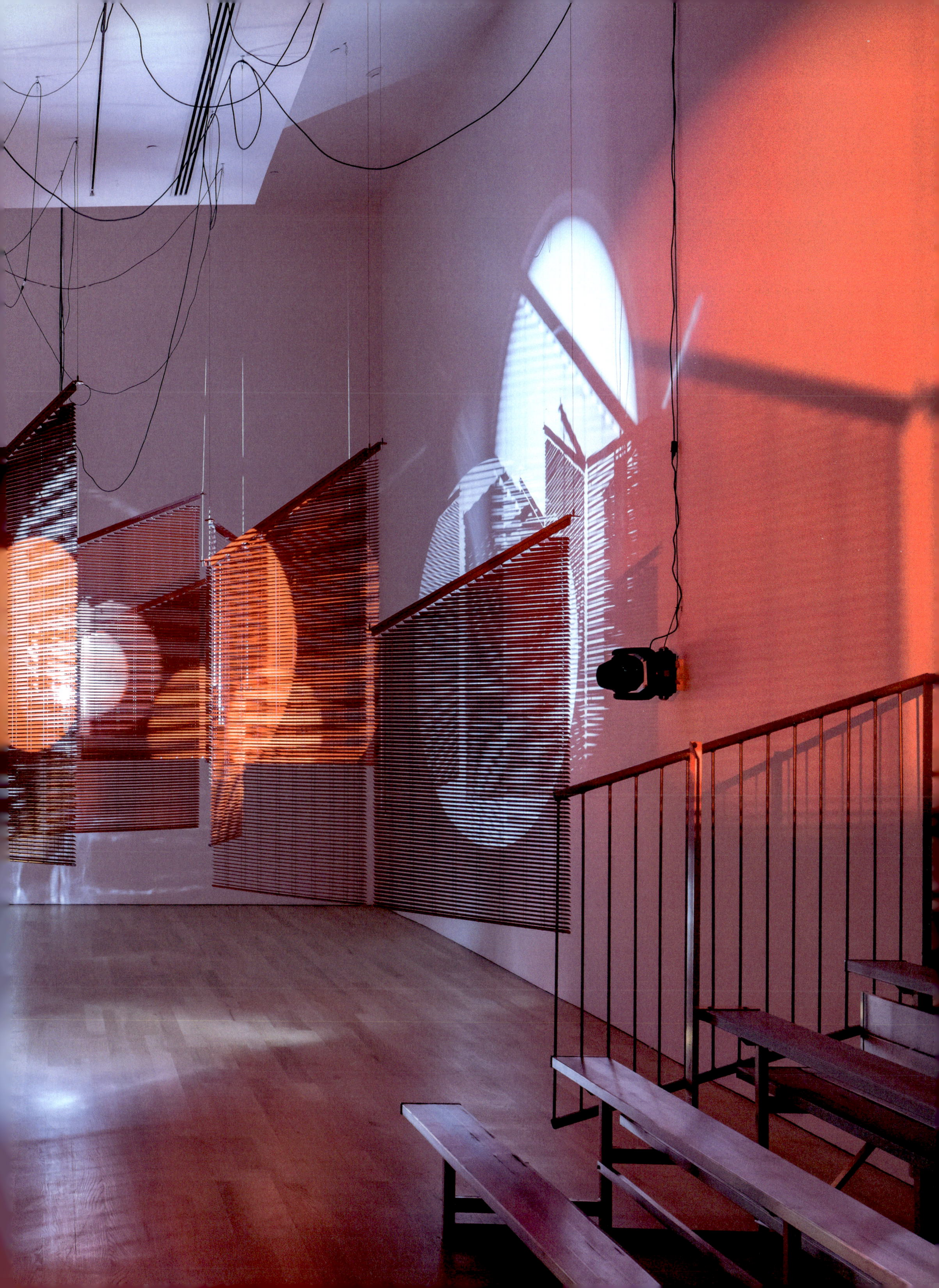

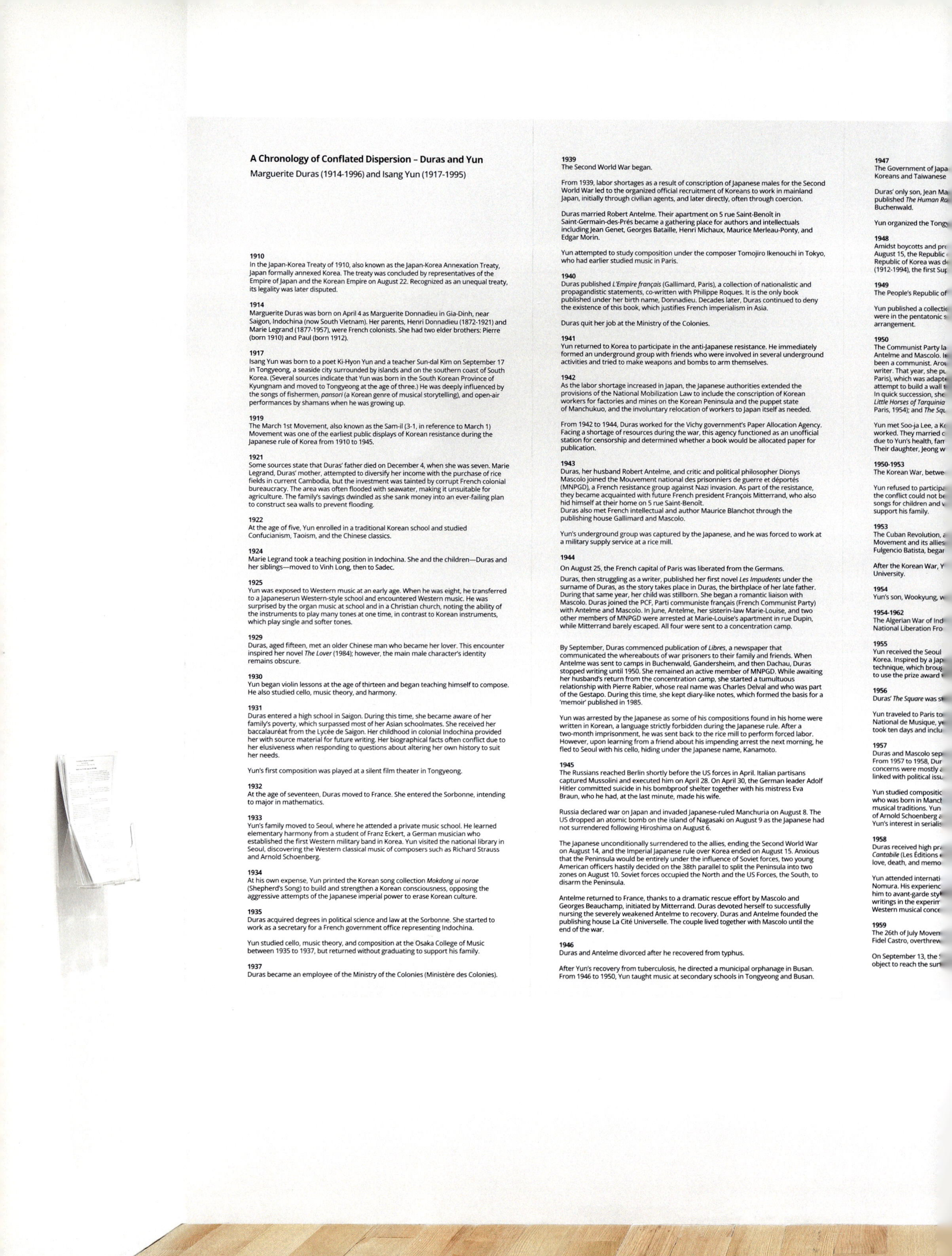

A Chronology of Conflated Dispersion – Duras and Yun

Marguerite Duras (1914-1996) and Isang Yun (1917-1995)

1910
In the Japan-Korea Treaty of 1910, also known as the Japan-Korea Annexation Treaty, Japan formally annexed Korea. The treaty was concluded by representatives of the Empire of Japan and the Korean Empire on August 22. Recognized as an unequal treaty, its legality was later disputed.

1914
Marguerite Duras was born on April 4 as Marguerite Donnadieu in Gia-Dinh, near Saigon, Indochina (now South Vietnam). Her parents, Henri Donnadieu (1872-1921) and Marie Legrand (1877-1957), were French colonists. She had two elder brothers: Pierre (born 1910) and Paul (born 1912).

1917
Isang Yun was born to a poet Ki-Hyon Yun and a teacher Sun-dal Kim on September 17 in Tongyeong, a seaside city surrounded by islands and on the southern coast of South Korea. (Several sources indicate that Yun was born in the South Korean Province of Kyungnam and moved to Tongyeong at the age of three.) He was deeply influenced by the songs of fishermen, *pansori* (a Korean genre of musical storytelling), and open-air performances by shamans when he was growing up.

1919
The March 1st Movement, also known as the Sam-il (3-1, in reference to March 1) Movement was one of the earliest public displays of Korean resistance during the Japanese rule of Korea from 1910 to 1945.

1921
Some sources state that Duras' father died on December 4, when she was seven. Marie Legrand, Duras' mother, attempted to diversify her income with the purchase of rice fields in current Cambodia, but the investment was tainted by corrupt French colonial bureaucracy. The area was often flooded with seawater, making it unsuitable for agriculture. The family's savings dwindled as she sank money into an ever-failing plan to construct sea walls to prevent flooding.

1922
At the age of five, Yun enrolled in a traditional Korean school and studied Confucianism, Taoism, and the Chinese classics.

1924
Marie Legrand took a teaching position in Indochina. She and the children—Duras and her siblings—moved to Vinh Long, then to Sadec.

1925
Yun was exposed to Western music at an early age. When he was eight, he transferred to a Japaneserun Western-style school and encountered Western music. He was surprised by the organ music at school and in a Christian church, noting the ability of the instruments to play many tones at one time, in contrast to Korean instruments, which play single and softer tones.

1929
Duras, aged fifteen, met an older Chinese man who became her lover. This encounter inspired her novel *The Lover* (1984); however, the main male character's identity remains obscure.

1930
Yun began violin lessons at the age of thirteen and began teaching himself to compose. He also studied cello, music theory, and harmony.

1931
Duras entered a high school in Saigon. During this time, she became aware of her family's poverty, which surpassed most of her Asian schoolmates. She received her baccalauréat from the Lycée de Saigon. Her childhood in colonial Indochina provided her with source material for future writing. Her biographical facts often conflict due to her elusiveness when responding to questions about altering her own history to suit her needs.

Yun's first composition was played at a silent film theater in Tongyeong.

1932
At the age of seventeen, Duras moved to France. She entered the Sorbonne, intending to major in mathematics.

1933
Yun's family moved to Seoul, where he attended a private music school. He learned elementary harmony from a student of Franz Eckert, a German musician who established the first Western military band in Korea. Yun visited the national library in Seoul, discovering the Western classical music of composers such as Richard Strauss and Arnold Schoenberg.

1934
At his own expense, Yun printed the Korean song collection *Mokdong ui norae* (Shepherd's Song) to build and strengthen a Korean consciousness, opposing the aggressive attempts of the Japanese imperial power to erase Korean culture.

1935
Duras acquired degrees in political science and law at the Sorbonne. She started to work as a secretary for a French government office representing Indochina.

Yun studied cello, music theory, and composition at the Osaka College of Music between 1935 to 1937, but returned without graduating to support his family.

1937
Duras became an employee of the Ministry of the Colonies (Ministère des Colonies).

1939
The Second World War began.

From 1939, labor shortages as a result of conscription of Japanese males for the Second World War led to the organized official recruitment of Koreans to work in mainland Japan, initially through civilian agents, and later directly, often through coercion.

Duras married Robert Antelme. Their apartment on 5 rue Saint-Benoît in Saint-Germain-des-Prés became a gathering place for authors and intellectuals including Jean Genet, Georges Bataille, Henri Michaux, Maurice Merleau-Ponty, and Edgar Morin.

Yun attempted to study composition under the composer Tomojiro Ikenouchi in Tokyo, who had earlier studied music in Paris.

1940
Duras published *L'Empire français* (Gallimard, Paris), a collection of nationalistic and propagandistic statements, co-written with Philippe Roques. It is the only book published under her birth name, Donnadieu. Decades later, Duras continued to deny the existence of this book, which justifies French imperialism in Asia.

Duras quit her job at the Ministry of the Colonies.

1941
Yun returned to Korea to participate in the anti-Japanese resistance. He immediately formed an underground group with friends who were involved in several underground activities and tried to make weapons and bombs to arm themselves.

1942
As the labor shortage increased in Japan, the Japanese authorities extended the provisions of the National Mobilization Law to include the conscription of Korean workers for factories and mines on the Korean Peninsula and the puppet state of Manchukuo, and the involuntary relocation of workers to Japan itself as needed.

From 1942 to 1944, Duras worked for the Vichy government's Paper Allocation Agency. Facing a shortage of resources during the war, this agency functioned as an unofficial station for censorship and determined whether a book would be allocated paper for publication.

1943
Duras, her husband Robert Antelme, and critic and political philosopher Dionys Mascolo joined the Mouvement national des prisonniers de guerre et déportés (MNPGD), a French resistance group against Nazi invasion. As part of the resistance, they became acquainted with future French president François Mitterrand, who also hid himself at their home on 5 rue Saint-Benoît.
Duras also met French intellectual and author Maurice Blanchot through the publishing house Gallimard and Mascolo.

Yun's underground group was captured by the Japanese, and he was forced to work at a military supply service at a rice mill.

1944
On August 25, the French capital of Paris was liberated from the Germans.

Duras, then struggling as a writer, published her first novel *Les Impudents* under the surname of Duras, as the story takes place in Duras, the birthplace of her late father. During that same year, her child was stillborn. She began a romantic liaison with Mascolo. Duras joined the PCF, Parti communiste français (French Communist Party) with Antelme and Mascolo. In June, Antelme, her sisterin-law Marie-Louise, and two other members of MNPGD were arrested at Marie-Louise's apartment in rue Dupin, while Mitterrand barely escaped. All four were sent to a concentration camp.

By September, Duras commenced publication of *Libres*, a newspaper that communicated the whereabouts of war prisoners to their family and friends. When Antelme was sent to camps in Buchenwald, Gandersheim, and then Dachau, Duras stopped writing until 1950. She remained an active member of MNPGD. While awaiting her husband's return from the concentration camp, she started a tumultuous relationship with Pierre Rabier, whose real name was Charles Delval and who was part of the Gestapo. During this time, she kept diary-like notes, which formed the basis for a 'memoir' published in 1985.

Yun was arrested by the Japanese as some of his compositions found in his home were written in Korean, a language strictly forbidden during the Japanese rule. After a two-month imprisonment, he was sent back to the rice mill to perform forced labor. However, upon learning from a friend about his impending arrest the next morning, he fled to Seoul with his cello, hiding under the Japanese name, Kanamoto.

1945
The Russians reached Berlin shortly before the US forces in April. Italian partisans captured Mussolini and executed him on April 28. On April 30, the German leader Adolf Hitler committed suicide in his bombproof shelter together with his mistress Eva Braun, who he had, at the last minute, made his wife.

Russia declared war on Japan and invaded Japanese-ruled Manchuria on August 8. The US dropped an atomic bomb on the island of Nagasaki on August 9 as the Japanese had not surrendered following Hiroshima on August 6.

The Japanese unconditionally surrendered to the allies, ending the Second World War on August 14, and the Imperial Japanese rule over Korea ended on August 15. Anxious that the Peninsula would be entirely under the influence of Soviet forces, two young American officers hastily decided on the 38th parallel to split the Peninsula into two zones on August 10. Soviet forces occupied the North and the US Forces, the South, to disarm the Peninsula.

Antelme returned to France, thanks to a dramatic rescue effort by Mascolo and Georges Beauchamp, initiated by Mitterrand. Duras devoted herself to successfully nursing the severely weakened Antelme to recovery. Duras and Antelme founded the publishing house La Cité Universelle. The couple lived together with Mascolo until the end of the war.

1946
Duras and Antelme divorced after he recovered from typhus.

After Yun's recovery from tuberculosis, he directed a municipal orphanage in Busan. From 1946 to 1950, Yun taught music at secondary schools in Tongyeong and Busan.

1947
The Government of Japa
Koreans and Taiwanese

Duras' only son, Jean Ma
published *The Human Ra*
Buchenwald.

Yun organized the Tong

1948
Amidst boycotts and pr
August 15, the Republic
Republic of Korea was d
(1912-1994), the first Sup

1949
The People's Republic of

Yun published a collecti
were in the pentatonic s
arrangement.

1950
The Communist Party la
Antelme and Mascolo. I
been a communist. Aro
writer. That year, she pu
Paris), which was adapt
attempt to build a wall
In quick succession, she
Little Horses of Tarquinia
Paris, 1954); and *The Squ*

Yun met Soo-ja Lee, a K
worked. They married
due to Yun's health, fam
Their daughter, Jeong w

1950-1953
The Korean War, betwe

Yun refused to particip
the conflict could not b
songs for children and
support his family.

1953
The Cuban Revolution,
Movement and its allies
Fulgencio Batista, begar

After the Korean War, Y
University.

1954
Yun's son, Wookyung, w

1954-1962
The Algerian War of Ind
National Liberation Fro

1955
Yun received the Seoul
Korea. Inspired by a Jap
technique, which broug
to use the prize award

1956
Duras' *The Square* was s

Yun traveled to Paris to
National de Musique, y
took ten days and inclu

1957
Duras and Mascolo sep
From 1957 to 1958, Dur
concerns were mostly
linked with political issu

Yun studied compositic
who was born in Manc
musical traditions. Yun
of Arnold Schoenberg
Yun's interest in serialis

1958
Duras received high pr
Cantabile (Les Éditions
love, death, and memo

Yun attended internati
Nomura. His experienc
him to avant-garde sty
writings in the experim
Western musical conce

1959
The 26th of July Movem
Fidel Castro, overthrew

On September 13, the
object to reach the sur

A Chronology of Conflated Dispersion – Duras and Yun, 2018

ᴚegistration Act, which defined Japanese

onys Mascolo, was born. Antelme
e, Paris), narrating his experience in

and played the cello.

ere created on the Korean Peninsula. On
shed in the South. The Democratic People's
er 9 in the North by Kim Il-sung
th Korea until his death.

ed.

titled *Dalmuri* (Lunar Halo). These songs
ongs and featured Western harmonic

onist, and she resigned, together with
owever, Duras stated that she had always
blished her reputation as a professional
raphical novel, *The Sea Wall* (Gallimard,
narrative investigates a mother's failed
rom flooding her farmland.
from Gibraltar (Gallimard, Paris, 1952); *The*
53); *Whole Days in the Trees* (Gallimard,
1955).

er at Busan Normal School where he
persistent opposition from Lee's family
ession as a musician.
r 20.

outh Korea, began on June 25, 1950.

and stated that he could not believe that
manner. During this period, he composed
. He also wrote film soundtracks to

del Castro's revolutionary 26th of July
arian government of Cuban President

everal universities including Seoul National

er 1.

t between France and the Algerian
independence from France.

st prestigious award conferred by South
osef Rufer's writing on the twelve-tone
nal frame to music, Yun was determined
e to study new forms of music.

amps-Elysées, co-directed by Claude Martin.

bin and Pierre Revel at the Conservatoire
in Korea. His journey to Paris from Seoul
ong Kong, and Istanbul.

ce-Observateur, a left-wing magazine. Her
d of groups or individuals, which she
xture of everyday individual experiences.

at the College of Music in Berlin. Blacher,
hina, advised Yun to retain his Asian
ve-tone technique from Josef Rufer, a pupil
writing on the technique that aroused

ich she followed with the novel *Moderato*
this period, the ideas of sexual desire,
g major themes in her later works.

tadt and met Nam June Paik and Yoshio
er of modern music at the time, exposed
rporation of Asian philosophy and
uraged Yun to integrate Eastern and

tionary organization then a party led by
dictatorship in Cuba.

nission became the first human-made

Filmmaker Alain Resnais asked Duras to write the screenplay for *Hiroshima Mon Amour*. The film received a lot of attention and led Duras to focus on writing for screen. Duras was later nominated for an Academy Award for Best Original Screenplay.

Yun's *Music for Seven Instruments* (1959) premiered at the International Vacation Courses for New Music in Darmstadt on September 4. Two days later, Herman Kruyt played *Five Pieces for Piano* (1958) at its premiere at the Gaudeamus Muziekweek in Bilthoven in the Netherlands. For this work, Yun compositionally drew upon the piano works of the Second Viennese School. Yun moved to Krefeld, Germany.

1960
Named for its number of signatories and published in 1960, the 'Manifesto of the 121' included Duras, Antelme, Jean-Paul Sartre, Alain Robbe-Grillet, Henri Lefebvre, and Alain Resnais. These 121 intellectuals refused to participate in the war against the Algerians, whom they felt were oppressed by the French.
Duras' *Moderato Cantabile* was adapted for film by director Peter Brook and starred Jeanne Moreau and Jean-Paul Belmondo. Moreau's character leads a boring life as the wife of a big steel manufacturer. Her life changes when she witnesses the murder of a woman by her lover. Her fascination with this violent love affair sparks a morbid relationship with a man played by Belmondo.
Duras began to exhibit signs of alcoholism and by the 1960s, had published eight novels.
At the International Society of Contemporary Music festival in Cologne, the legendary Novák Quartet (led by Dušan Pandula) from Prague premiered Yun's *String Quartet III* (1959).

1961
Organized and carried out by Park Chung-hee, the May 16 Military Coup d'état took place in South Korea.

In Darmstadt, Michael Gielen conducted the premiere of Yun's *Symphonic Scene* (1960), which was inspired by the painting style of Jackson Pollock. In September, Yun's wife Soo-ja joined him in Germany. Despite Yun's emerging popularity, he was in a financially precarious situation. He supported his wife and himself using the proceeds from a South Korean Foundation for the Development of Culture prize and a job as an East Asian music expert for a radio station.

1962
Francis Travis directed Yun's orchestral piece *Bara* (1960) in Berlin, merging the twelve-tone technique with Korean Buddhist musical traditions. The title is taken from *Bara-chum* (Dance with the Cymbals), a Korean temple dance, performed in strides before the altar portrait of Buddha and transmitted to the present day. *Bara* (or para) is the name of a Korean percussion instrument, the cymbal. This slightly curved metal disc is mostly employed in pairs and occurs in a specific Korean Buddhist ceremony.

While Yun's early works were generally well-received, he faced several obstacles. Performers had difficulty interpreting his music, and he encountered rejections and a few negative reviews. Based on these incidents, Yun consciously simplified his notation.

1963
Yun visited the Great Tomb of Gangseo in North Korea, an ancient decorated tomb from the Goguryeo dynasty (37 BC – 668 AD) thought to have been painted around the sixth or seventh century. The mural depicts four guardian deities—the Azure Dragon of the East, the White Tiger of the West, the Vermillion Bird of the South, and the Black Tortoise of the North. The deities are believed to relate to the four cardinal directions, the four seasons, and the twenty-eight major constellations. They are said to ward off evil influences and ensure the balance of yin and yang energy. Painted without any background decoration, the deities assume a commanding presence on the walls. Vigorously executed in realistic strokes, they are regarded as some of the finest works in East Asian painting.

1964
Duras collaborated with Gérard Jarlot for the screenplay of the telefilm *Sans merveille*. She published *The Ravishing of Lol Stein* (Gallimard, Paris).

Yun's daughter and son joined their parents in Germany. After receiving a Ford Foundation Grant for artists working in Berlin, Yun decided to settle in the city.

1965
Duras staged *Whole Days in the Trees*. She published *The Rivers and the Forests, The Square, La Musica* (Gallimard, Paris), and *The Vice-Consul* (Gallimard, Paris).

Yun's *Der Traum des Liu-Tung* (The Dream of Liu-Tung, 1965) premiered in Berlin. The opera has a prelude, four dream images, and a postlude. The libretto is based on a fourteenth-century Chinese didactic drama by Ma Chi-Yuan about a Confucian scholar's conversion to Taoism.

1966
The premiere of Yun's *Réak* for large orchestra (1966) was done under the direction of Ernest Bour in Donaueschingen. In *Réak*, Yun imparted a ritualistic character that evokes the mood of Korean court music in combination with his personal musical language using a main tone and sound complex techniques.
Asian musical instruments including the Korean bak (a wooden clapper) and a Thai gong were featured. Yun studied and lectured at the Aspen and Tanglewood festivals in the US for two months.

1967
On June 17, Yun was kidnapped from West Berlin by the South Korean secret service. He was taken to Seoul via Bonn, condemned for espionage, and threatened with life imprisonment by the Park Chung-hee government. Yun, along with the poet Cheon Sang-byeong, painter Yi Eungno, and scores of other innocent people, were jailed, tortured, and forced into confessions of communist subversion in what became known as the East Berlin Incident. According to the Korean Central Intelligence Agency (KCIA), 194 people were involved, mostly intellectuals, artists, scholars, and elites.
In October, Yun received permission to compose in his unheated prison cell.

1968
In early May, during the student occupation protests, Duras signed a petition published in *Le Monde* supporting the students. On May 20, the Students-Writers Action Committee was created; Duras, Antelme, Mascolo, and Blanchot joined. It is thought that one of the most famous slogans from this period—'Sous les pavés, la plage' (Under the paving stones, the beach)—was coined by Duras.

During his time in prison cell, Yun worked successively on three pieces. The opera *Butterfly Widow* (1967/68), which Yun had started composing in Germany, was

completed on February 5. It is based on a C
transmigration of souls.
He also wrote *Riul* (Law), for clarinet and pia
violoncello. *Images* for flute, oboe, violin an
room where he was transferred to after a p
Yun's 1963 visit to the Great Tomb of Gangs
southwest of Pyongyang. Yun's visit was cru

1969
The US' Apollo 11 was the first manned mis

From June to July, following the dissolution
Lettres nouvelles published five anonymous
Students-Writers Action Committee. Duras an
Mascolo contributed three.
Duras' feature-length film *Destroy, She Said*
the same title. The student movement and

After international protests led by Igor Stra
Karajan, and the efforts of his friends and t
the end of February, returning to West Berl
released earlier. He then taught compositic
Hanover till 1971.

1970
In protest against substandard labor condi
year old worker and workers' rights activist
death in public. His suicide led to the forma
Korea.

The 1970s was a period of filmmaking for D
Neauphle-le-Château, where she lived alon
Duras published *Abahn Sabana David* (Gallir
Blanchot. Here, she described Jews as the r
submissive to any state power but pursuin
perspectives towards the Jewish diaspora a

1971
From 1971 to 1973, Duras wrote screenplay
the Ganges, and *Jaune le soleil*. Jeanne More
role—acted in *Nathalie Granger*. Both actor
Duras once stated that *Nathalie Granger* is
she discovered that the previous owner of
terrifying. Duras also noted that people ter
situation which resonates with the notion c
Scholar Emma Wilson translated one of he
also inscribed, the need for retreat, a whol

Yun became a West German citizen. *Namo*
premiered in Berlin on May 4. The title is dr
and the piece references the singing style c
Spirits (1969/70) premiered in Kiel under Ha
Nuremberg on October 22

1972
President Richard Nixon spent eight days i
Chairman Mao Zedong and signed the Sha

Wolfgang Sawallisch conducted the premie
1972 Olympics in Munich. It is based on a K
often associated with *pansori*, or Korean na
charged narrative of *Shim Cheong*—who sa
a sea ritual, yet is reincarnated—one wond
this repertoire at the postwar Olympic Gan
Professor at the Hochschule der Künste in

1973
The 1973 oil crisis began when members o
Exporting Countries proclaimed an oil emb

Duras published *India Song* (Gallimard, Pari

Yun began supporting campaigns for dem
of North and South Korea, when Kim Dae-J
who later became president of South Kore
officers in Tokyo. Yun was a composer-in-re

1975
The Vietnam War, which started on Novem
Saigon on April 30, 1975.

Duras directed the film version of *India Son*
actress—played the mysterious central fen
promiscuous wife of the French Vice-Consu
be a militant feminist; she signed *Le Manife*
abortion) along with Duras, Moreau, and Si
Duras wrote an article for *Vogue* on Seyrig,
(1966) and *Baxter, Vera Baxter* (1977). Althou
passion, and loss—is supposed to be set in
mansion (le Palais Rothschild). Duras chose
which she had visited in her teens, just as s
screenplay for *Hiroshima Mon Amour*. Anot
non-synchronic approach, what Duras onc
actor in *India Song* speaks. Voices only com
actors' performances, while the piano walt
throughout.

Up until this point, Yun's compositions had
and were inspired by Asian ideas and tech
Asian influence. After 1975, Yun began ado
sonata for his compositions.

1976
Duras adapted *Whole Days in the Trees* and
film. In the latter, the plot returns to *India S*

THE ARCHITECTURE OF OPACITY

by Philippe Vergne

1 For a detailed analysis of Haegue Yang's dictionary of forms, ideas, and references, see Doryun Chong's *A Small Dictionary for Haegue Yang* (2008) and *A Less Small Dictionary (for HY)* (2013), both published in *Haegue Yang, Anthology 2006–2018, Tightrope Walking and Its Wordless Shadow* (Milan: Skira Editore, 2019), pp. 66–123.

About five years ago in a café in Seoul, Haegue Yang mentioned in the "detour" of a sentence that the blinds that have been so central to her work have been related to the condition of authoritarianism that she grew up under in the Korea of the early 1970s. The blinds obliterated the transparency of windows and therefore protected citizens from the indiscretions of a regime that valued censure and spying. The blinds made everybody a shadow, a blurry character with not much information to share, with not much information to transmit. The blinds canceled images and movements. Since this conversation that might seem obvious to many, but was not for me at the time, I have reframed my gaze on Haegue Yang's work, and started to contemplate how much strategies, materials, and circumstances of opacity, of interrupted transmission, of untold history, contradicted politics, or hidden intimacy are at the center of her practice.

Yang's symphony and choreography of blinds are an architecture, a vulnerable architecture, to use her words, of opacity. Vulnerable, because of the materiality, of their fragility, and due to the fact that they only partly affect transparency and visibility. In many cases, the notion of visibility in Haegue Yang's work is not limited to visuality. She formalizes a true phenomenology of perception in which all of the senses are called to task. When it comes to her work, one perceives with one's entire body and senses: one sees, one hears, one touches, one feels, one smells, one moves or is moved. *Series of Vulnerable Arrangements – Blind Room* (2006) perfectly formalizes this. A vulnerable architecture that does not shy away from the decorative; scents dispatched in the installation; gusts of winds coming from the climatology of domestic fans; sunsets of artificial lights; office/house chairs. I have often looked at *Series of Vulnerable Arrangements – Blind Room* and her murals as the matrix of her body of work, or the one that gives access to not only her materials, but the intellectual directions, the cultural routes that she follows and opens.

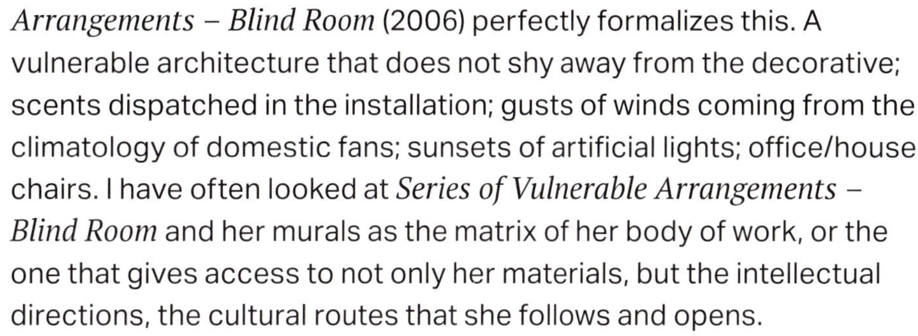

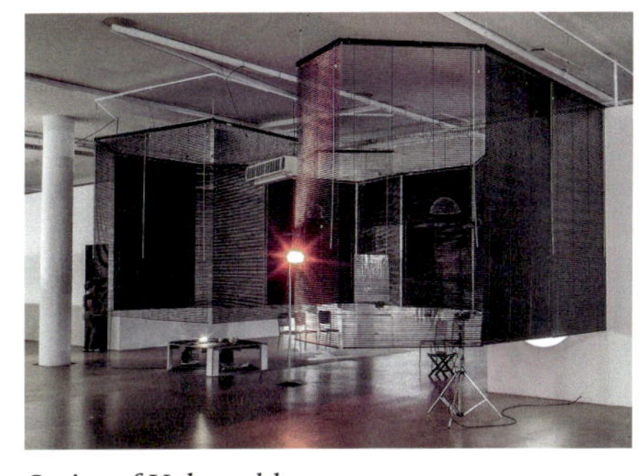

Series of Vulnerable Arrangements – Blind Room, 2006, 27th São Paulo Biennial, Ciccillo Matarazzo Pavilion, São Paulo, Brazil, 2006

Before even entering an analysis of the works presented at The Bass exhibition titled *In the Cone of Uncertainty*, it is important to stress how methodical Haegue Yang's work is, and how much she has over the years established a very clear and deliberate language of forms and ideas. Her work is a neologism. She has elaborated vocabulary and syntax that she keeps exploring and enriching as the work develops. Specific objects and materials (blinds, light bulbs, electrical cords, artificial plants, furniture, clothing racks, domestic fans, laundry racks, origami) have been combined with a set of literary, philosophical, and cultural references (Marguerite Duras, Hannah Arendt, Petra Kelly, Kim San, Marcel Broodthaers, Igor Stravinsky, Oskar Schlemmer, to name a few)[1] in order to assemble critical tools and forms that the artist articulates, like elements of languages according to the different communities and circumstances that she encounters with her works. These elements are the data of a metalanguage invented by Yang.

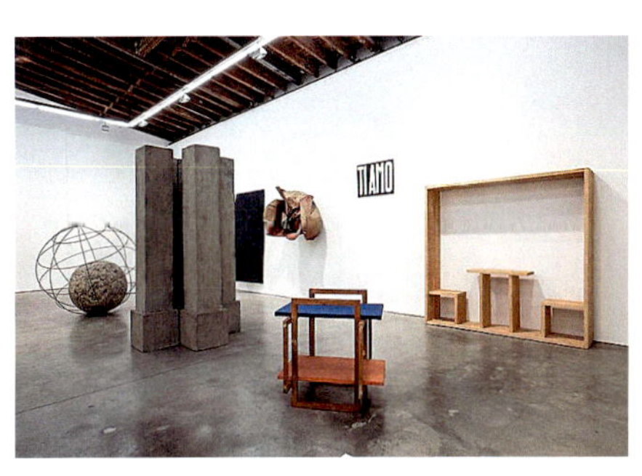

Michelangelo Pistoletto, *Minus Objects*, 1965–66

Yang's approach evokes the way the Italian artist Michelangelo Pistoletto established, very early on, through a set of objects and forms, the *Minus Objects* (1965–66) that feed and inform, to this day, the development of his work. For Pistoletto, these objects constitute the smallest common denominators of his work, and each of them embodies a set of ideas and values that he stood and stands by aesthetically, culturally, and politically, from his positioning vis-à-vis American Pop Art to his connection to the liberation movements of the late 1960s in postwar industrial Italy. In a way, the *Minus Objects* liberated Michelangelo Pistoletto from the necessity of endlessly inventing new forms to carry his work. Similarly, Yang's "dictionary" or "vocabulary" frees her from the need to invent new objects, new forms, new ideas, as she travels an intense rhythm of exhibition and a genuine and prolific need to explore deeper the ideas that sustain her works. In this way, her interest in objects, ready-made objects or material, even if "ready-made assistés" is more deeply ontological and rhetorical than it is Duchampian. Her forms, ready-made or not, are metonymic, or vehicles that allow her to "write her work" and betray the core content of the work.

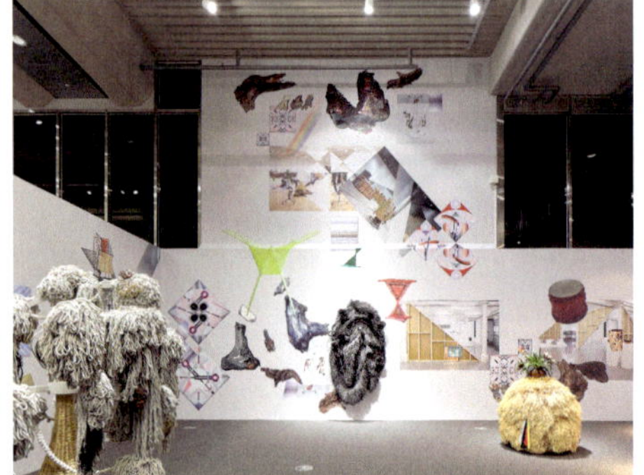

Field of Teleportation, 2011, *Homo Faber: Craft in Contemporary Sculpture*, Asia Culture Center, Gwangju, South Korea, 2019

The same applies to her wallpaper and mural works, which she began making in 2010–11. The wallpaper works and the framed collage works share the same ethos as the sculptures of the installation. And as with the blinds, they start with quotidian material, different kinds of papers, taken away from their initial function and destination. The materials, echoing the ad hoc nature of the installation, are industrially made, and commercially available. They range from security envelopes to graph paper and self-adhesive vinyl film, from origami paper to sandpaper.

Similar to Yang's installation work, as the wallpaper works develop they become more and more layered and complex; evolving from a hard-edge, straightforward simplicity to compositional intricacy. Hence *Trustworthy Wave #1* (2010) and *Trustworthy Wave #9–#12* (all 2010) are the simple horizontal layering of security envelope paper and graph paper, composing an all-over pattern of landscape-like imagery. Their pictoriality is systematic in a style that could, at first glance, evoke an afterimage, a memory, of Sol LeWitt's minimal and serial work. But a closer look reveals the nature of their materiality and what they are made of. The graph paper signifies rigor, calculus, system, and an aesthetic of investigation in which discipline is deeply anchored in Yang's approach to her work, her research around and within the topics she embraces, the communities she engages with, and the themes she elects to explore and study. The security envelopes bring us to the notion of opacity that Yang explores with the blinds. Like the blinds, they conceal information and create a nonporous, infra-thin barrier and separation between the public realm and a private, intimate one. They protect us from indiscretion, as much as they interfere with transparency of information. They also belong to the world of global circulation of goods, information, and individuals. Not unlike Yang's sculptures, the envelopes pass through contexts and cultures and, despite their opaque nature, their DNA is to connect people and communities, to bring people together, exchanging voices and ideas.

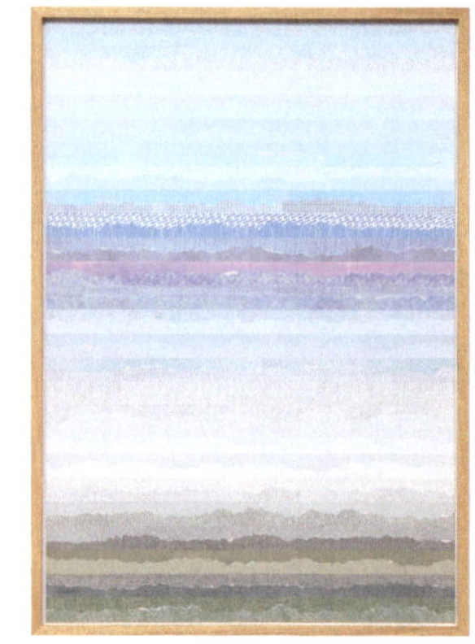

Trustworthy Wave #9, 2010

From these modest beginnings, the collages came to embrace more pictorial qualities, as if the artist, from the identification of the language, were taking pleasure in exploring the decorative potential of the material involved. *Central Composition in Explosion – Trustworthy #184* (2012–13) exemplifies such playful exuberance. A composition of eleven frames geometrically organized on

2 *The Responsive Eye* was an exhibition organized in 1965 by The Museum of Modern Art in New York and curated by William C. Seitz. The exhibition brought together painting and sculptures exploring optical effects and illusions. Among the artists represented in the exhibition were Yaacov Agam, Josef Albers, Enrico Castellani, Bridget Riley, and Victor Vasarely.

a wall, this work brings together abstract and concentric collaged compositions made of security envelopes and graph paper. The aesthetic model to which each unit seems to refer belongs to a family that includes the 1920s constructivism of Lázsló Moholy-Nagy and Alexander Rodchenko, as well as the illusionistic Op Art work of Bridget Riley. In both cases, these artists believed in the dynamic of art toward progress and the trust in a "responsive eye,"[2] or the retinal ability to perceive motion, or the illusion of motion from the static stimuli of paintings and collages. But one cannot overlook the affinity and synonymity that Yang's collages share with the artwork produced by Emma Kunz in the 1930s. A telepathic healer, a spiritualist from Switzerland, Kunz created, with the help of a pendulum, large-scale mandala-like geometric pictures on graph paper that she described as the expressions or the measurements of the cosmos equilibrium and the energy field for her meditative, restorative, and transcendental practice, as well as her holistic world view.

More than faith in progress and modernity, these works, and eventually Haegue Yang's own work, imply a true belief that art has a healing, holistic impact on the world, or serves as a tool to better approach, understand our present, our history, and to take responsibility. It shows trust in a "responsible eye" and the ambition to conceive of works of art that address, if not redress, issues that frame our time and our history; an ambition for the work of art to be an agent of change, to be active, and to invite an active response from viewers. Both aesthetically and philosophically, Haegue Yang's works share commonality with the way Brazilian artist Lygia Clark (1920–88) was moving through the confines of geometry and painting. For instance, Haegue Yang's *Central Composition in Explosion – Trustworthy #184* shares with Lygia Clark's *Planes in Modulated Surface 4* (1957) the use of unconventional material (wood and Formica for Clark), a spiraling composition around a central point that simulates or suggests movement and transformation of the geometric composition. Both seem, through these aesthetic decisions, to share doubts, if not frustration, with traditional pictorial models. In the case of Clark, this would lead her to experiment with interactive sculptures based on a deconstruction of plane surfaces in her painting. These sculptures, the *Bichos*, made of metal plates joined by hinges, are organic, active sculptures that invite viewers, spectators, to interact with them, to fold and unfold them in gestures close to the logic of origami-making so dear to Haegue Yang.

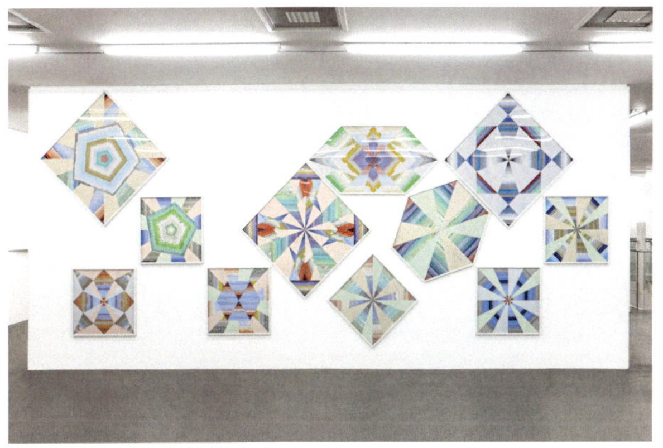

Central Composition in Explosion – Trustworthy #184, 2012–13, Musée de la Ville de Strasbourg et l'Aubette 1928, Strasbourg, France, 2013

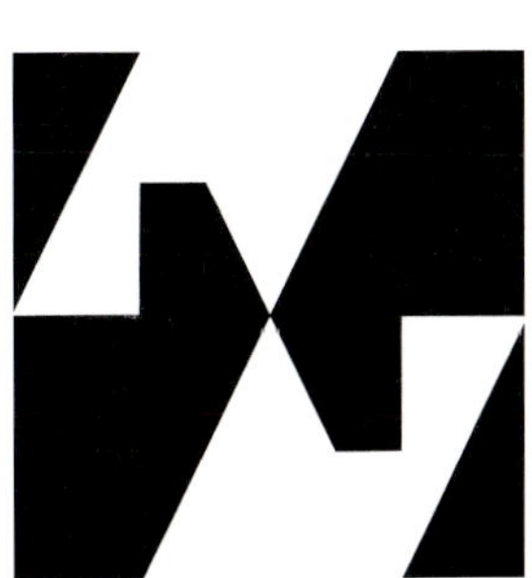

Lygia Clark, *Planes in Modulated Surface 4*, 1957

A logical extension or an echo of Yang's "doubts" in the traditional model resonates with her interest in the kinetic possibilities of her series *Rotating Notes* (2010–13), wall-mounted rotating boards on which the artist has attached personal images and texts that turn into blurry abstract patterns when the board rotates, helped by the gentle push of a viewer.

This implication of the visitors goes further and deeper in many of Haegue Yang's sculptures, for instance in *Sonic Dances* (2013–15) or *Dress Vehicles* (2011–18), conceived and built to invite the participation of audience members by moving them in the exhibition space and becoming, together with the sculpture, the protagonists of series of movements choreographed by the artist, who thus affects their perception both of their bodies and of the space they inhabit and activate.

Beyond what might be a formal (and serendipitous) connection, these points of contact show how deeply connected Yang is to the history or the memory of radical avant-garde international movements that were porous and open to confronting art, society, and life (later in her career, Clark privileged therapy and healing over art-making and developed a therapeutic practice based on the relationship of objects and the memories of trauma). They also show how interested she is in merging modernist and vernacular traditions, between Clark and origami, Oskar Schlemmer and crochet work, Igor Stravinsky and the ornamental, and the disruptive and non-Western oriented and feminine exuberance of the Pattern and Decoration movement. This creative tension is never more visible than in the visual tension created by the juxtaposition of her mural works with her sculptural works. It might be even possible to contemplate the idea that Haegue Yang's mural and wallpaper works visually trace the genealogy of her work in general. The mention of Oskar Schlemmer and of Igor Stravinsky is far from gratuitous, as they are figures often "called back," rather than quoted, by Haegue Yang. Igor Stravinsky's *Le Sacre du Printemps* (1913) is played in the installation titled *Warrior Believer Lover* (2011), and Schlemmer's costumes for the *Triadic Ballet* are the base for Yang's moving Sonic Sculptures called *Boxing Ballet* (2013–15). This work is surrounded by the wall pieces *Trustworthy #211–#221* (all part of *Boxing Ballet*) and directly lifted from the *Triadic Ballet*'s décor. In this perspective, Haegue Yang's wallpaper and mural have to be considered as set décor for a performative space which is that of the exhibition.

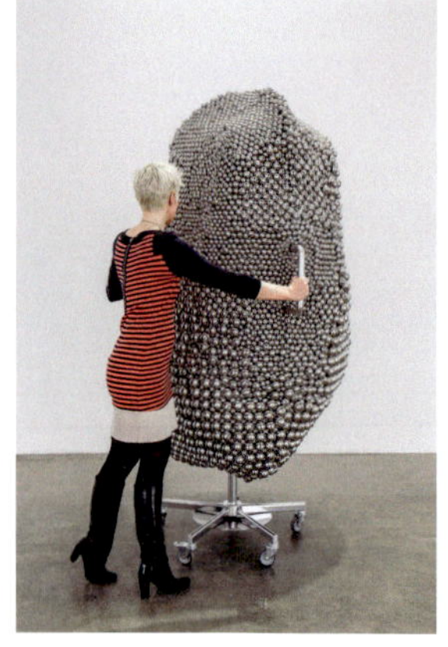

Sonic Nickel Dance, 2013, Galerie Chantal Crousel, Paris, France, 2013

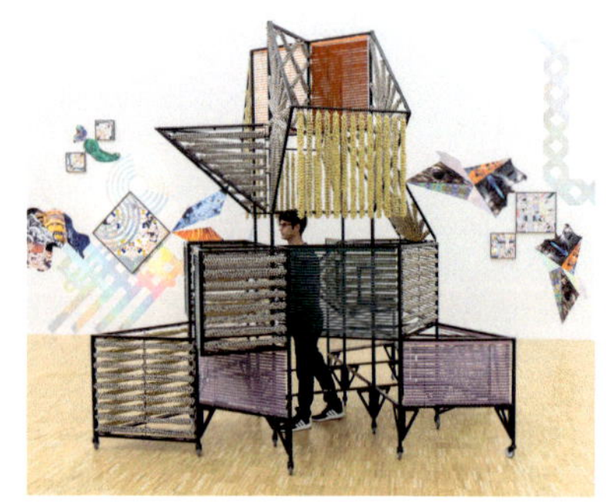

Sonic Dress Vehicle – Hulky Head, 2018, *Tightrope Walking and Its Wordless Shadow*, La Triennale di Milano, 2018

Whether one contemplates a connection with Emma Kunz or with Lygia Clark, or a connection with Oskar Schlemmer and Marguerite Duras—what is striking is that Yang stages and revives moments of historical transition accompanied by aesthetic ones in her installations: the end of a world order at the beginning of the twentieth century; an intimate transition marking the last gasps of colonization; forms meant to process the trauma of dictatorship. Would the movements implied in Yang's sculpture be ones toward liberation?

The wallpaper *Eclectic Totemic* (2013, see pages 72–77) seems so central to this idea. Most of her totemic figures are present and represented in towering floor-to-ceiling wallpaper, fractured portraits that invite the graphic-design memory of the likes of Alexander Rodchenko and her ability to fracture and recompose the past in a nonhierarchical manner, to evacuate nostalgia and take liberties with history to better encapsulate the present, her present. Looking back with nostalgia would only be a way to silence the present when it needs to scream. But looking back does not define her methodology, far from it: looking ahead does. What veritably defines her approach is a nonhierarchical and anachronistic transversality, where past and present references collide, where modern and traditional merge, and where vernacular modes of expression feed on high art across chronologies and cultural geographies.

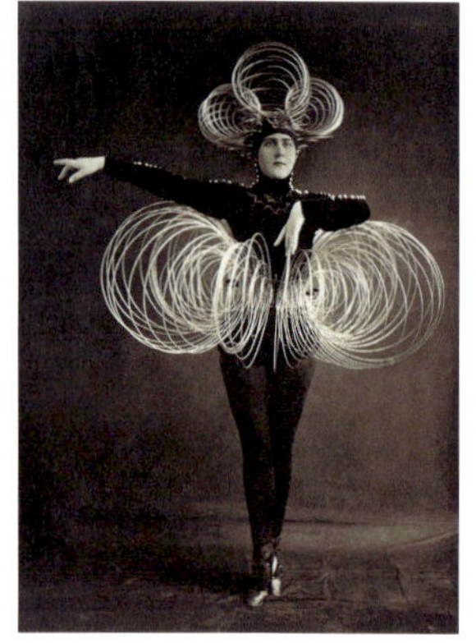

Triadic Ballet (detail), 1926

Incubation and Exhaustion (2018, see pages 94–99) is a "delirious" wallpaper rendering of this methodology. To clarify, by delirious I do not imply any form of madness, but an acute and restless ability to process disorder and incoherence in order to produce a form of knowledge that transcends traditional modes of representation, of thoughts, and of speech; a non-verbal acuity.

Incubation and Exhaustion projects the viewers in an immersive vortex of light and darkness, human and non-human, nature and robotic devices, industrial, folk, and paganistic cultures; it is a "folly" about our "folie" and its looming dangers on humans and on the environment. It is about delirious and "inconvenient truths" assembled in discontinuous blocks.

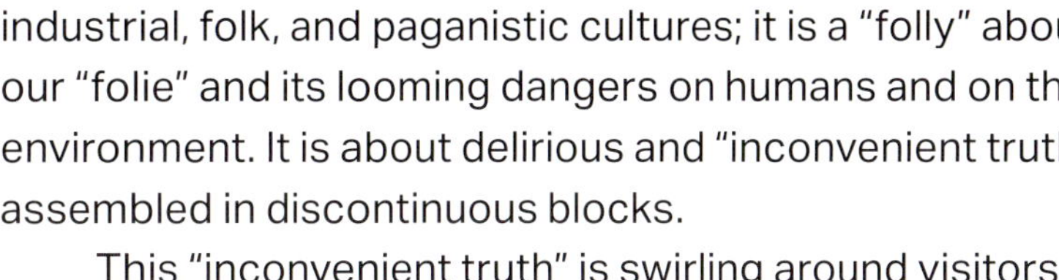

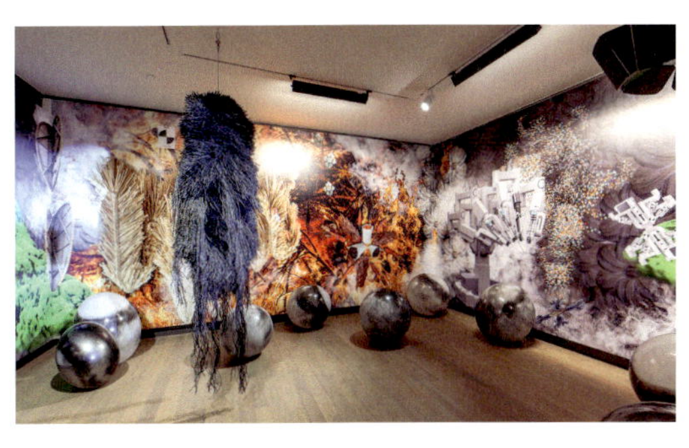

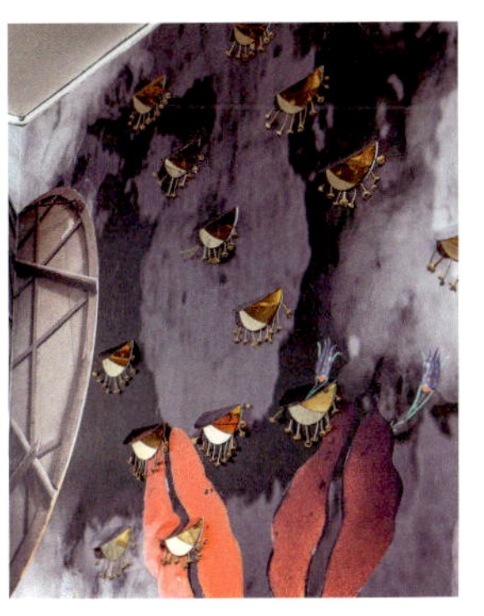

Incubation and Exhaustion – Version Istanbul, 2019, 16th Istanbul Biennial, Turkey, 2019

This "inconvenient truth" is swirling around visitors in a vortex down-spiraling The Bass staircase to reach the "eye" of *Coordinates of Speculative Solidarity* (2019, see pages 104–107), a mural mapping ocean currents, hot air and cold air areas, and heavenly, paradisiac views that anticipate an environmental darkness and violent deterritorialization, not even to come, but already upon us, and somehow still opaque to many. Such opacity is not produced by blinds or by security envelopes. This opacity is of our own making; sui generis. Could Yang's work, with all its apparent playfulness, shiny and bright materiality, be a "whistle-blower," warning us, without being didactically ideological, about what lies ahead?

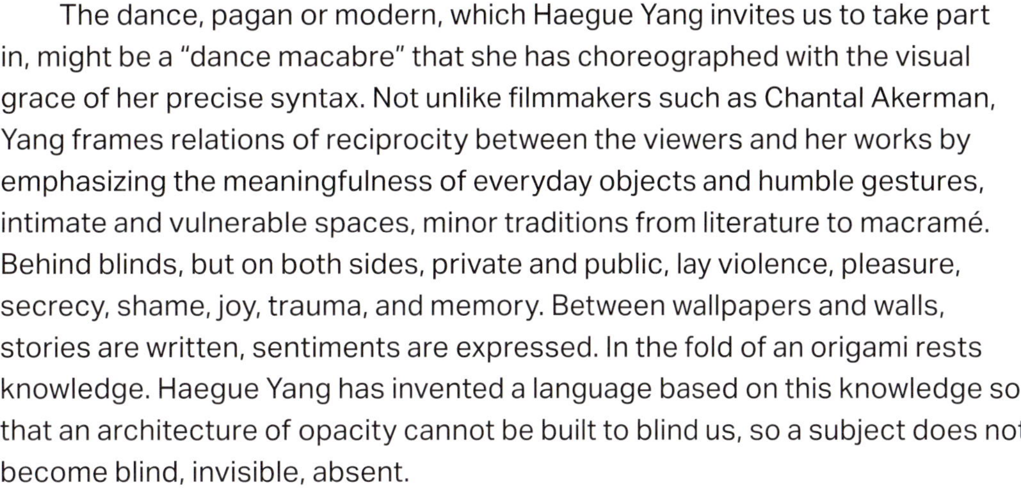

The dance, pagan or modern, which Haegue Yang invites us to take part in, might be a "dance macabre" that she has choreographed with the visual grace of her precise syntax. Not unlike filmmakers such as Chantal Akerman, Yang frames relations of reciprocity between the viewers and her works by emphasizing the meaningfulness of everyday objects and humble gestures, intimate and vulnerable spaces, minor traditions from literature to macramé. Behind blinds, but on both sides, private and public, lay violence, pleasure, secrecy, shame, joy, trauma, and memory. Between wallpapers and walls, stories are written, sentiments are expressed. In the fold of an origami rests knowledge. Haegue Yang has invented a language based on this knowledge so that an architecture of opacity cannot be built to blind us, so a subject does not become blind, invisible, absent.

A few years ago, in 2015, I bought a bracelet designed by Monday Edition and inspired by Yang's Sonicwears, sold at the shop of the Leeum, Samsung Museum of Art in Seoul. This little piece of inexpensive jewelry was made, among other elements, of little bells. These bells, as one would wear the bracelet, were as loud as they were small. The bracelet disrupted the voluptuous silence of tasteful adornment. It defied muteness. It made noise, warning us that something was coming. Some people did not like it, while others smiled and played with it. Silence was broken and people started to talk to each other. Haegue Yang certainly smiled.

Introduction to the Genealogy of Wallpaper and Mural Works, 2011–19

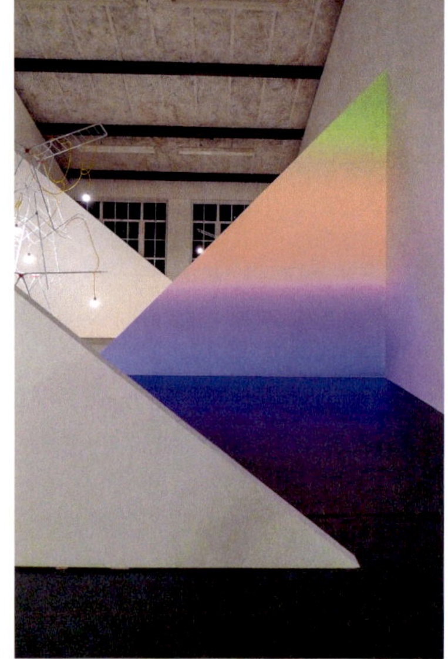

Intro Motion Ditch, Art Sheffield, S1 Artspace, Sheffield, UK, 2010

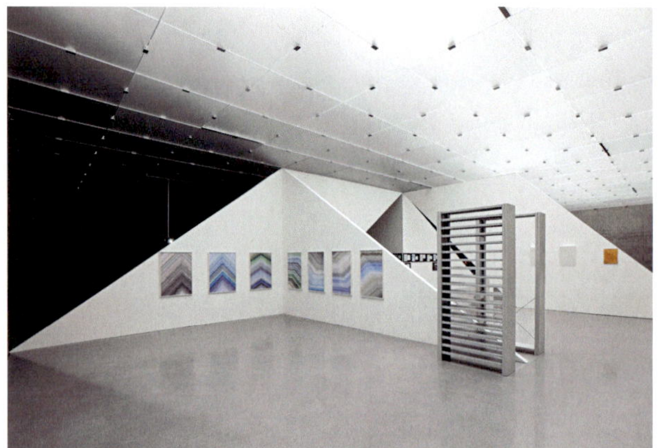

Arrivals, Kunsthaus Bregenz, Austria, 2011

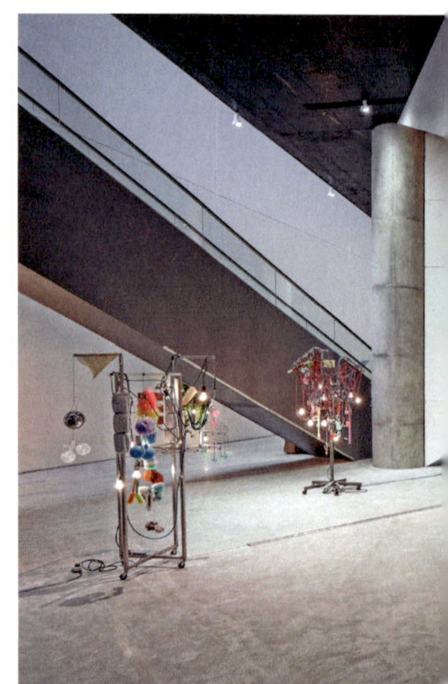

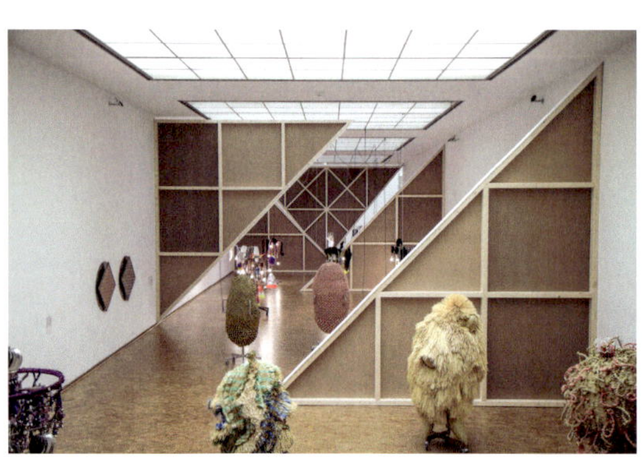

ETA 1994–2018. 2018 Wolfgang Hahn Prize, Museum Ludwig, Cologne, Germany, 2018

Concurrent with her growing interest in movement, Haegue Yang developed a gradual yet pronounced fascination with the concept of "flatness." In Yang's practice, flatness is defined as both a material state and an inherently dynamic process. Her investigation into the multiple characteristics of flatness led Yang to produce a volume of related and evolving mural and wallpaper works.

As she had previously demonstrated by running origami objects through a press in her *Non-Foldings* series, flatness could be achieved by compression. It could also be thematized by translating three-dimensionality into a flat modality, as evidenced by her *Carsick Drawings*, in which the artist's horizontal lines served as seismographic visual records of the bumpiness of the road her bus was driving on, transmitted by passing vehicles.

An important aspect of Yang's concept of flatness, however, is that within a seemingly flat surface, several hidden layers are compressed and have the potential to unfold and fold as well as to oscillate between these two states. A fascination with latent energy is present in many aspects of Yang's practice. One can look back through her career to multiple precursors and alternative articulations of this concept. The venetian blind, for example, is a recurring trope and conceptual pivot point in Yang's work.

Since 2006, she has used blinds to geometrically filter space and vision in her exhibitions, often coupled with the construction of shaped walls to create a partial and graphic covering/opening of the gallery-goer's view into the space. This obstruction can be overcome by walking into the space and shifting one's viewpoint, activating the viewer's body in the product of their vision.

Triangularly shaped walls prolong the path to the end of the room, and one is naturally enticed to go around the objects to uncover the view. How these walls then restrict and widen the visual field is dependent on the viewer's location and movement. Yang considers the shaped walls as discrete elements, rather than a singular body of work, that build a folded experience out of space in a physical, visual, and metaphorical way.

The viewer's movement is responsive to the elements in the exhibition, triggered by a shift in their perspective, similar to the effect of venetian blinds. In this sense, the installation holds both a bodily and representational quality: the dynamics between the obscuring and revealing of sight significantly shift whilst traversing the exhibition. The cutting, covering, or opening effects also have a strong graphic impact.

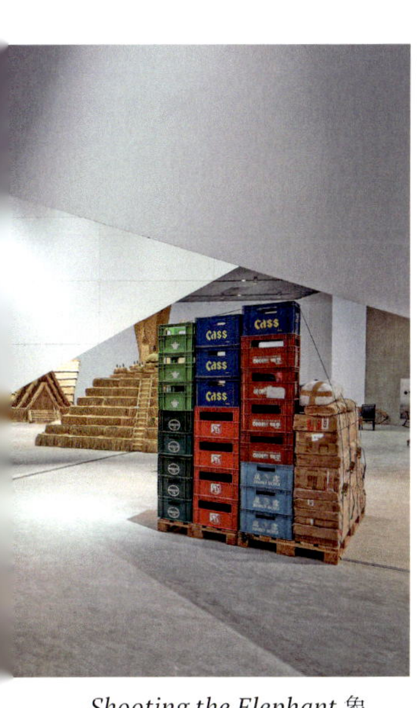

Shooting the Elephant 象 Thinking the Elephant, Leeum, Samsung Museum of Art, Seoul, South Korea, 2015

Geometric incisions, shutting down or partially opening up one's view, resonate with other works such as the *Trustworthies* and her venetian blind installations, while building a contrast to her organic and anthropomorphic sculptural practice including her Light Sculptures and *The Intermediates*.

Parallel to the shaped walls, Yang's wallpapers and murals can be read as installed experiences that represent and translate physical space. The interplay between sculptural and graphic elements in works such as *Field of Teleportation* and *Multiple Mourning Room* can be seen as a stage and synthesis in her ongoing experimentation with the dynamic character of "flatness" in that they approximate an experience of travel across space and time. Yet, these installations escape the conventional understanding of material reality by building an alternative "environment of layered flats," compressing and extending space with physical and graphic interventions.

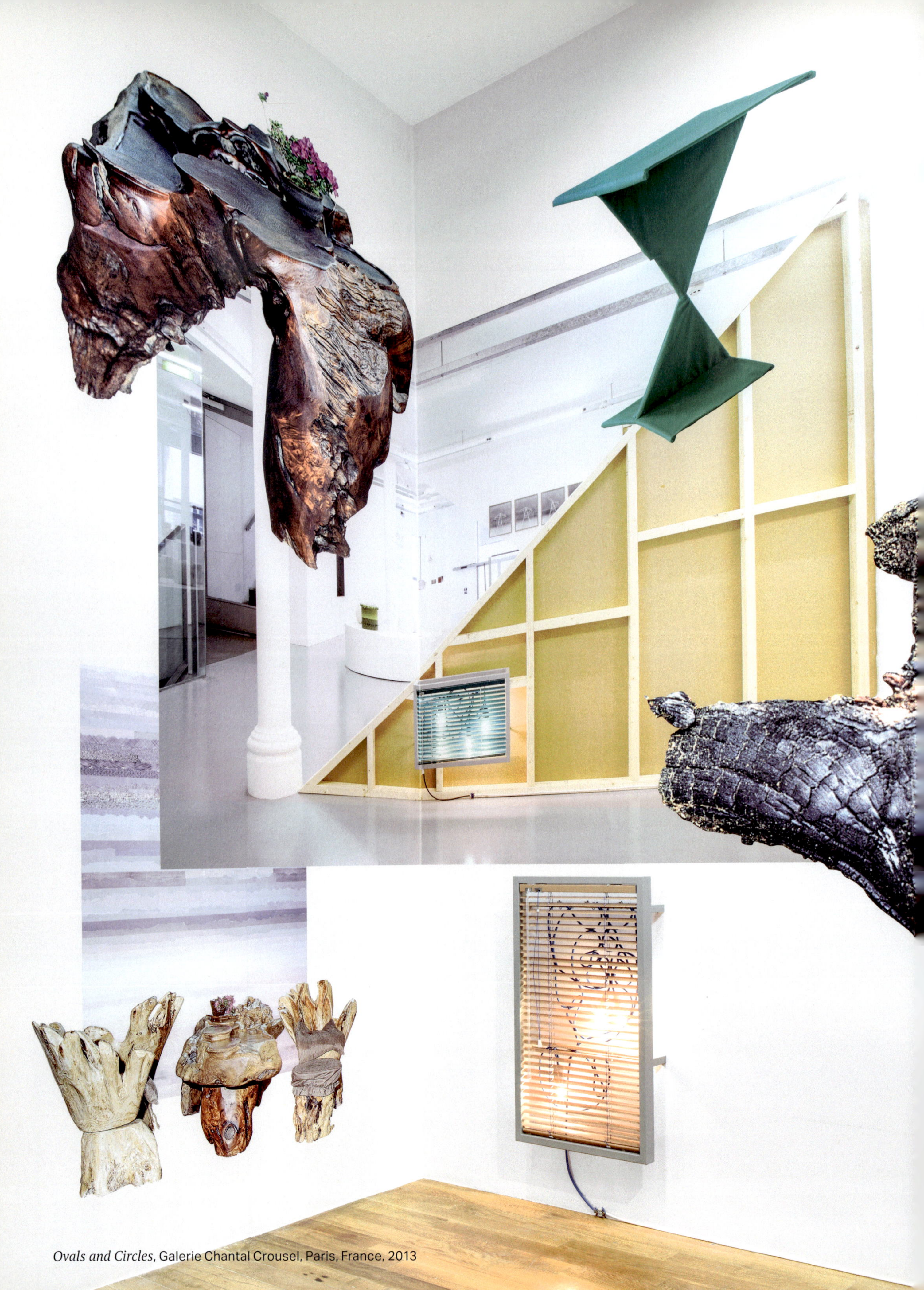

Ovals and Circles, Galerie Chantal Crousel, Paris, France, 2013

Field of Teleportation, 2011

In collaboration with
Studio Manuel Raeder
Digital color print
Dimensions variable

Field of Teleportation, one of the earliest in Yang's wallpaper series, was created in collaboration with Berlin-based graphic designer Manuel Raeder while they worked together closely for *Haegue Yang: Wild Against Gravity*. This catalogue was produced for two different solo shows in 2011: *The Art and Technique of Folding the Land* at the Aspen Art Museum in the US and *Teacher of Dance* at Modern Art Oxford in the UK. Notions of movement played a crucial role in both exhibitions, yet manifested differently in each, through dance at Modern Art Oxford and teleportation at the Aspen Art Museum.

A nonhierarchical, indeterminate, yet layered surface, *Field of Teleportation* is populated by elements that are suspended in time and space. Inhabiting this supernatural microcosm in flux are motifs drawn from artworks, such as cutouts of Yang's own sculptures and graphic works, and artifacts drawn from the artist's interests, such as root carvings and driftwood. Various images of the artist's works and relics are literally "teleported" away from their original configuration and context. Stripped of gravity, scale, weight, or depth, the objects in this memory vortex compose a scene of distinctive parts, creating an idiosyncratic and anachronistic field that also serves as a quasi-archive.

Field of Teleportation invites the viewer into a two-dimensional surface in which perspectives and dimensions unfold arbitrarily. These resulting "flat layers"—partially created by the photographic compression of three-dimensional objects into flat space—are informed by Yang's study of mystic G. I. Gurdjieff's sacred dances and Taoist movements, both deeply connected with nature. Yang further connects the wallpaper to the concept of a cultural diaspora, a long-standing interest reflected in her research and work on the biographies of prominent diasporic figures. Just as a diaspora is scattered and divided, the wallpaper's contents have been literally dispersed or atomized.

The Art and Technique of Folding the Land, Aspen Art Museum, Aspen, CO, USA, 2011
ARCO Madrid, Spain, 2012
Ovals and Circles, Galerie Chantal Crousel, Paris, France, 2013
Anachronistic Layers of Dispersion, Henry Art Gallery, Seattle, WA, USA, 2013
The Great Acceleration, Taipei Biennial 2014, Taiwan, 2014
Homo Faber: Craft in Contemporary Sculpture, Asia Culture Center, Gwangju, South Korea, 2019

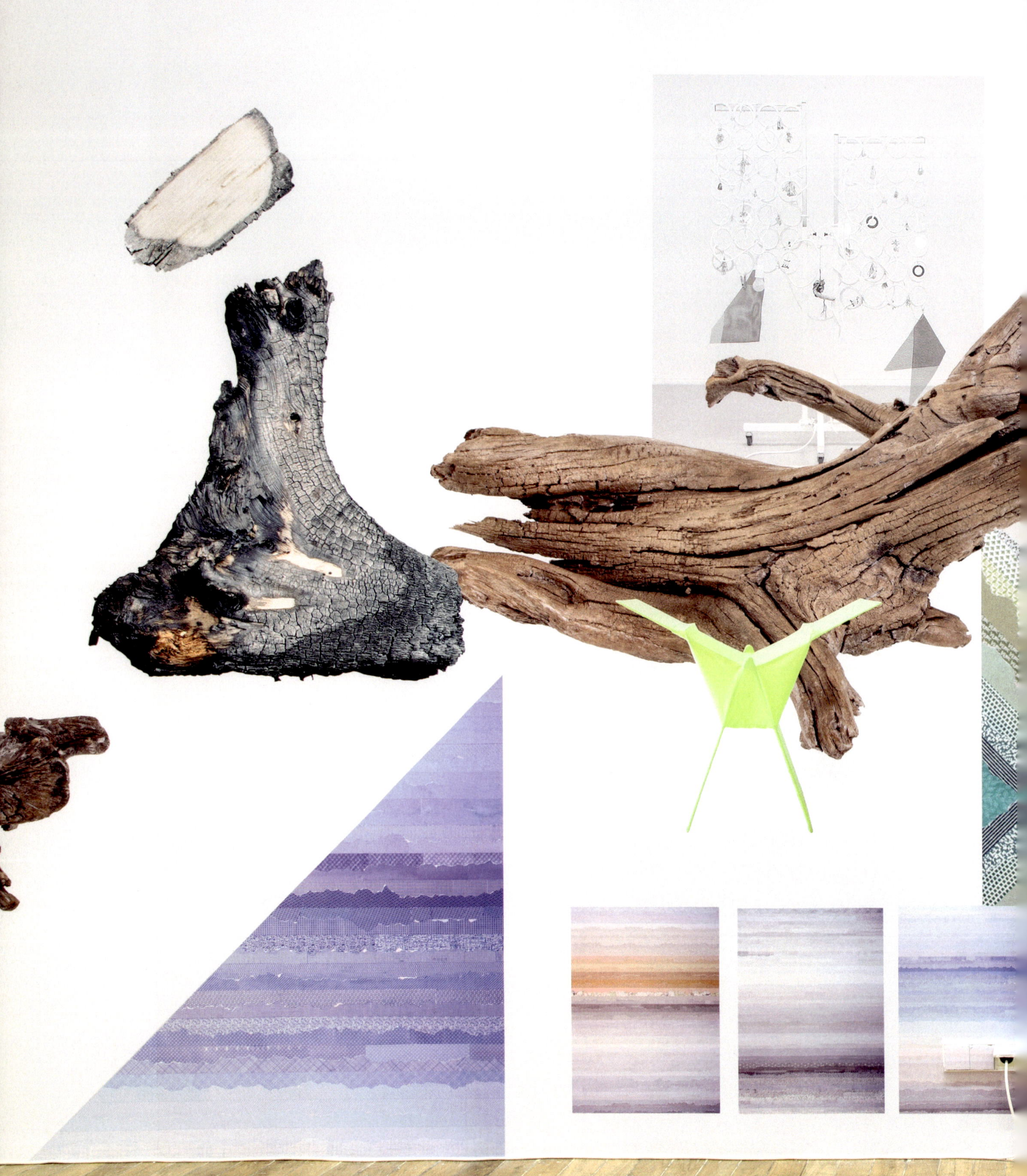

Ovals and Circles, Galerie Chantal Crousel, Paris, France, 2013

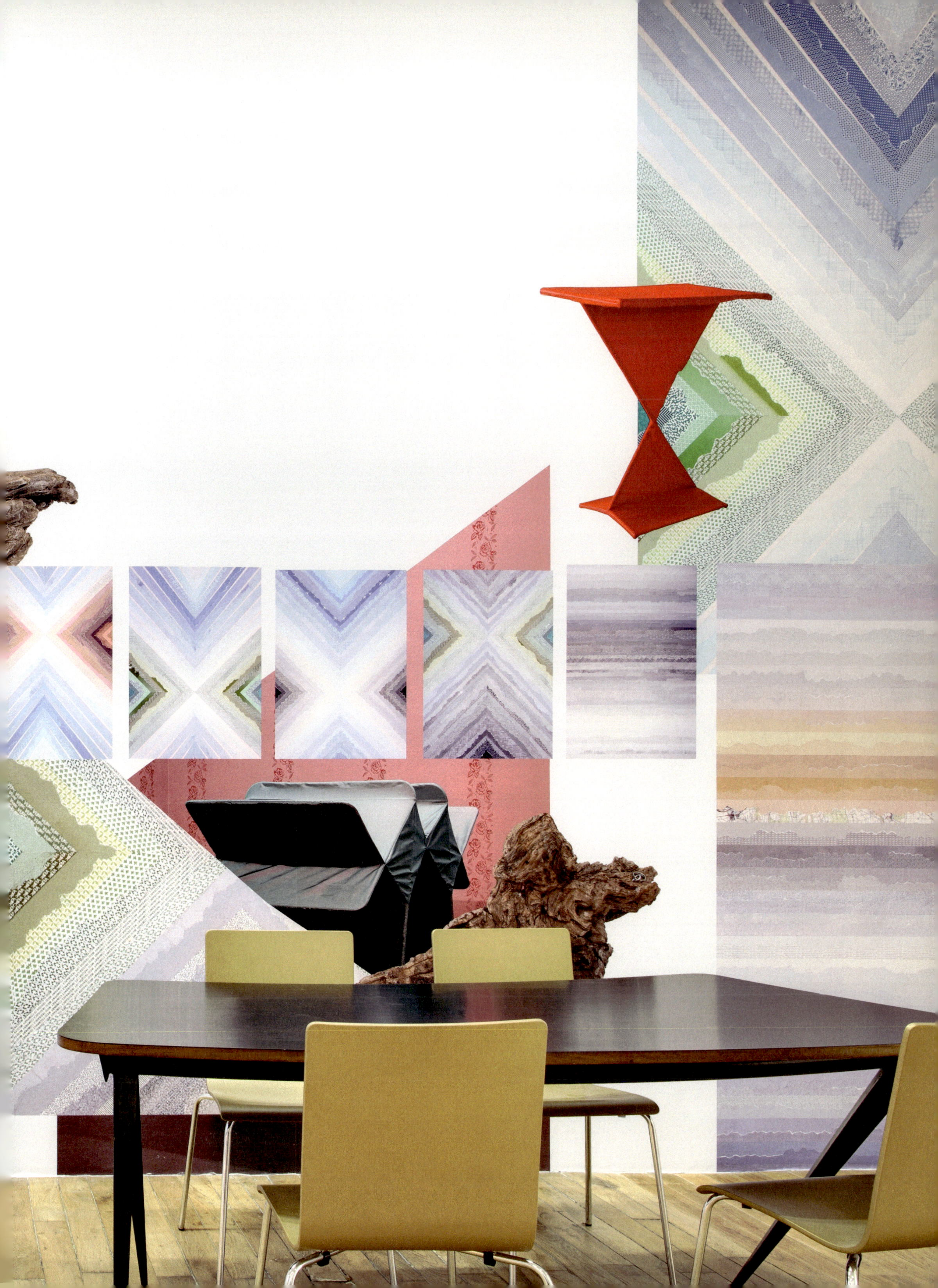

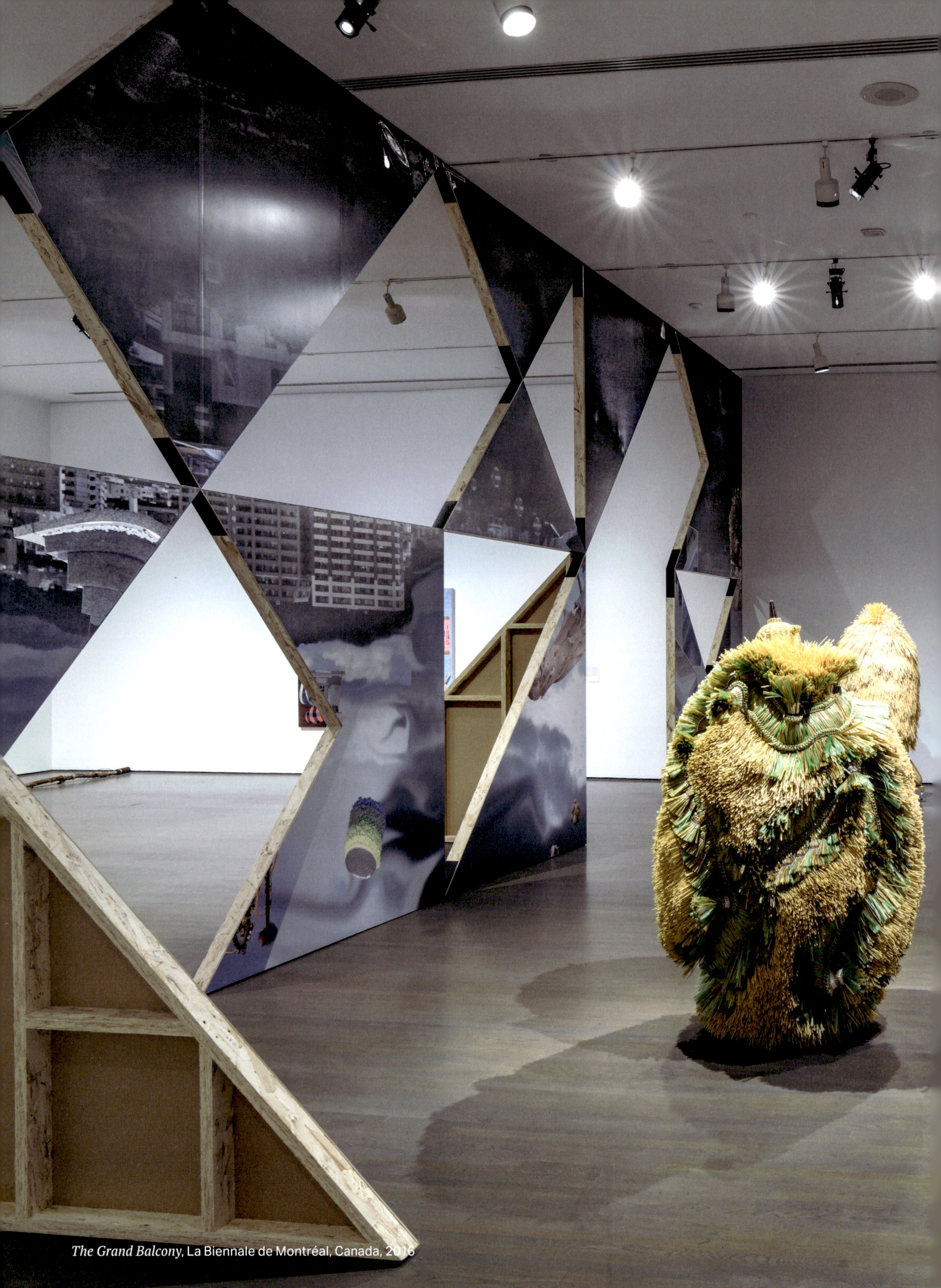

The Grand Balcony, La Biennale de Montréal, Canada, 2016

Multiple Mourning Room, 2012

In collaboration with
Studio Manuel Raeder
Digital color print
Dimensions variable

Yang's wallpaper *Multiple Mourning Room*, also produced in collaboration with Studio Manuel Raeder, was first exhibited as part of her debut solo exhibition at Greene Naftali, New York, in 2012. Titled *Multi Faith Room*, the exhibition referred to the airport-designed prayer rooms furnished to accommodate all religious practices, a response to an increasingly common lifestyle of permanent transience. Suggesting a culture of shamanistic tourism and a separation of identity from place, and using a landscape as background, *Multiple Mourning Room* marked a departure from Yang's wallpaper of the previous year, *Field of Teleportation*, yet continued her exploration into her so-called "layered flats," or 3D objects compressed into 2D space. In this disorienting phenomenological field, associations between the objects are upended, catalyzing associative relationships.

In dreams, the size, shape, gravity and luminosity of objects is often malleable and random. Floating across Hiroshima's inverted cityscape are a variety of real objects appearing as illusory, flexible phantasms, as if recalled in moments before sleep. Works by Yang, including *Can Cosies*, *Trustworthies*, and furniture sculptures appear as avatars of themselves, in both truncated and whole form, as if only partially remembered; they float and drift alongside volcanic rock fertility statues from South Korea's Jeju Island, furniture sculptures, Shinto gravestones, and root carvings. Organic forms, twisted by man-made, natural, or digital means, appear still or as moving at impossibly high speeds. These shadowy non-representations of real objects appear in surrealistic high definition, projecting an evocative and uncanny effect.

To date, *Multiple Mourning Room* has been the most widely exhibited of Yang's wallpaper works. Notably, the presentation at ICA Boston expanded the work to fit the extraordinary height and shape of the museum's wall by presenting a mirrored, corrected view of the landscape above the original reversed scenery.

Multi Faith Room, Greene Naftali, New York, NY, USA, 2012
Art Wall: Haegue Yang, The Institute of Contemporary Art, Boston, MA, USA, 2013
Vom Eigensinn der Dinge, KAI 10 | Raum für Kunst, Düsseldorf, Germany, 2013
Shooting the Elephant 象 Thinking the Elephant, Leeum, Samsung Museum of Art, Seoul, South Korea, 2015
The Grand Balcony, La Biennale de Montréal, Montréal, Canada, 2016
Triple Vita Nestings, Institute of Modern Art, Brisbane, Australia, 2018
Triple Vita Nestings, Govett-Brewster Art Gallery, New Plymouth, New Zealand, 2018
Kunst Handwerk, Kunsthaus Graz, Austria, 2019

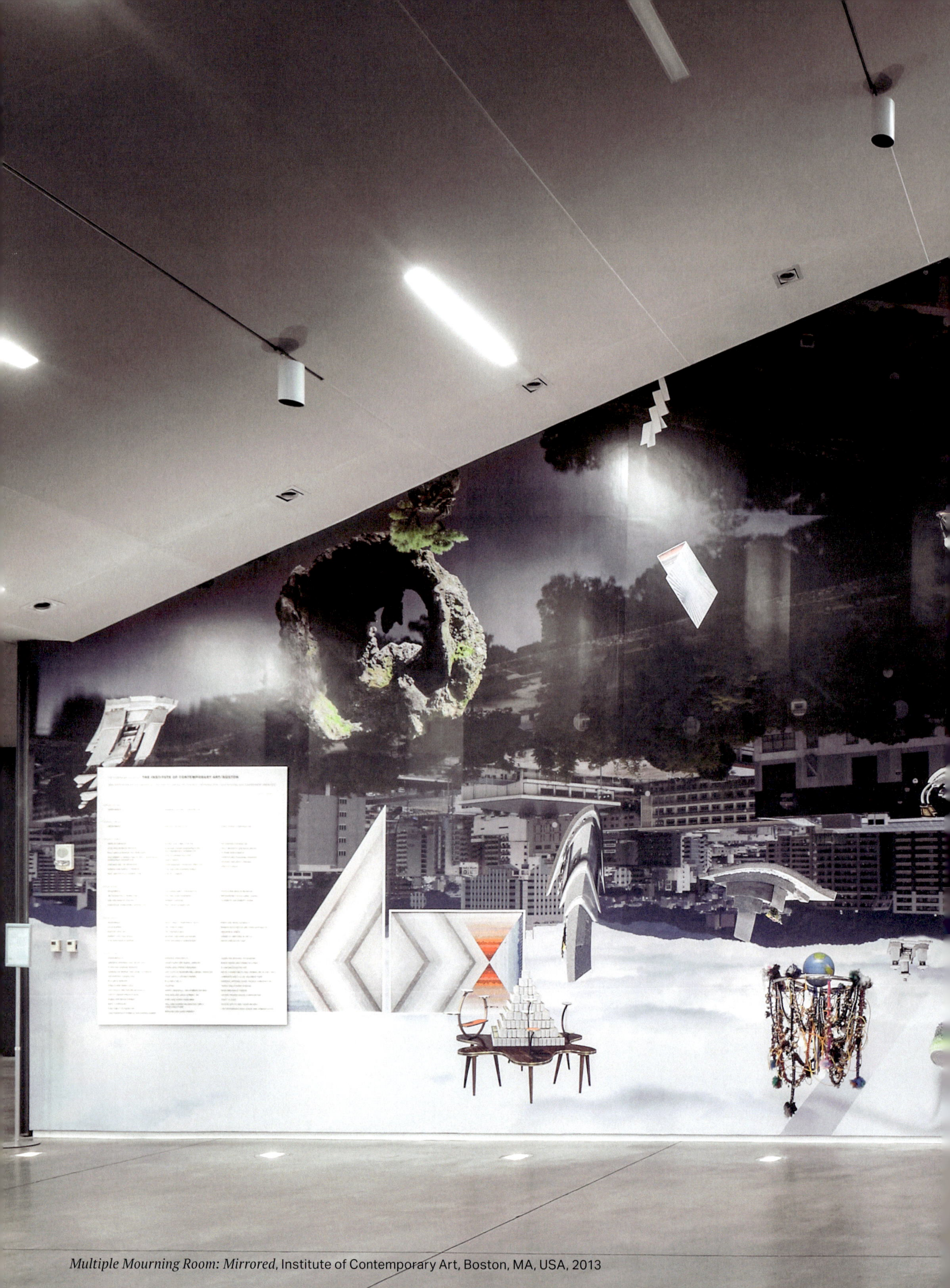

Multiple Mourning Room: Mirrored, Institute of Contemporary Art, Boston, MA, USA, 2013

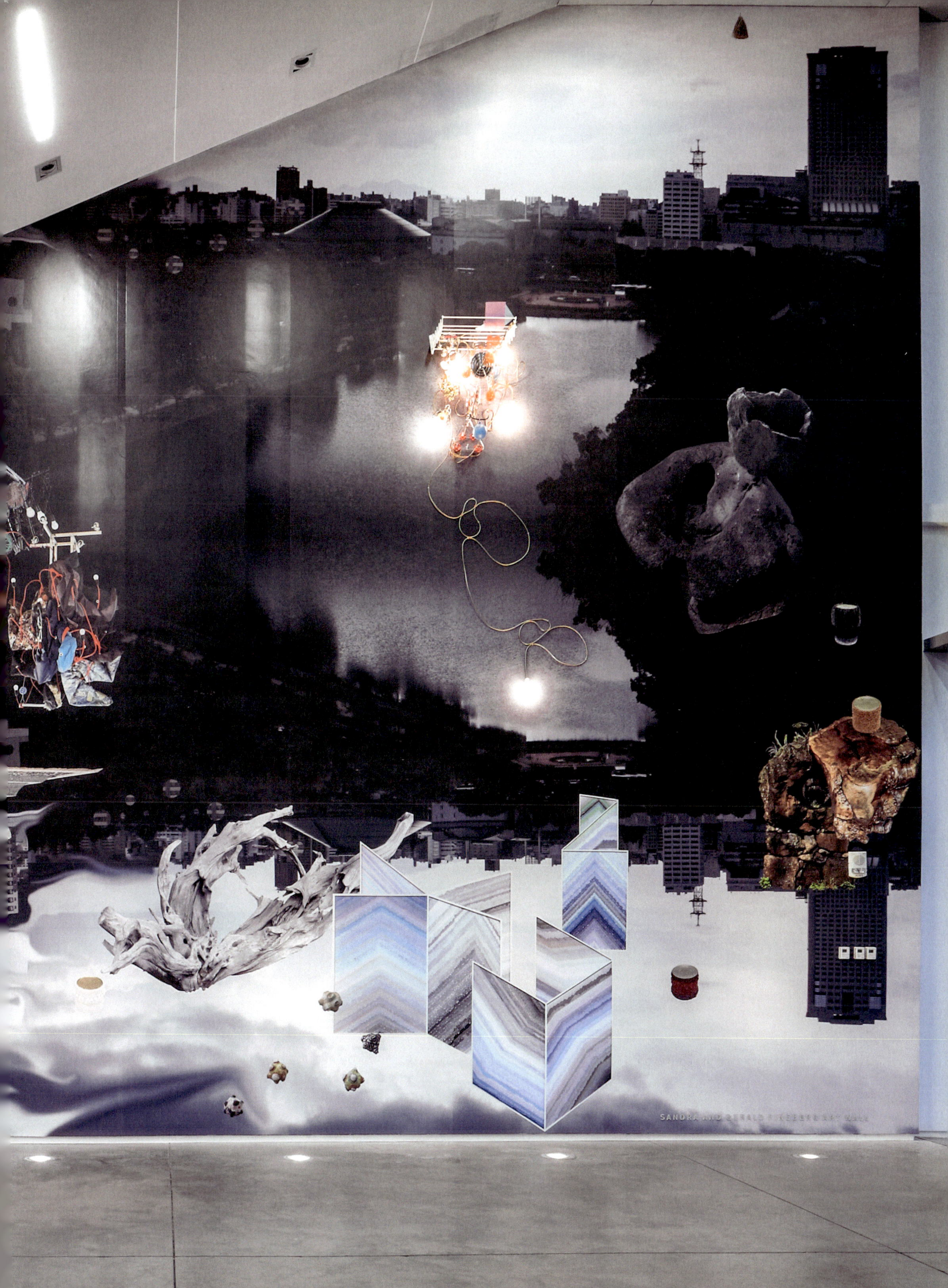
SANDRA

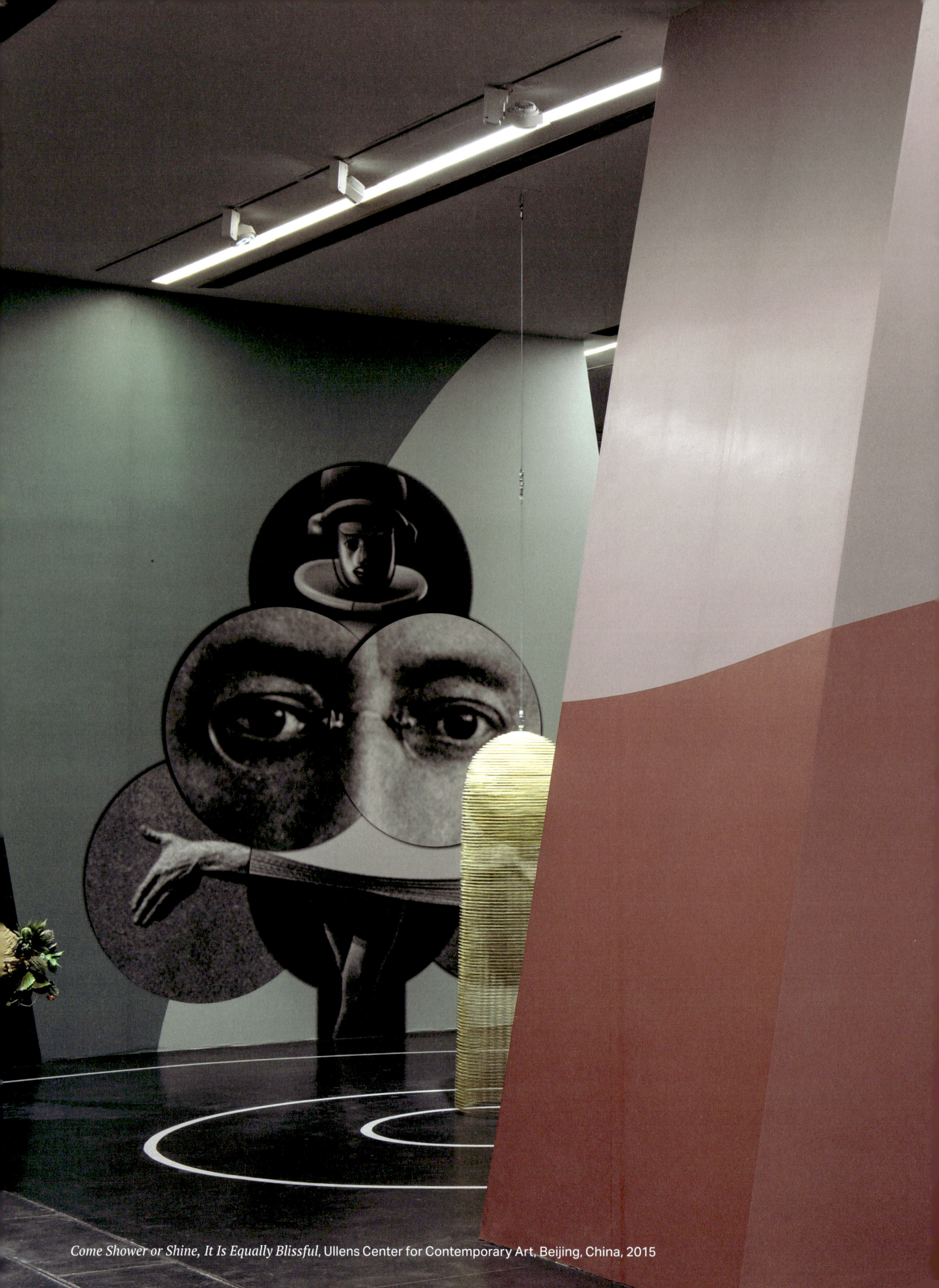

Come Shower or Shine, It Is Equally Blissful, Ullens Center for Contemporary Art, Beijing, China, 2015

Eclectic Totemic, 2013

In collaboration with OK-RM (Oliver Knight and Rory McGrath, London)
Digital color print
Dimensions variable

The third wallpaper, *Eclectic Totemic*, was again driven by a collaboration, this time with duo OK-RM, who were commissioned to design the catalogue *Family of Equivocations* for Yang's eponymous solo exhibition at Aubette and Musée d'Art Moderne et Contemporain, Strasbourg, in 2013. At the designers' suggestion, the wallpaper mobilizes Yang's rarely visible, yet rich variety of references, including historical and literary figures as motifs. The collection of modern art of the museums of Strasbourg, particularly works by Sophie Taeuber-Arp and her artist companion Jean Arp, the latter of whom was born in Strasbourg, served as further inspirational input.

The result was five totems, compelled by the hybridity of Yang's seemingly disparate source material, including fragments of images of Romain Gary, George Orwell, Marguerite Duras, Petra Kelly, Igor Stravinsky, a figurine from Oskar Schlemmer's *Triadic Ballet*, a bear, an elephant, a clown, a brick wall, etc. With their looming, impressive scale, the totems appear as giants standing in the room, yet their physicality is constituted by a Frankenstein-like assemblage that stands against the backdrop of an abstract landscape in colors and shapes quoting sculptures and paintings by Arp and Taeuber-Arp. Spanning three large walls, the figures create a jumble of references to the modern Western avant-garde, dances and costumes, and other formal or symbolic languages, weaving the associated cultural heritages together.

Two years later, *Eclectic Totemic* was exhibited again, this time on three massive columns at the Ullens Center for Contemporary Art (UCCA), Beijing, instead of on walls. The columns were shaped as slanting boxes in different directions, while the wallpaper rendered each of them as a giant, but flat figuration, which coexisted alongside the physical sculptures. The entire gallery space was constructed to evoke an archaic tomb, complete with cave paintings and funerary objects.

Family of Equivocations, Aubette 1928 and Musée d'Art Moderne et Contemporain, Strasbourg, France, 2013
Come Shower or Shine, It Is Equally Blissful, Ullens Center for Contemporary Art, Beijing, China, 2015

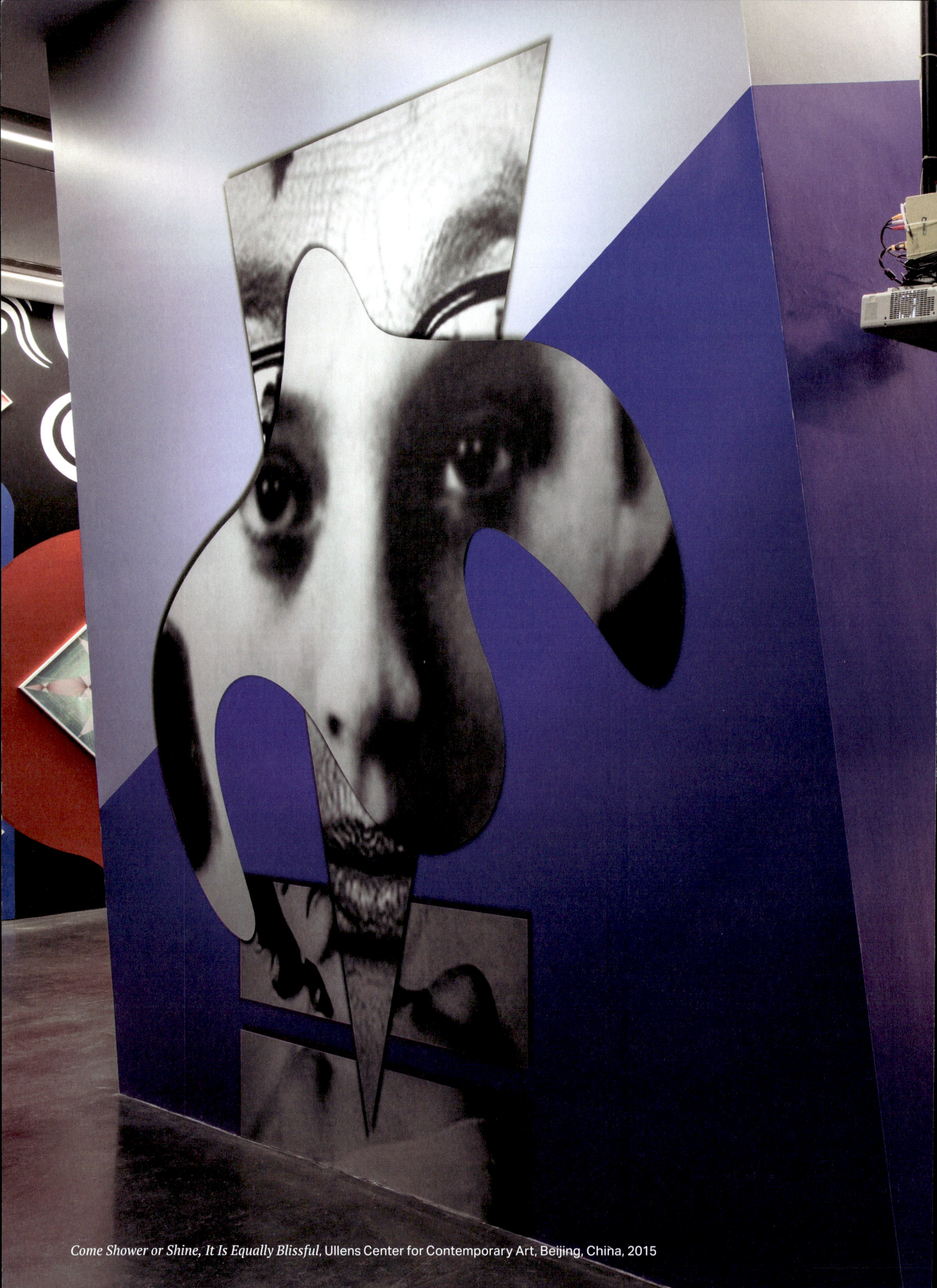

Come Shower or Shine, It Is Equally Blissful, Ullens Center for Contemporary Art, Beijing, China, 2015

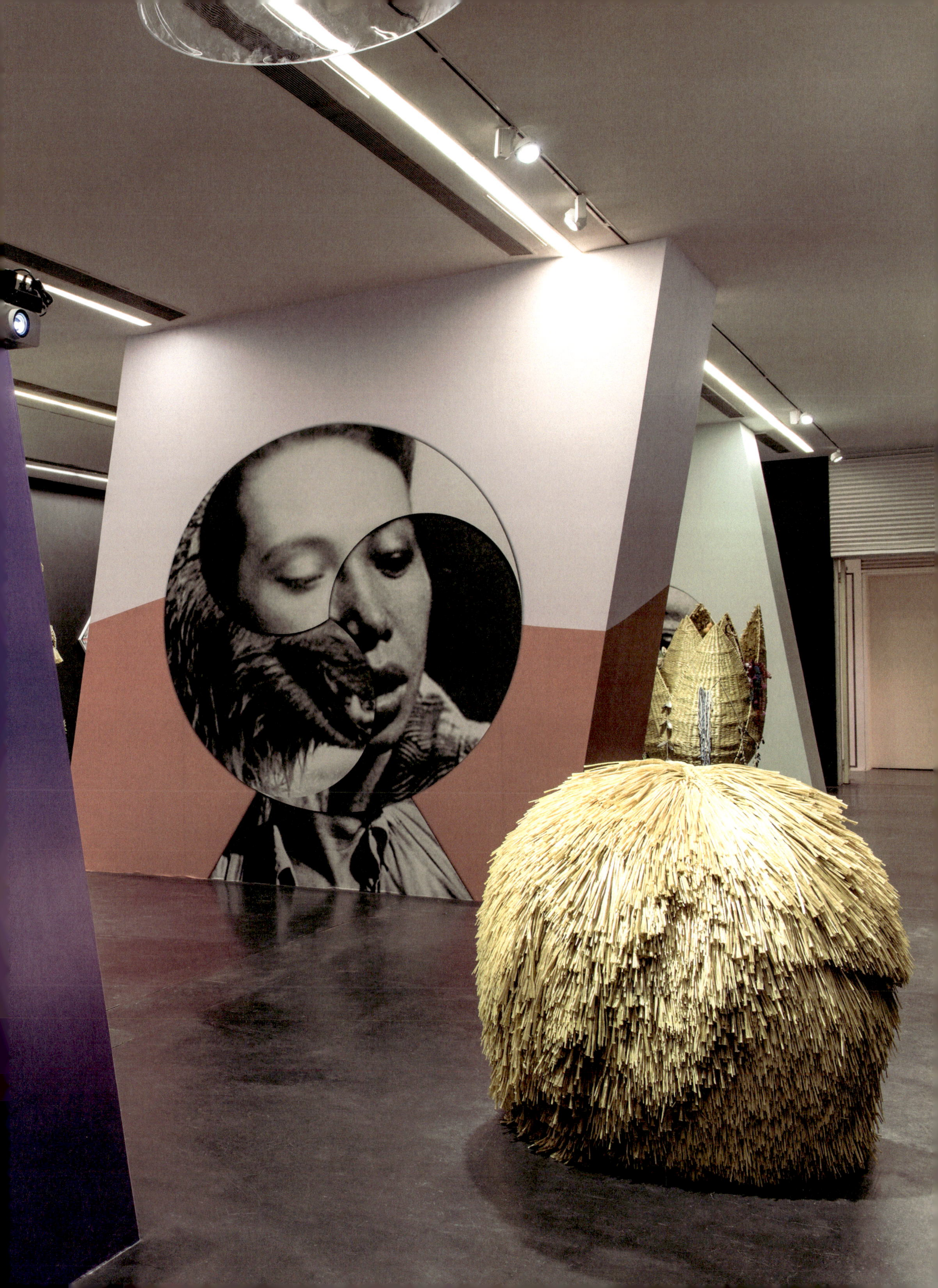

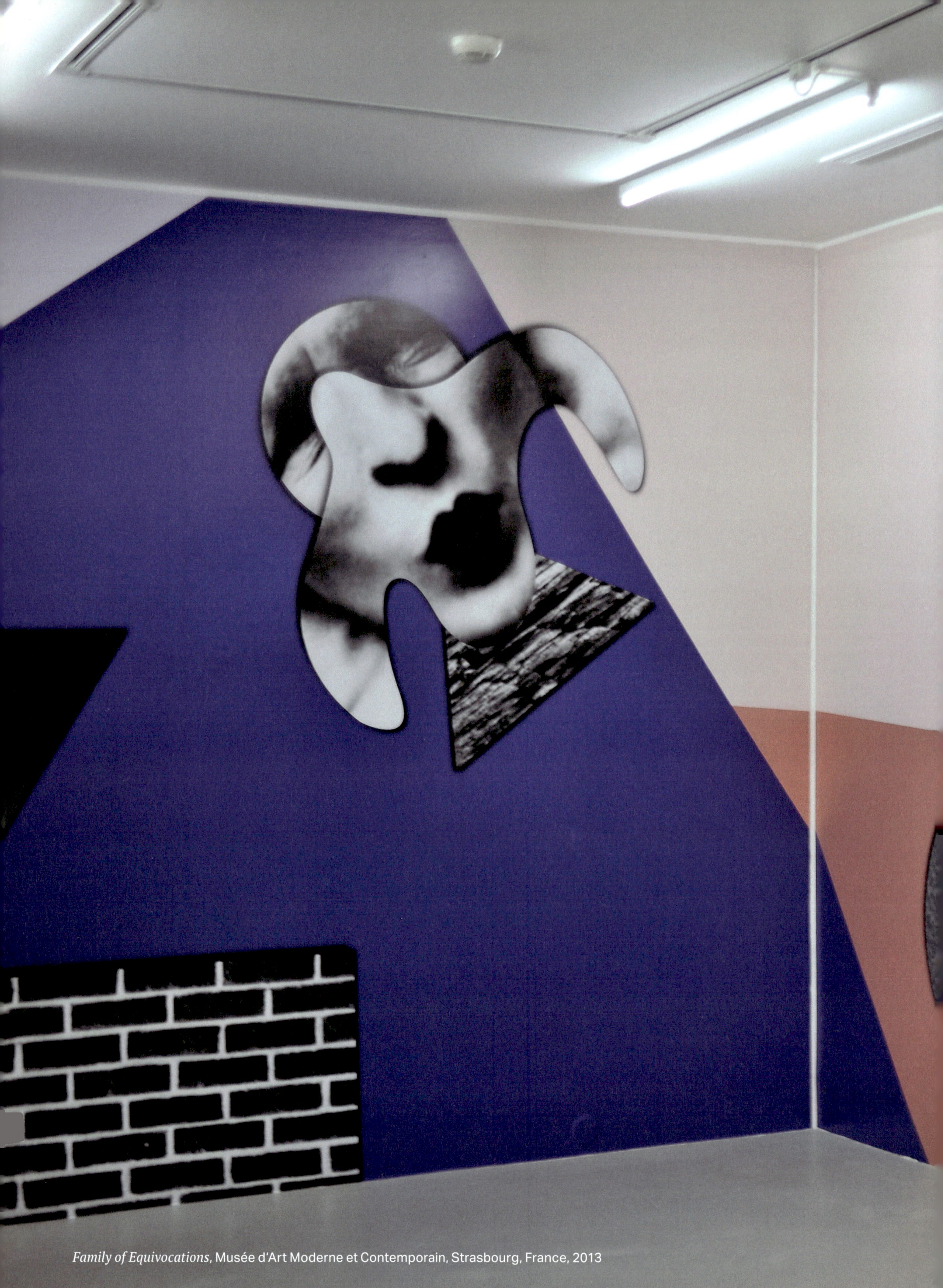

Family of Equivocations, Musée d'Art Moderne et Contemporain, Strasbourg, France, 2013

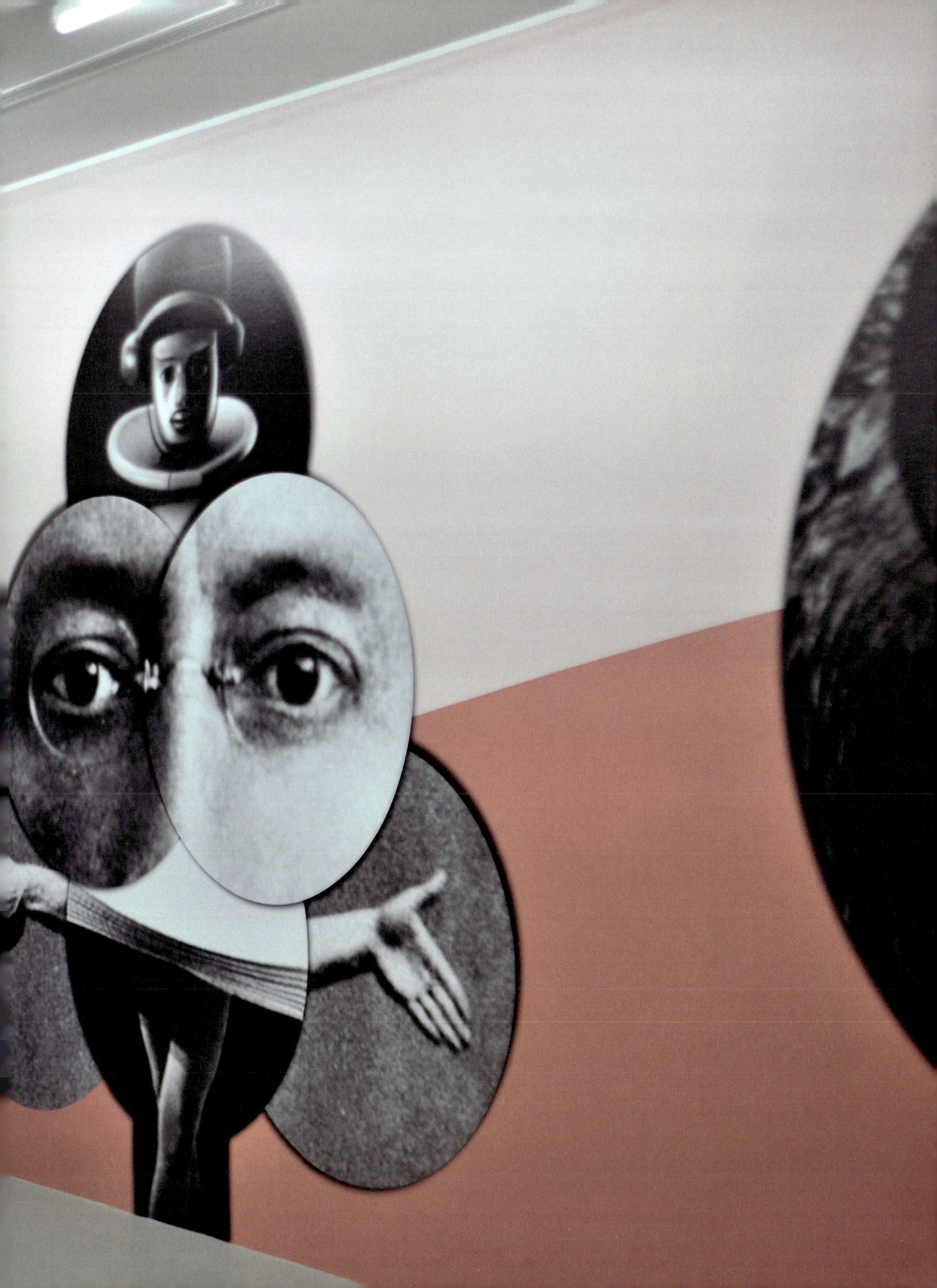

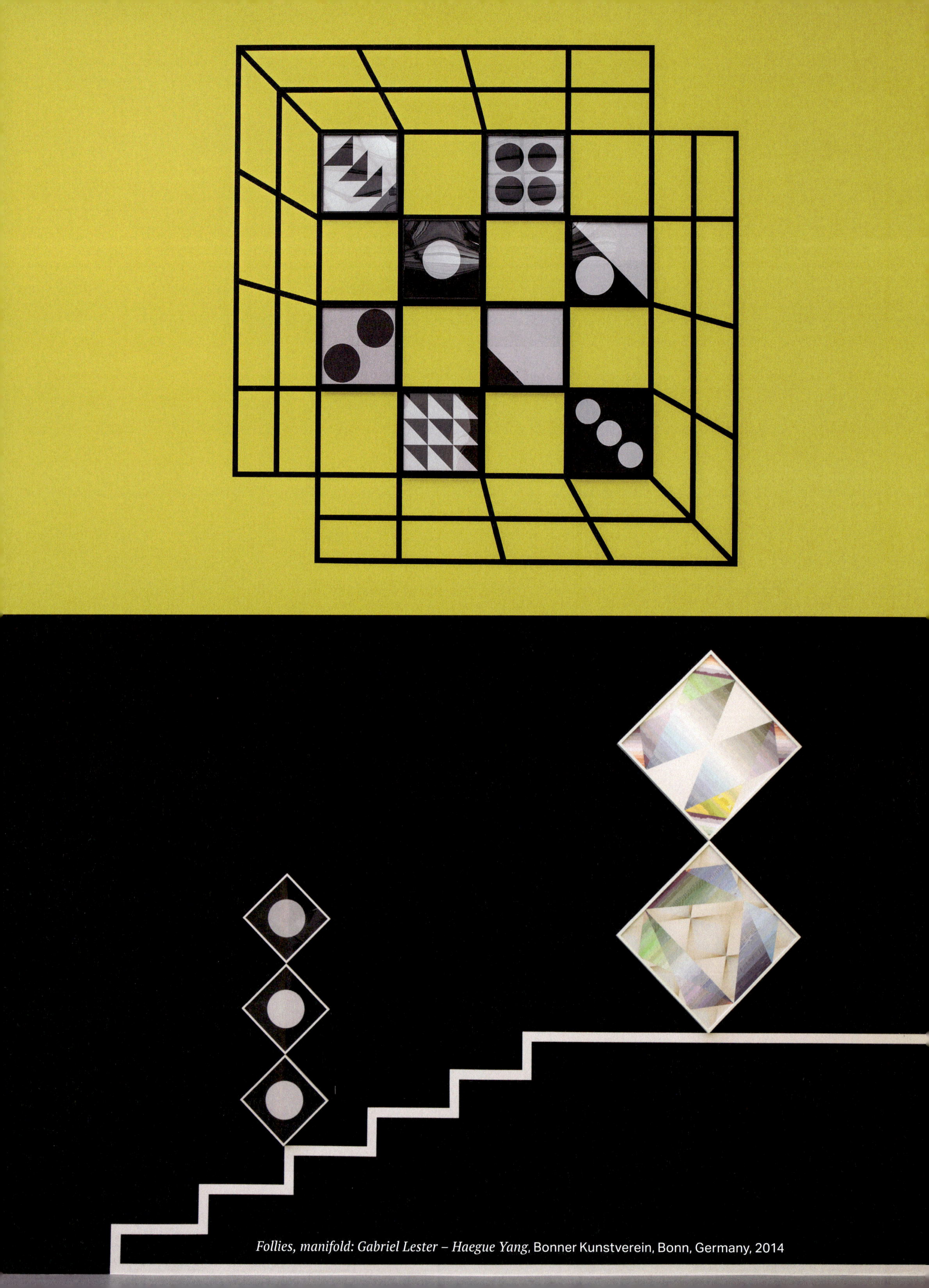

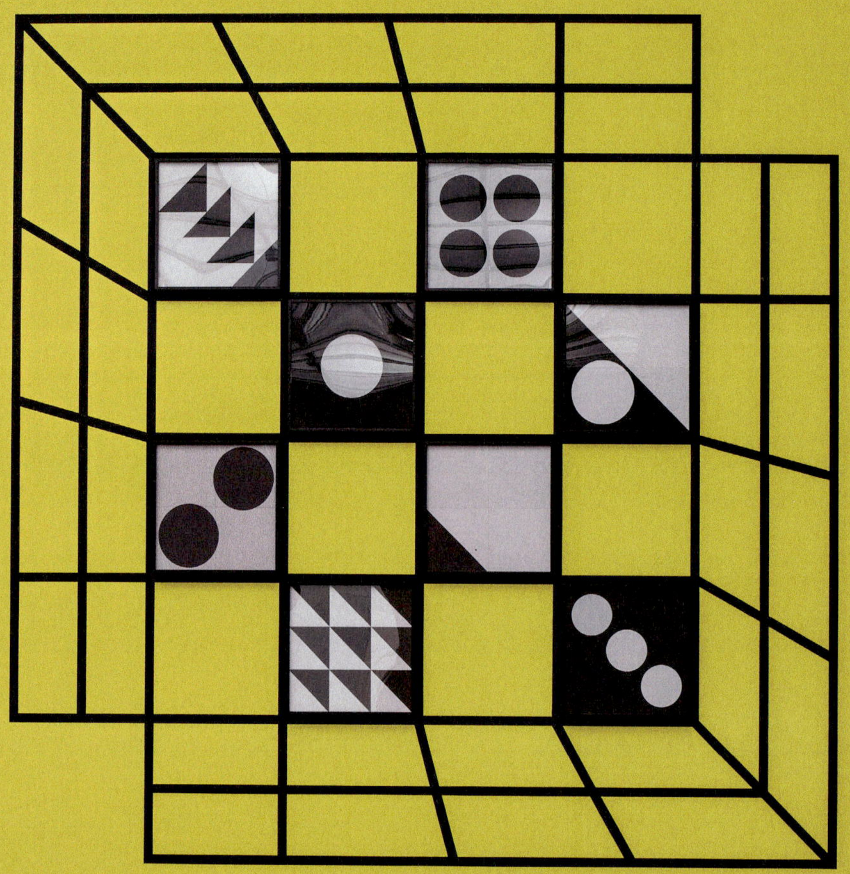

Follies, manifold: Gabriel Lester – Haegue Yang, Bonner Kunstverein, Bonn, Germany, 2014

Trustworthies #211–#221 (part of *Boxing Ballet*), 2013

Various security envelopes, graph paper and sandpaper on cardboard, spray paint on paper, framed, vinyl tape
41 parts, 142.2 × 102.2 cm;
102.2 × 102.2 cm;
100 × 72 cm;
72.2 × 72.2 cm;
41.2 × 41.2 cm;
33.2 × 33.2 cm

Oskar Schlemmer conceived the iconic dance work *Triadic Ballet* (1922) during his time at the Bauhaus as a way to connect his ideas about choreographed geometry to space, using the human body as a new artistic medium and designing costumes with restrictive corset-like frames and appendages for dancers so they resembled figurines. Gradually reconciling the Western avant-garde, Yang revisited Schlemmer's ballet and devised *Boxing Ballet*. As her interest in the body in motion grew, Schlemmer's sculptural costumes served as model inspirations of static counterpoints to naturalistic movement.

Colored walls served as a device to translate the time-based ballet into a spatial installation-based configuration and narrate the shifting moods of the three acts of the original ballet—yellow, pink, and black (also present in Schlemmer's original). Framed collages from her *Trustworthy* series (since 2010), flat works incorporating security envelopes applied inside out, likewise draw reference to geometric ornamentation and graphic abstraction and hinge on formal tenets of the Bauhaus order such as concepts of balance. Displayed in choreographed arrangements on the colored walls, they serve not only as novel actors, but, accompanying the figures in the *Boxing Ballet*, extend the modernist aesthetic of the room both as scenic elements and active protagonists. Vinyl tape on the floor delineates movement, divides the room, and references graphic elements in the original ballet.

Trustworthies previously expressed movement only within their compositions. This newborn constellation of mural-like complexity enabled each collage to perform: unfurl, persist on the brink of expansion, fold out horizontally, or stack to become a giant totemic figure. Employing the entire wall surface as a field, like a wallpaper, the narrative potential of the *Trustworthies* was amplified and expanded. Additionally, they incorporated an increasing variety of materialities, such as sandpaper, the artist's own graph paper designs from *Grid Bloc A3* (2013), and origami paper.

Journal of Echomimetic Motions, Bergen Kunsthall, Norway, 2013
Follies, Manifold: Gabriel Lester – Haegue Yang, Bonner Kunstverein, Bonn, Germany, 2014
Shooting the Elephant 象 Thinking the Elephant, Leeum, Samsung Museum of Art, Seoul, Korea 2015
In the Cone of Uncertainty, The Bass Museum of Art, Miami Beach, FL, USA 2019

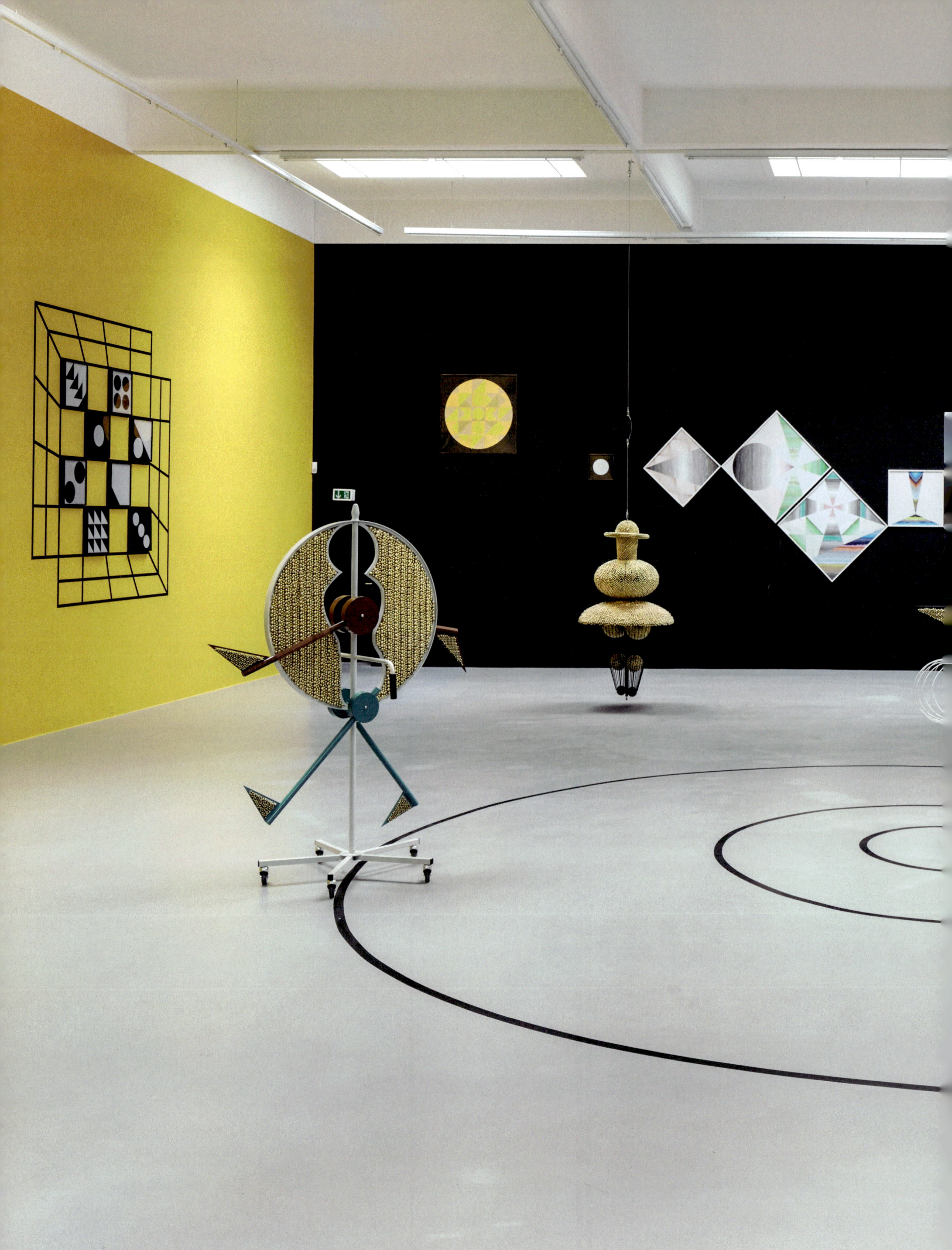

Follies, Manifold: Gabriel Lester – Haegue Yang, Bonner Kunstverein, Bonn, Germany, 2014

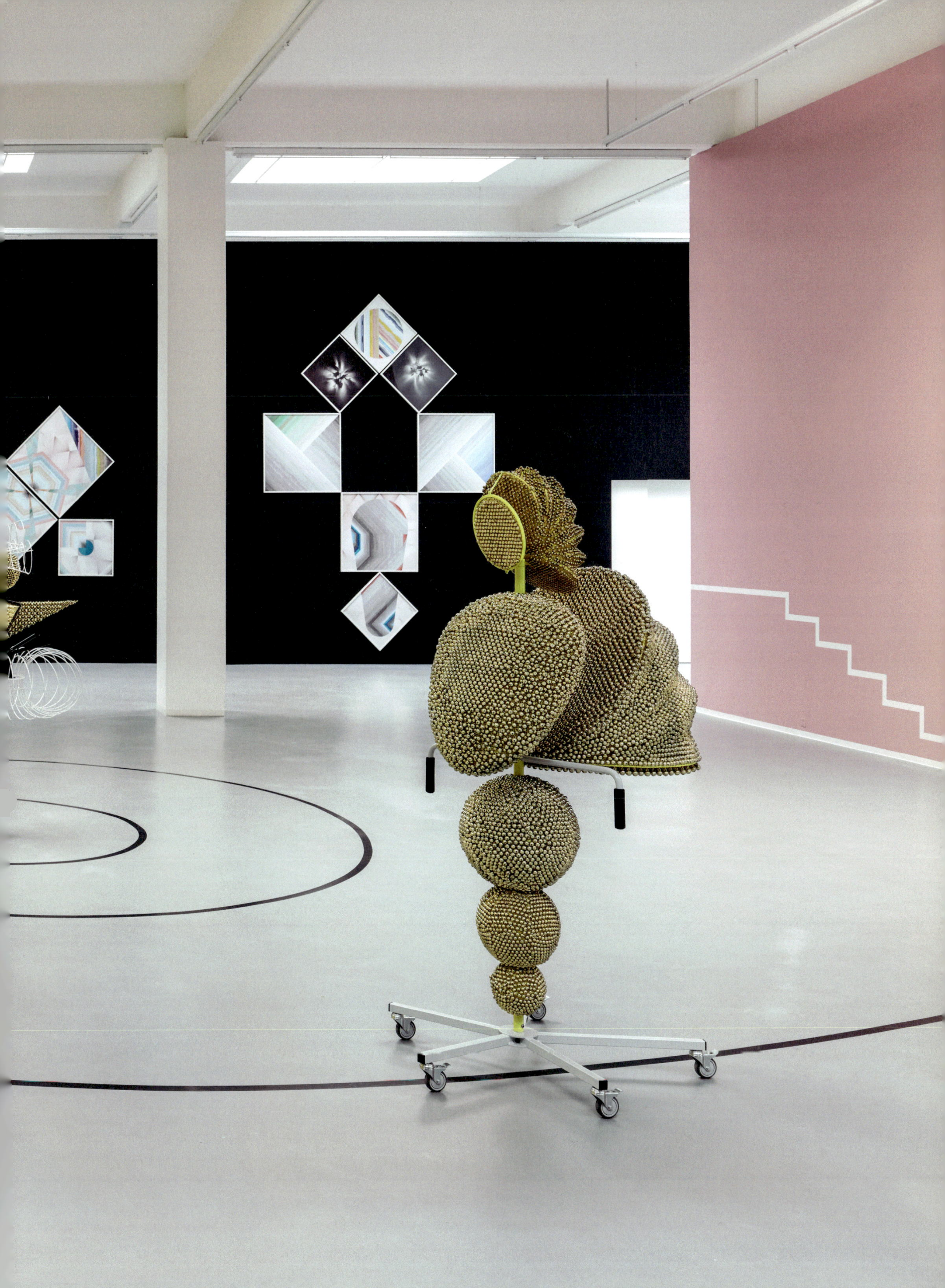

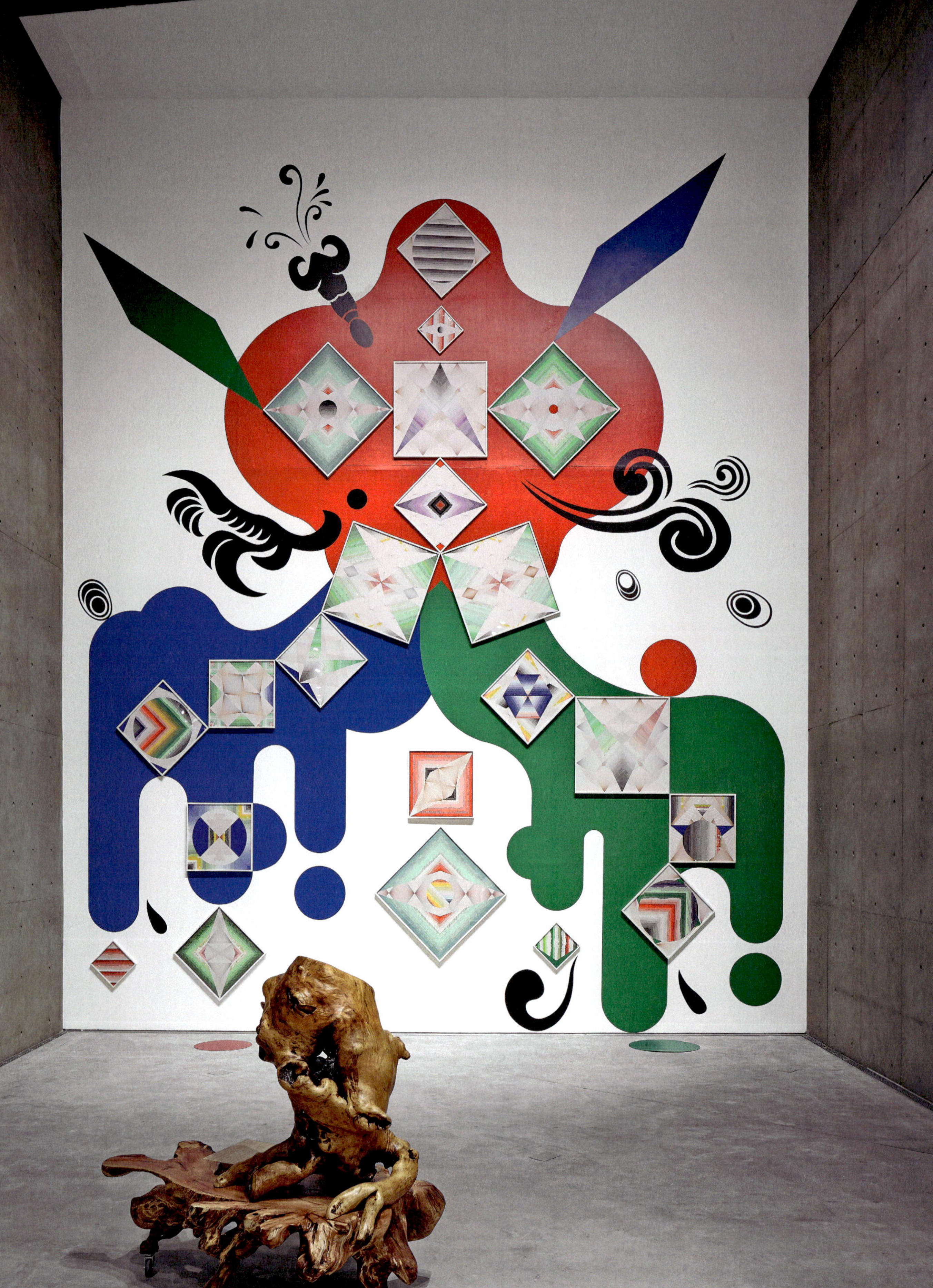

Shooting the Elephant 象 Thinking the Elephant, Leeum, Samsung Museum of Art, Seoul, South Korea, 2015

Hovering Lion Dance – Trustworthy #240, 2015

Various security envelopes, graph paper, and origami paper on cardboard, framed, self-adhesive vinyl film
21 parts, 102.2 × 102.2 cm; 72.2 × 72.2 cm; 36.2 × 36.2 cm

Hovering Lion Dance – Trustworthy #240 (hereafter referred to as *Hovering Lion Dance*) was conceived following years of continuous development as well as numerous productions of *Trustworthies*. The ten-meter-high, mostly hidden wall in the postmodern building of the Leeum, Samsung Museum of Art, was a seminal inspiration, its enormous height recalling the tradition across cultures of large rock faces with carved reliefs, displaying animistic reverence to mountains, rivers, and the sea.

Made of twenty-one framed *Trustworthies* hung in a rhythmic sequence, *Hovering Lion Dance* is an imposing vertical composition, with distinctive shapes cut from vinyl adhesive sheets in vibrant primary colors. If the vinyl shapes build the body of the creature, the framed *Trustworthies*, with their crystalline compositions, geometrically map its inner life. At once striving towards the verticality inherent to effigies or stewards that protect individuals and society, it also harnesses primal energy by evoking floating imagery from Buddhist or Taoist traditions.[1]

When *Hovering Lion Dance* was shown for the first time, the monumental size and minimalistic blankness of the adjacent exposed concrete wall provided an allegorical contrast and plausible habitat for the figurative creature. In the Far East, the lion is a non-native species, and therefore often thought to be capable of projecting a supernatural power, thusly popular among the repertoire of folk dances in Korea, Japan, and China. Whether confronting us directly or gazing over the human world from above, the strong graphic presence of a lion in ascent exudes eeriness, provoking introspection into a power of foreign origin within native or indigenous nature-culture.

The vinyl graphics of *Hovering Lion Dance* were rearranged at the Ullens Center for Contemporary Art (UCCA), Beijing, in a horizontal configuration as if to squeeze and stretch the mythical figure inside the painted black wall, rather than its bold graphic shapes on an airy backdrop.

1 Cliff-carved Buddhas and Bodhisattvas are broadly found in regions of Buddhist belief. One example is the Bamiyan Buddhas in Kabul, Afghanistan. The first cliff-carved Buddha appeared in Korea around the seventh century during the Baekje Kingdom period in the Seosan and Taean regions.

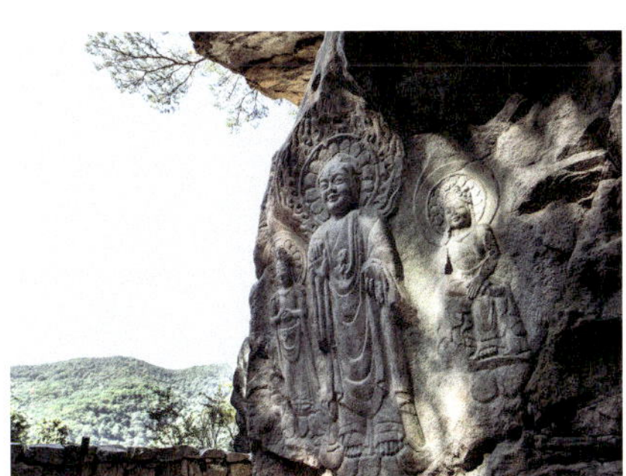

Shooting the Elephant 象 Thinking the Elephant, Leeum, Samsung Museum of Art, Seoul, South Korea, 2015
Come Shower or Shine, It Is Equally Blissful, Ullens Center for Contemporary Art, Beijing, China, 2015

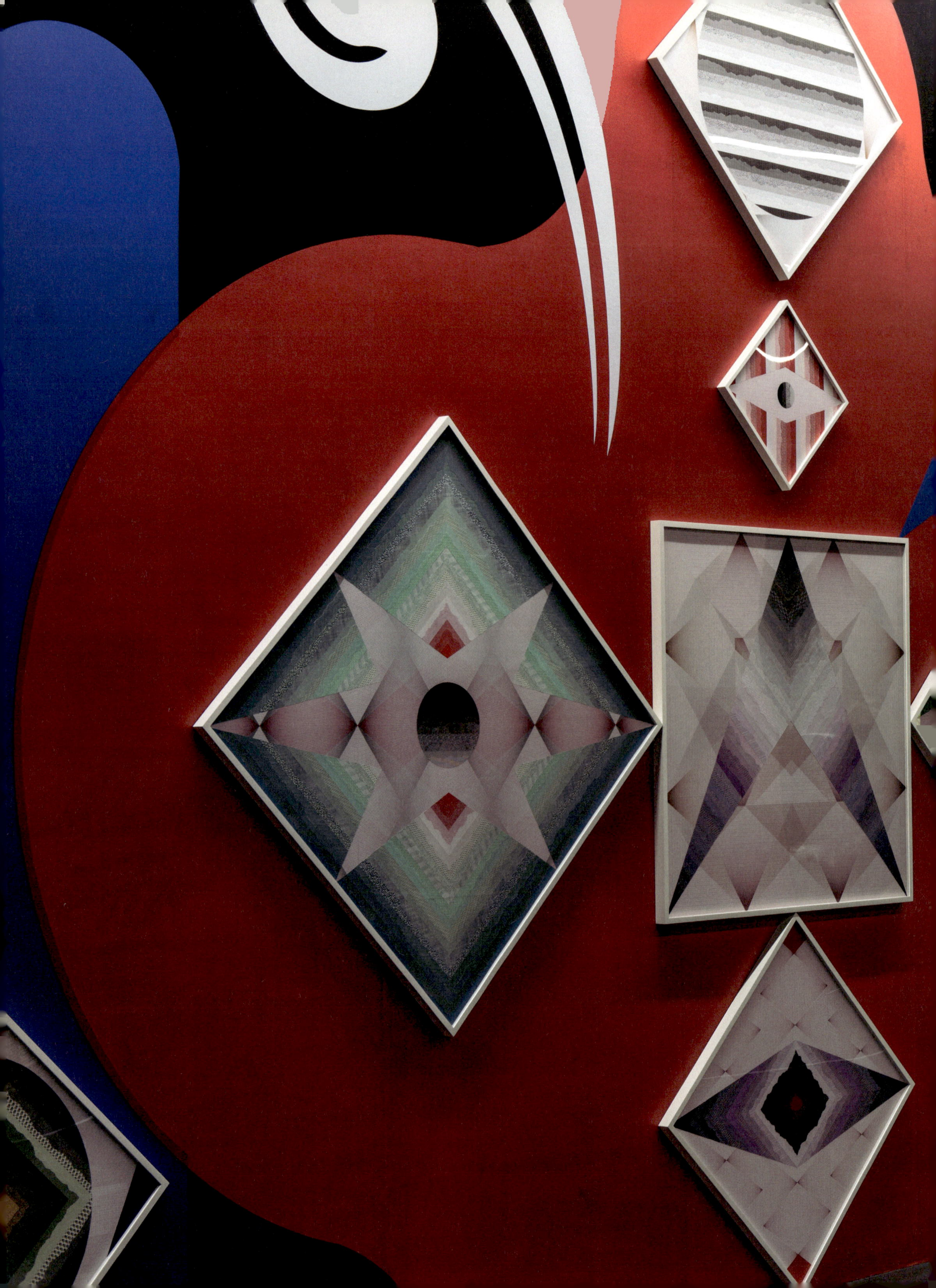

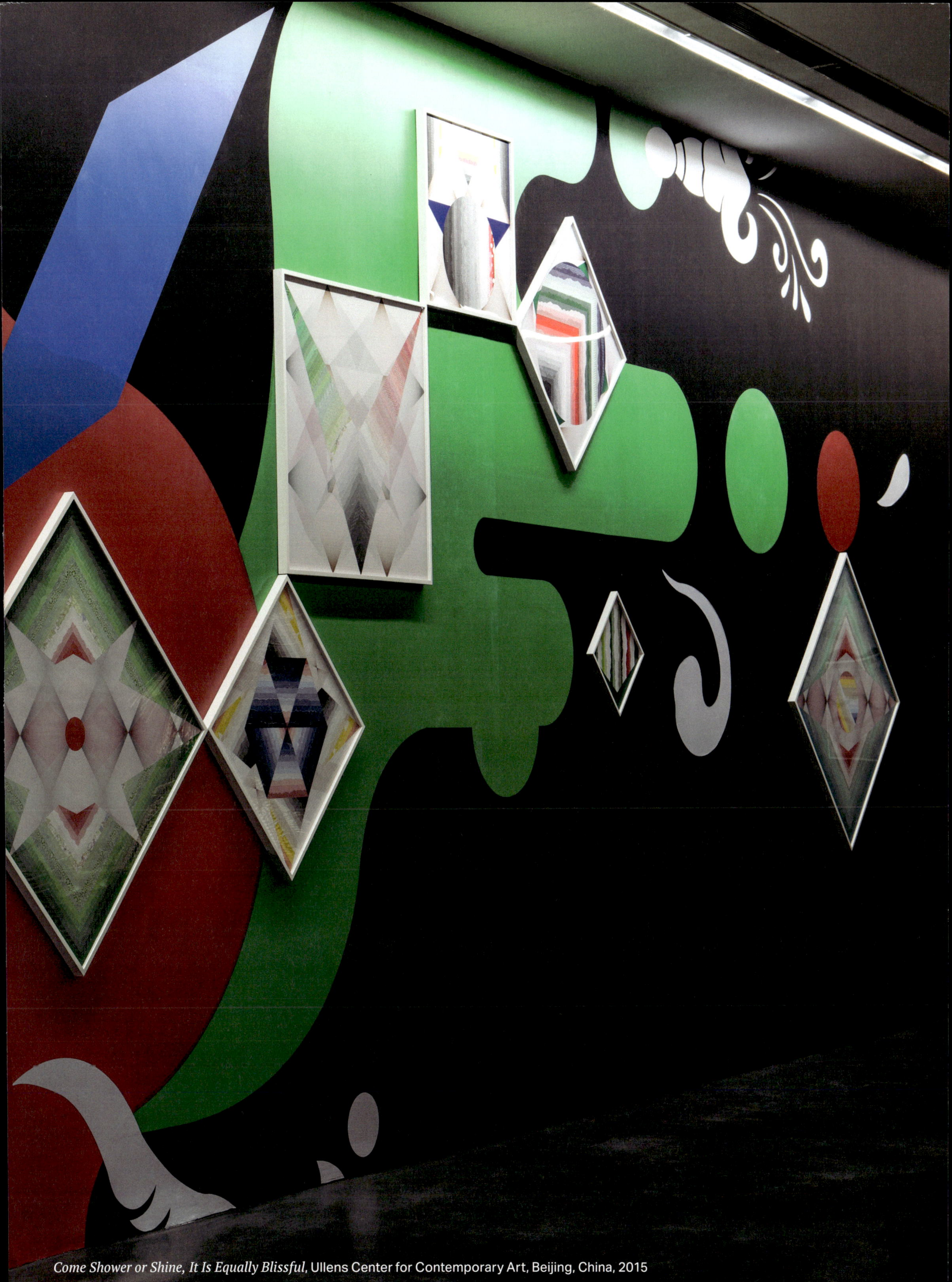

Come Shower or Shine, It Is Equally Blissful, Ullens Center for Contemporary Art, Beijing, China, 2015

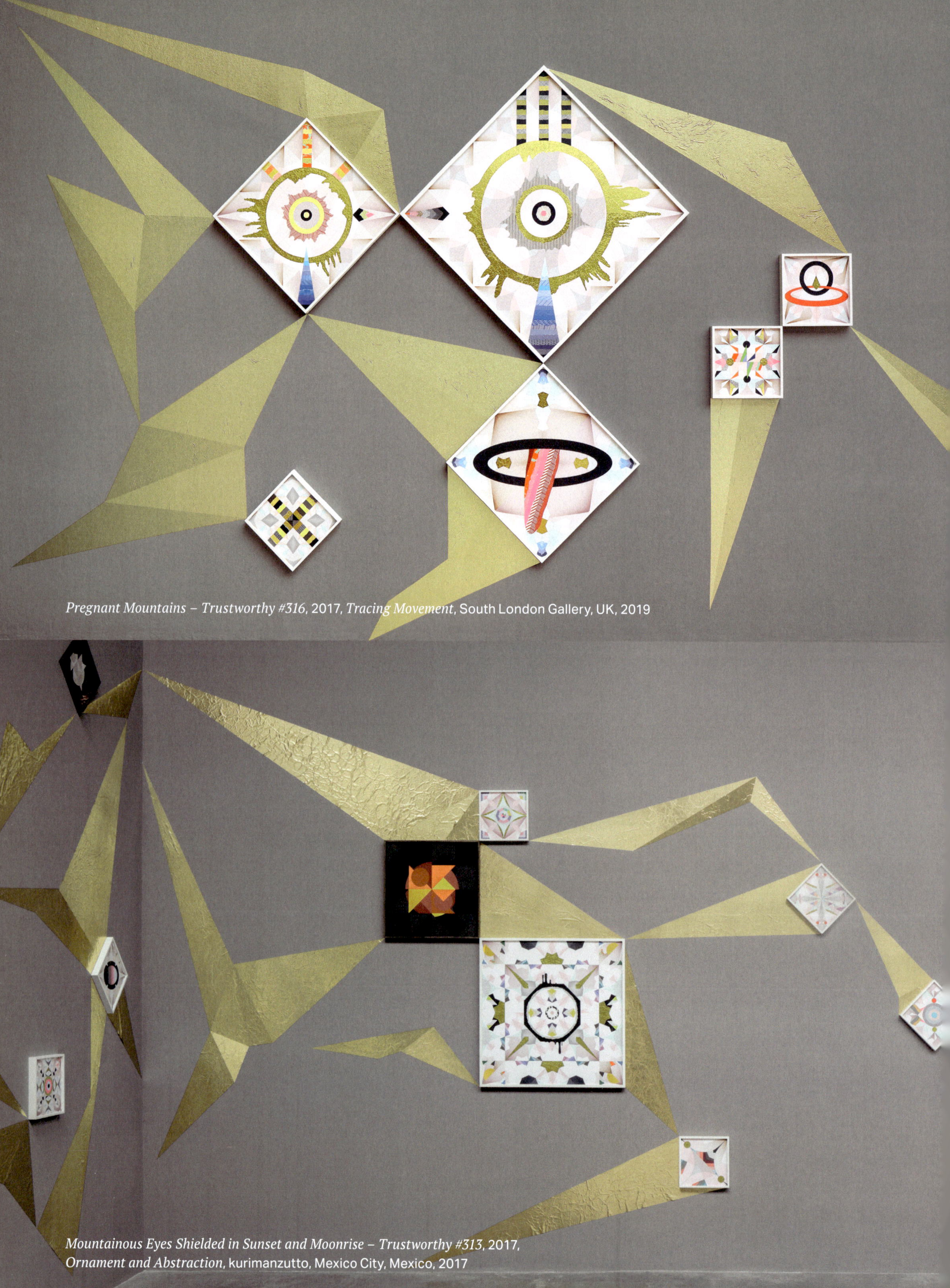

Pregnant Mountains – Trustworthy #316, 2017, *Tracing Movement*, South London Gallery, UK, 2019

Mountainous Eyes Shielded in Sunset and Moonrise – Trustworthy #313, 2017, *Ornament and Abstraction*, kurimanzutto, Mexico City, Mexico, 2017

Trustworthies #313–#316, 2017

Mountainous Eyes Shielded in Sunset and Moonrise – Trustworthy #313
13 parts

Lightning Gleam in the Lunar Mountains – Trustworthy #314
7 parts

Big-eyed Tongue-tied Mountains beneath Solar and Lunar Orbs – Trustworthy #315
11 parts

Pregnant Mountains – Trustworthy #316
7 parts

Various security envelopes, graph paper, origami paper, and sandpaper on cardboard, framed, self-adhesive vinyl film

86.2 × 86.2 cm;
57.2 × 57.2 cm;
29.2 × 29.2 cm

The development and composition of these *Trustworthies* was guided by Yang's approach to her first solo exhibition in Mexico, in which she reconsidered both ornamentation and the Western canon of abstraction simultaneously. The shared ground between folk craftsmanship and industrial fabrication often associated with the post-Fordist world is evident in her work and furthermore in this exhibition, titled *Ornament and Abstraction*. Referencing modernist architect Adolf Loos's essay *Ornament and Crime* (1910) and her critical reading of it, Yang ambitiously aims to embrace these seemingly oppositional fields: the modern strategy for a liberation from ornamentation and the spirituality inherent in ethnic ornamentation. In both, Yang proposed a concept of labor divorced from profit. The shaped walls with holographic elements emerge here again as both structural and formal incisions in the overall installation.

On a dark-gray backdrop against the gallery's semi-reflective floor, reaching lines like thin triangular legs of golden vinyl connect and cinch each frame within a mountainous silhouette, forming an illogical perspectival space. As if each *Trustworthy* were a mesmeric mineral, they share an almost spiritual impulse toward mechanical expansion. The hard geometric lines of the mural contrast with the organic spines of *The Intermediates* in the foreground. The arrangement of four mural-like pieces was inspired by pre-Columbian gold artifacts from the ancient Muisca civilization, which considered metal to be a sacred substance. The use of gold vinyl—reminiscent of fool's gold—in this piece is especially significant, as the artist often uses rather pseudo- or quasi-materials, instead of real and truthful substances, such as the substitution of synthetic for real straw in *The Intermediates*.

Ornament and Abstraction, kurimanzutto, Mexico City, Mexico, 2017
Tracing Movement, South London Gallery, London, UK, 2019 (only *Trustworthies #313, #315, #316*)

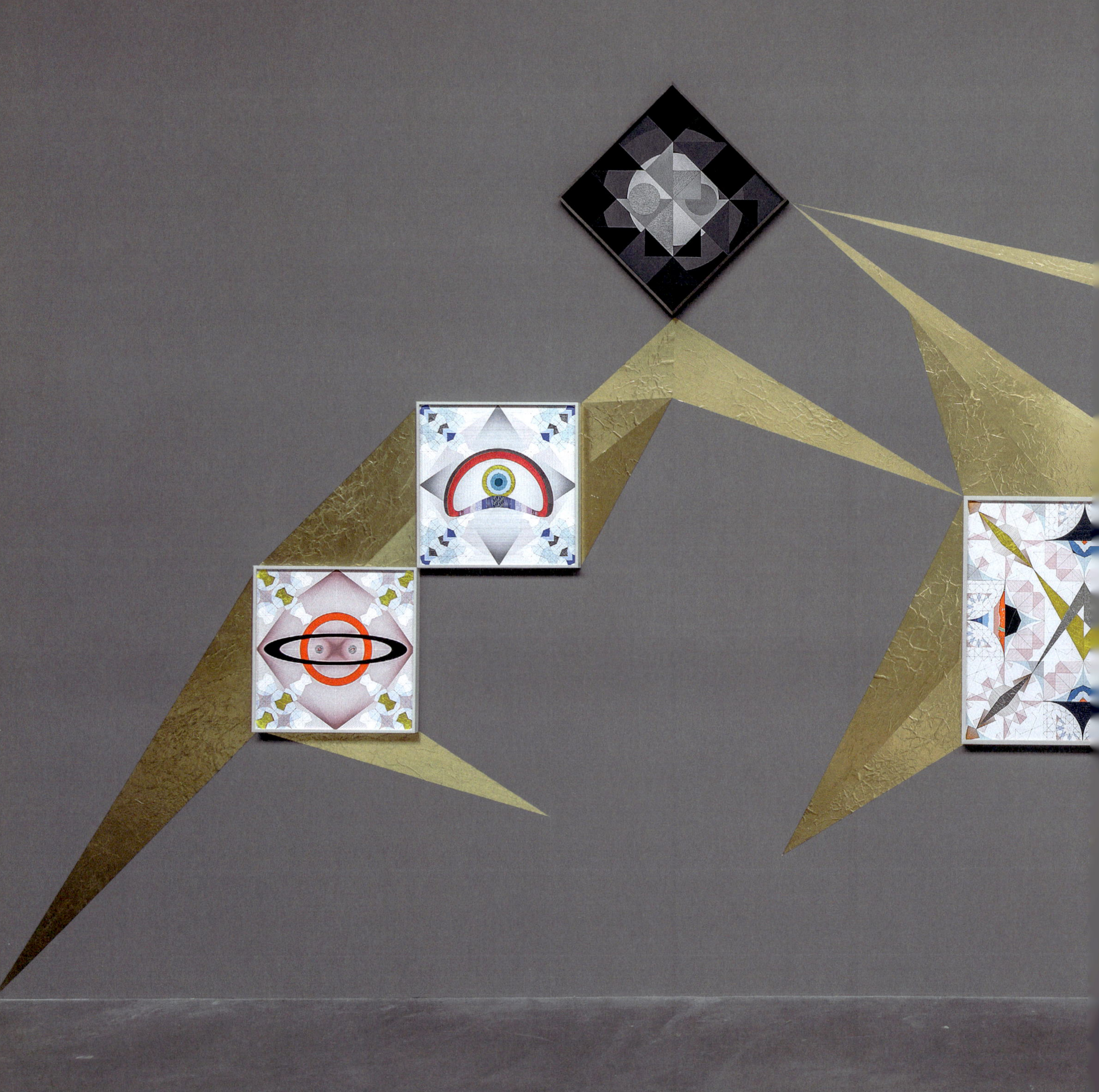

Lightning Gleam in the Lunar Mountains – Trustworthy #314, 2017, *Ornament and Abstraction*, kurimanzutto, Mexico City, Mexico, 2017

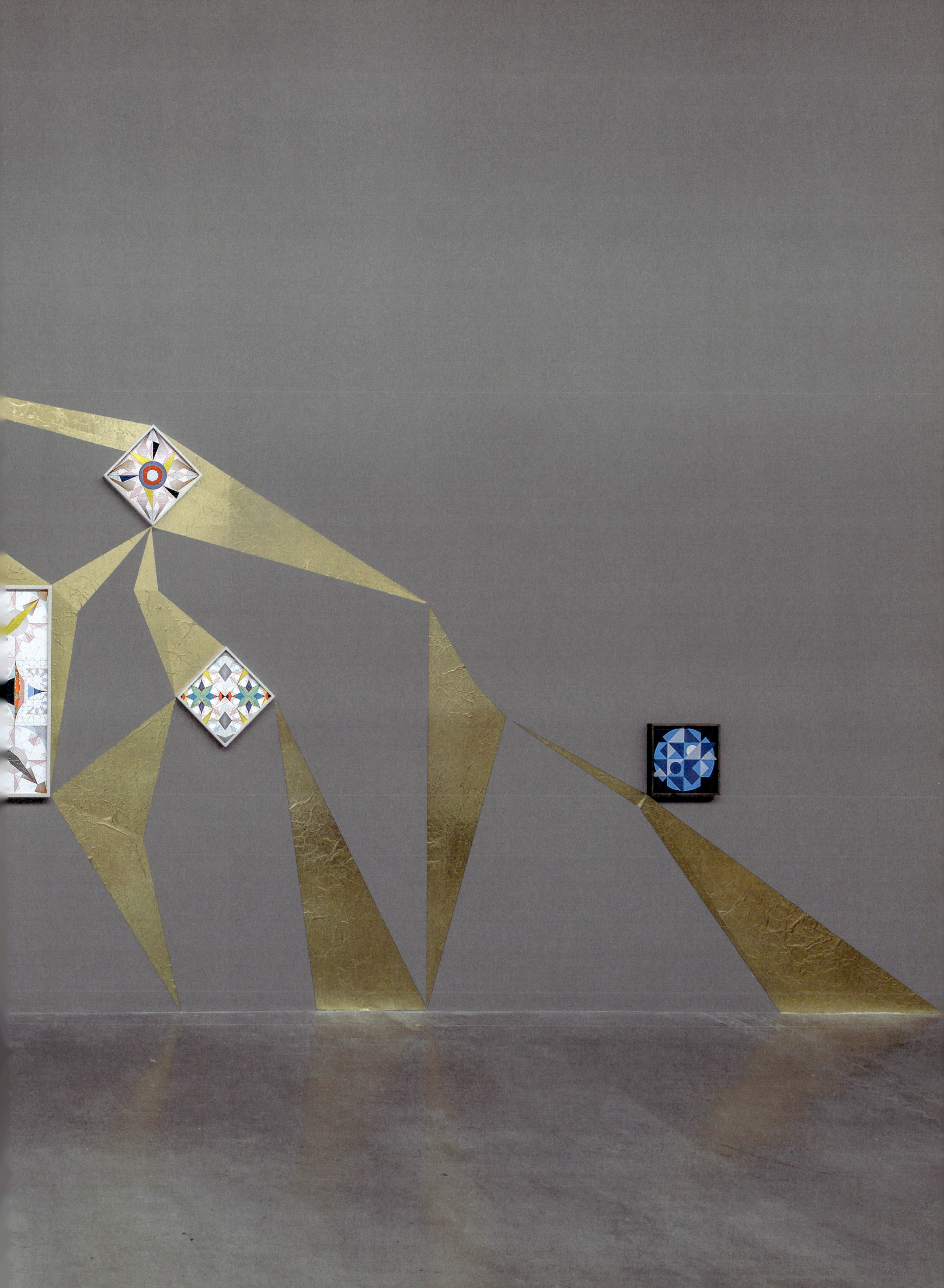

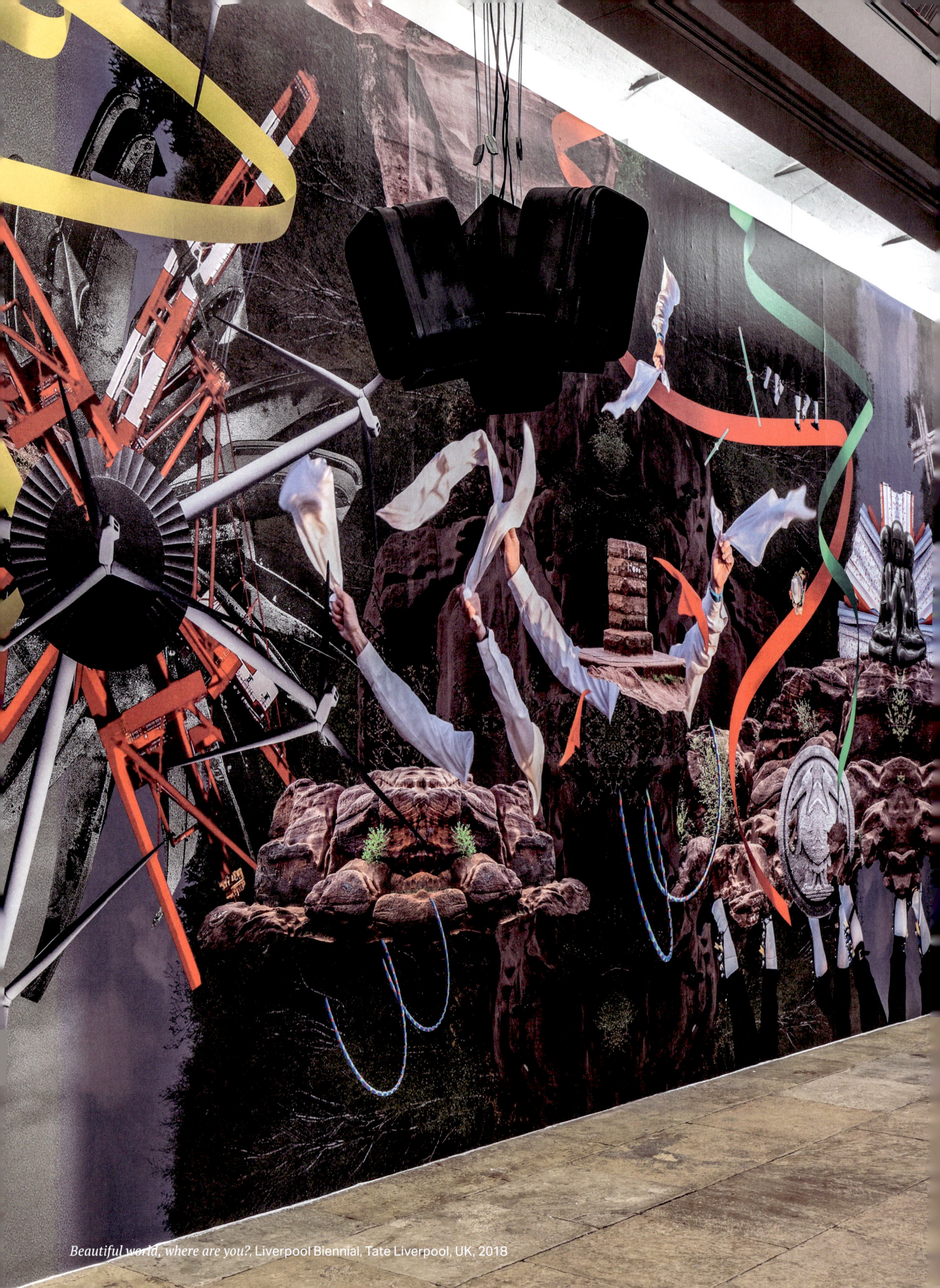

Beautiful world, where are you?, Liverpool Biennial, Tate Liverpool, UK, 2018

Dockside Rock and Roll, 2018

In collaboration with Mike Carney
Digital color print
Dimensions variable

For the Liverpool Biennial, Yang for the first time incorporated site-specificity into a wallpaper. *Dockside Rock and Roll* allows a reading of Liverpool's modern and ancient history, while also indirectly addressing a post-globalized, decentralized, and overly connected society, in which time and place are destabilized. The synthetic woven sculptures *The Intermediates* (2015–ongoing) inhabit terrarium-like islands filled with generic display objects such as fake rocks and artificial vegetation. They appear both alien and native to their environment. Ribbons drawn from the ceiling of the Wolfson Gallery to the pillars resemble maypoles from traditional English Mayday rituals with roots in pagan festivities, yet are upside-down with abnormal colors referring to the Korean traditional textile Saekdong. Speakers suspended from the ceiling broadcast British Library recordings from natural and urban spaces accompanied by ASMR sounds, which are used to trigger a physical sensation, bridging the various physical and visual elements.

Set against a gray background color that matches iron elements in the gallery and also resembles a gloomy mirrored Liverpool landscape, the wallpaper combines numerous local references; folk traditions and brutal industrial history seamlessly coexist. Spiritual sites such as Thurstaston rocks from the Wirral Peninsula seem psychedelic rather than sacred through multiple mirrorings. Overlapping shipyard power cranes and wind turbines are disorienting. The gloved hands and hips of female Morris dancers—a dance that has been evolving for more than 500 years—and arms grasping handkerchiefs of male dancers intersect, juxtaposed with Art Deco details from Liverpool's restored docklands and iconic Queensway Tunnel ventilation tower. Isolated from their original context to form a (sur)real world, these recognizable motifs spar in a confrontation between local urban mythical and actual worlds, suspended into a colorful all-over composition. Commenting on the hybridity in modern-day society, Yang acknowledges the vitality of such traditions and rituals by layering together multiple histories.

Beautiful world, where are you?, Liverpool Biennial, Tate Liverpool, UK, 2018

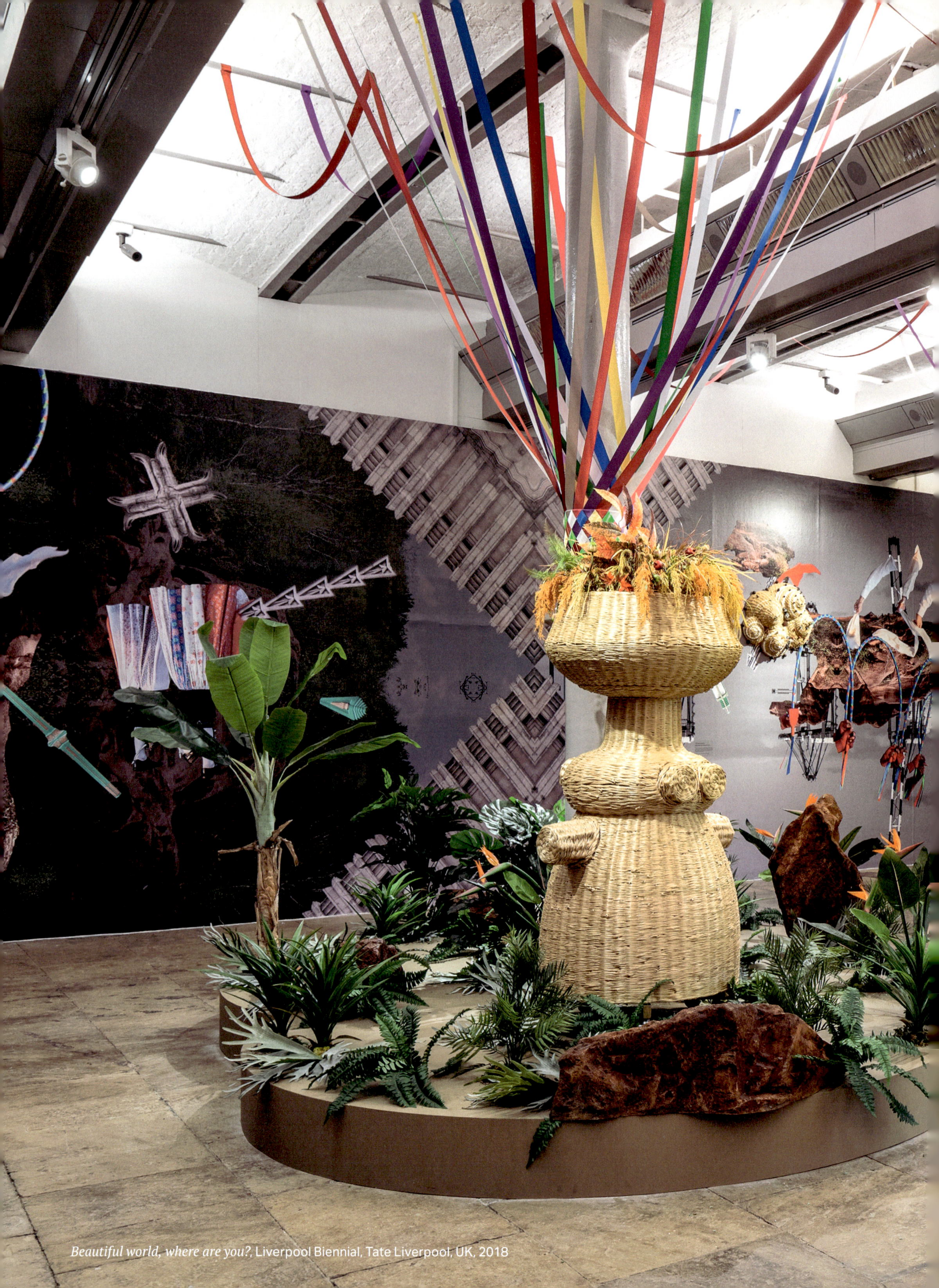

Beautiful world, where are you?, Liverpool Biennial, Tate Liverpool, UK, 2018

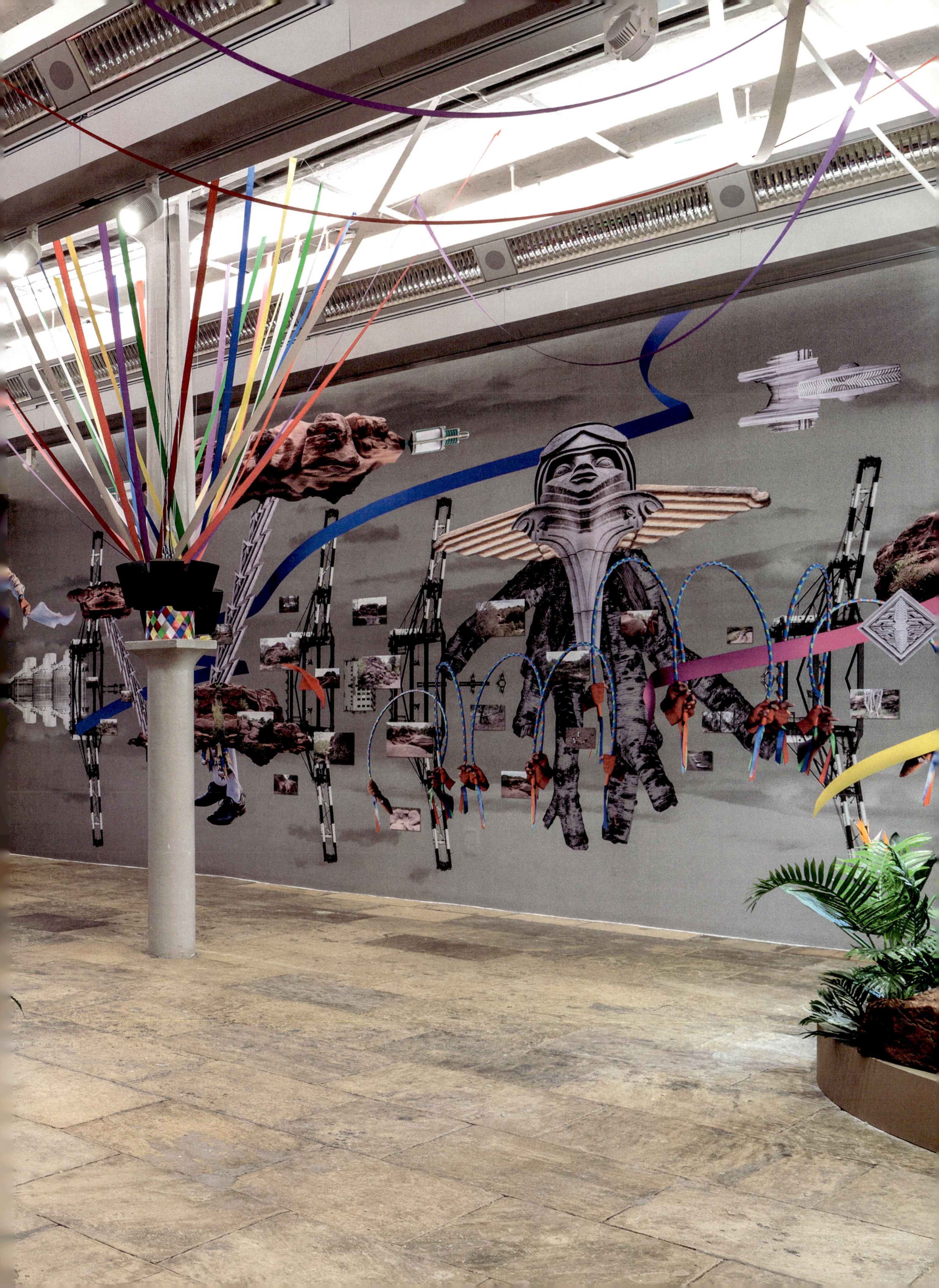

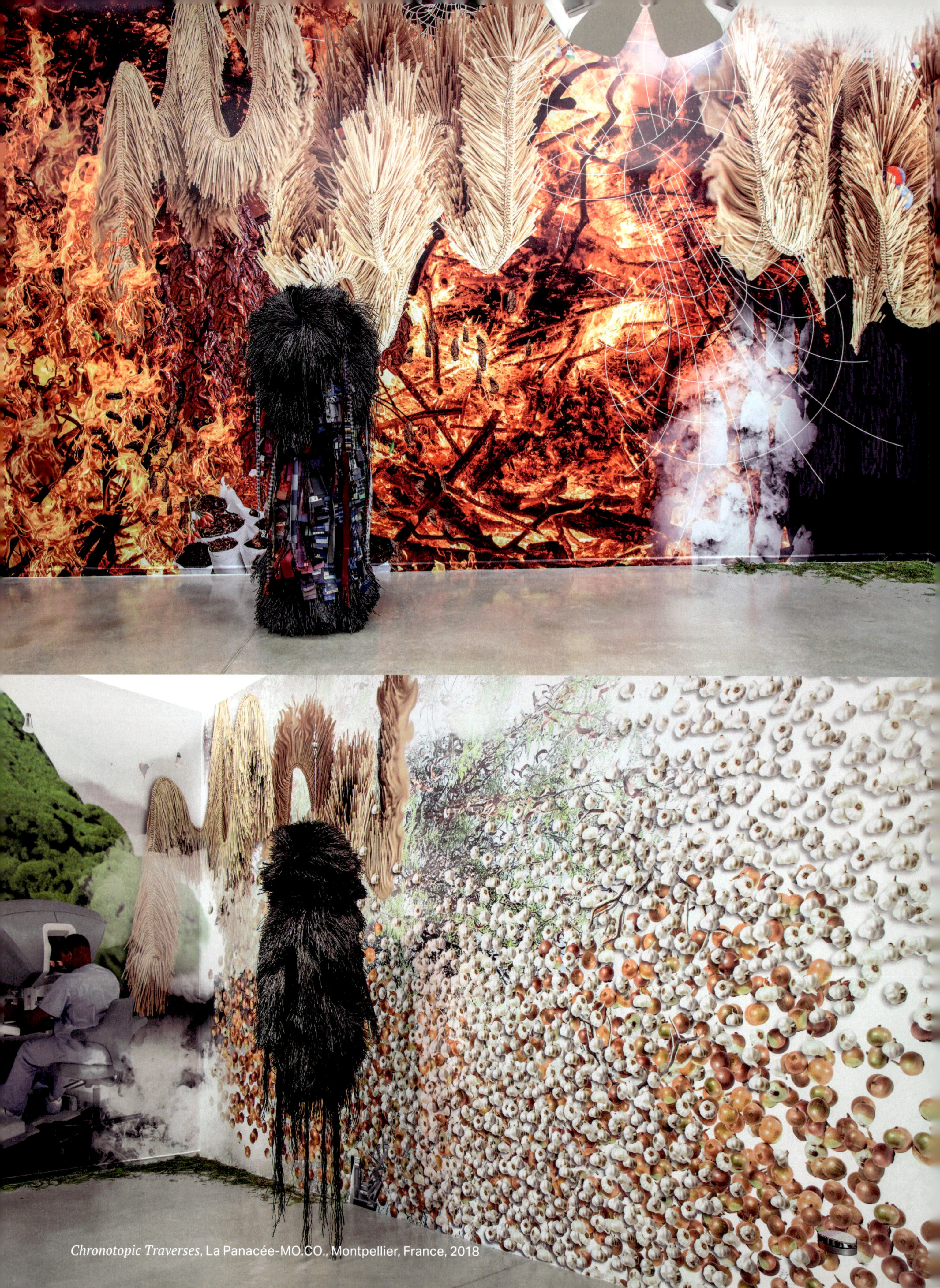

Chronotopic Traverses, La Panacée-MO.CO., Montpellier, France, 2018

Incubation and Exhaustion, 2018

In collaboration with Studio Manuel Raeder
Digital color print
Dimensions variable

Gathered together as a result of Yang's initial investigation into Occitan culture and modern local industries, and her long-standing interest in European pagan culture and folklore, the motifs in *Incubation and Exhaustion*, commissioned for her solo exhibition *Chronotopic Traverses* at La Panacée-MO.CO. and shown with a variety of sculptures, originate from various places and eras. Composed of anachronistic or even oppositional parts, their placement echoes natural diametrical cycles and binaries, such as day and night, blooming and burning, old and new, and human and non-human. Flames, patches of murkiness, and ambiguous clouds or fog build transitions in the oscillating cycle. Yang's affinity for common grocery items—like chilies, garlic and onions—is evident, segueing into an image of a false pepper tree (Schinus molle). Branches and leaves that Yang found at the yard of La Panacée scattered in the corners of the space and enriched with essential oil blur the illusionary and the real. The high-end surgical robot, separating surgeons from patients, serves as both a representation of the current high tech industrial development in Montpellier and mimics the amputation and connection between the motifs in the wallpaper.

The natural and technological imagery forsakes order and compartmentalized readings of terms such as folkloric, historic, modern, and contemporary. This nonhierarchical and anachronistic aspect of *Incubation and Exhaustion* addresses place and time as a conglomerate, time as flux, and enables us to embark on an immersive journey, juxtaposing and merging contradictions to reveal the complexities of common knowledge and phenomena seemingly beyond our grasp of reality.

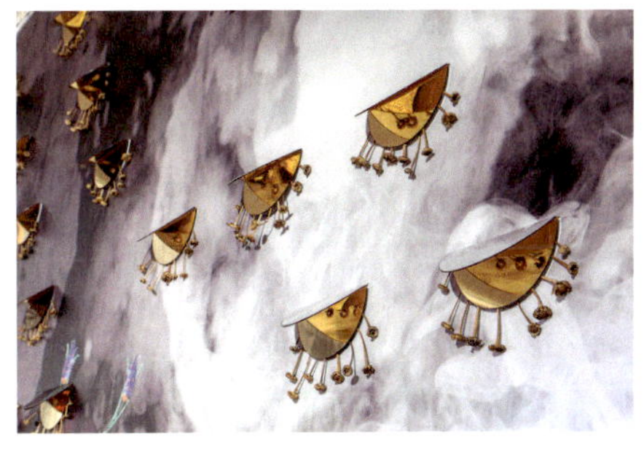

Incubation and Exhaustion – Version Istanbul, 2019, 16th Istanbul Biennial, Turkey, 2019

For the Istanbul Biennial, images of winged angels, pomegranates, and "broken" tulips are added. The raised semicircular cuts and adapted Secchi disks address the constant reconstruction of multiple layers of ancient civilizations in Istanbul. Scenographic elements such as moving lights, scent, fog, exercise balls, and sound complete the immersive setting.

Chronotopic Traverses, La Panacée-MO.CO., Montpellier, France, 2018
Taipei Dangdai, Taiwan, 2019
And Berlin Will Always Need You: Art, Craft and Concept Made in Berlin, Gropius Bau, Berlin, Germany, 2019
When The Year 2000 Comes, Kukje Gallery, Seoul, South Korea, 2019
The Seventh Continent, 16th Istanbul Biennial, Turkey, 2019

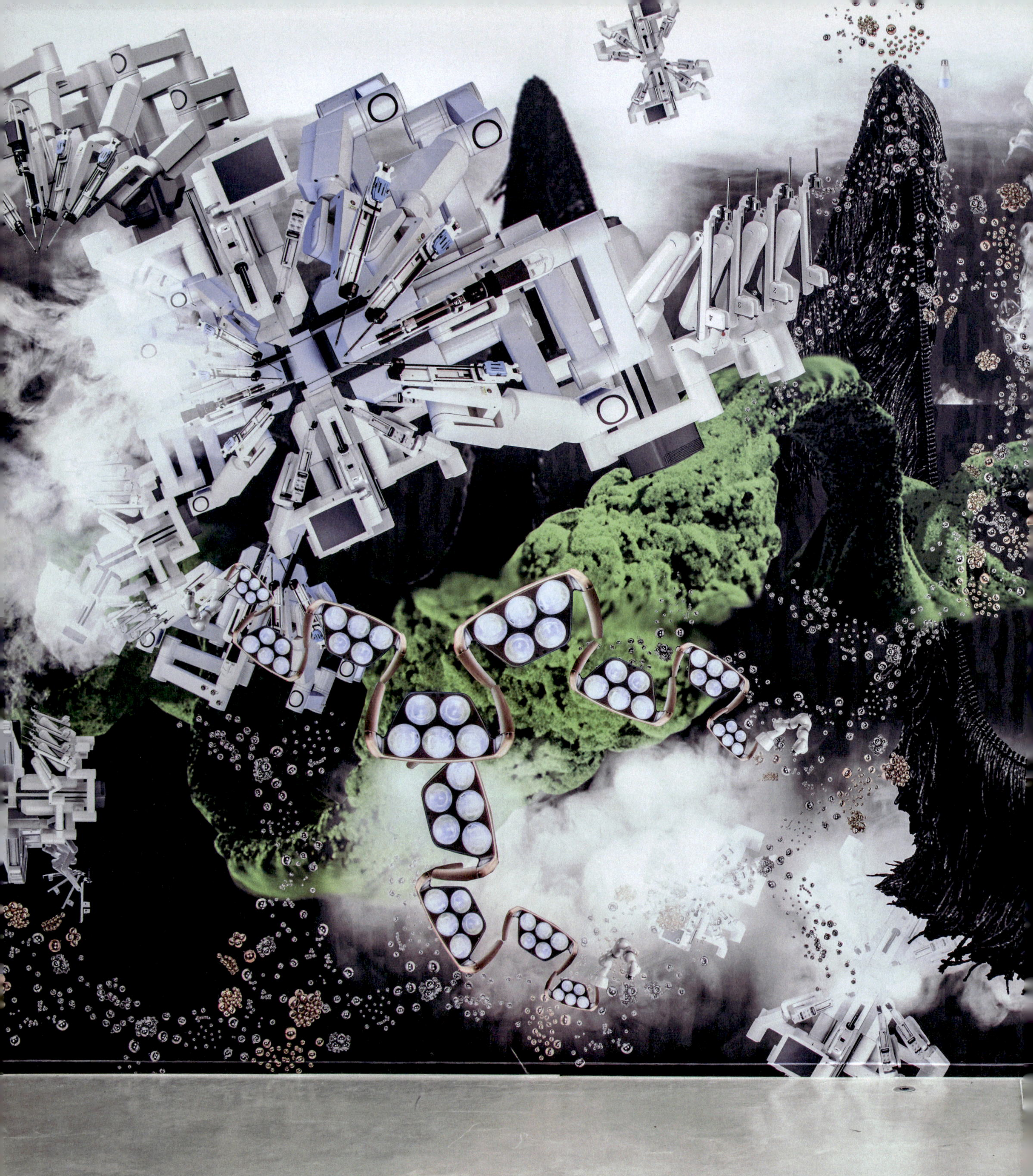

Chronotopic Traverses, La Panacée-MO.CO., Montpellier, France, 2018

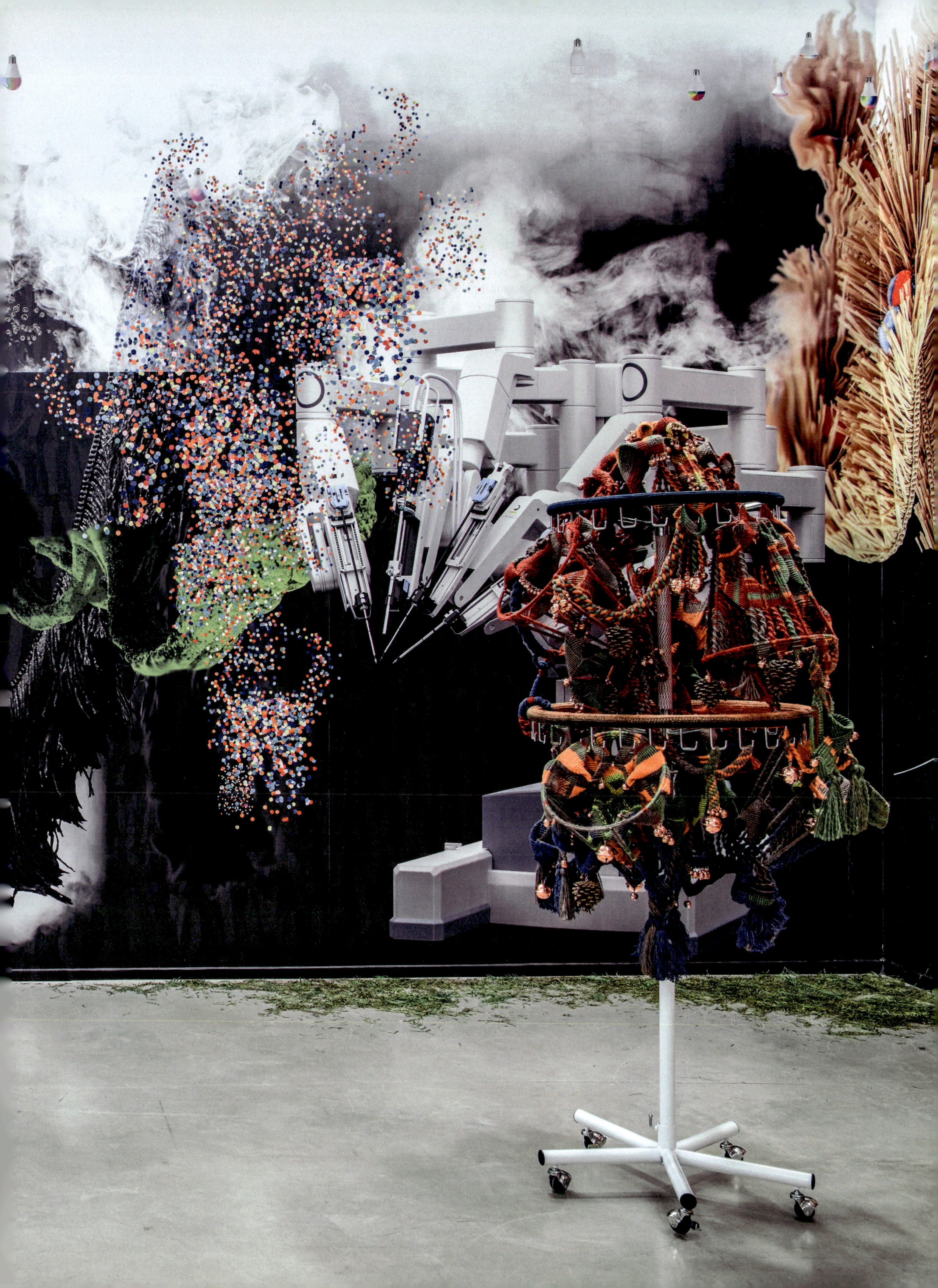

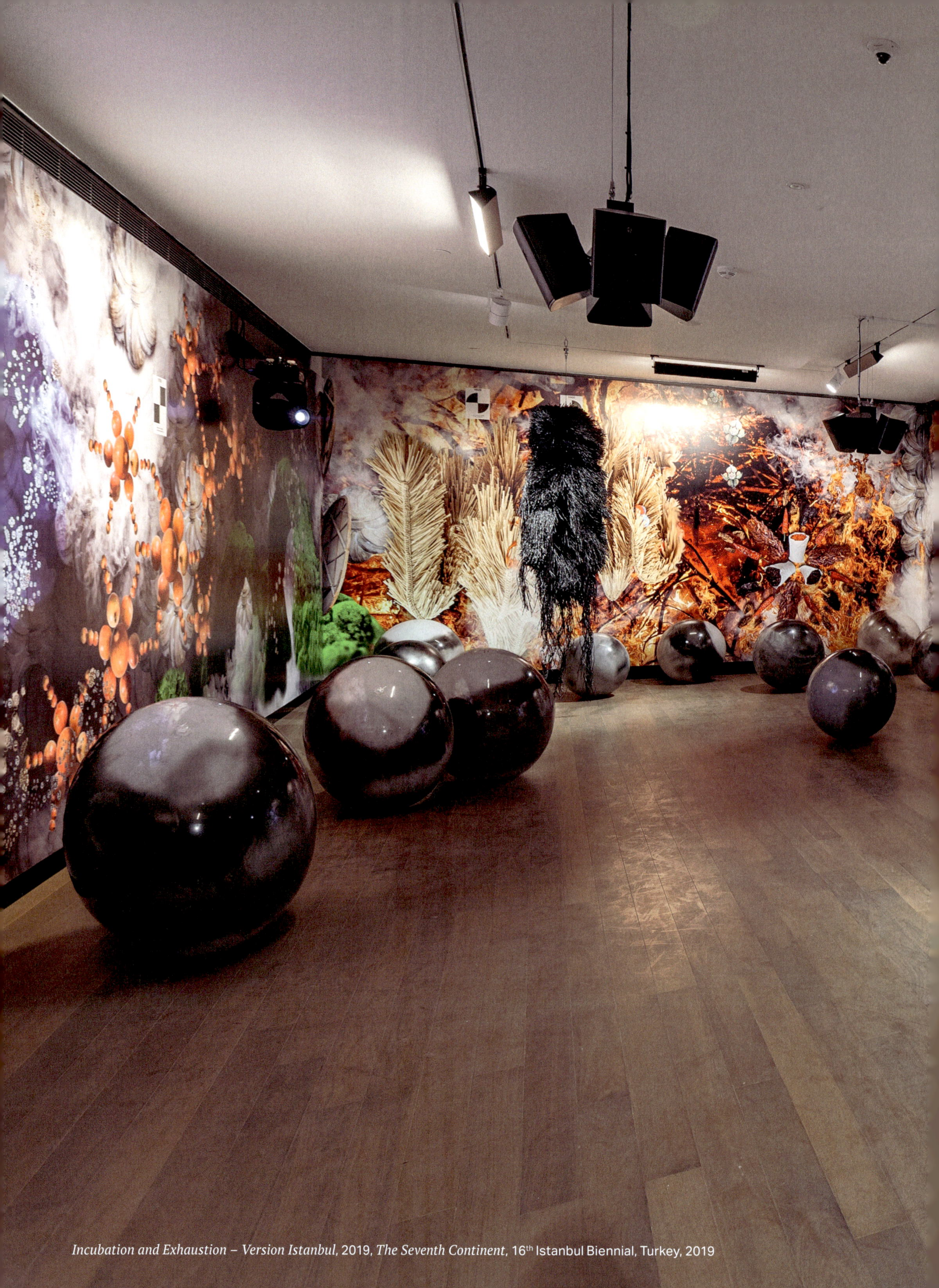

Incubation and Exhaustion – Version Istanbul, 2019, *The Seventh Continent*, 16th Istanbul Biennial, Turkey, 2019

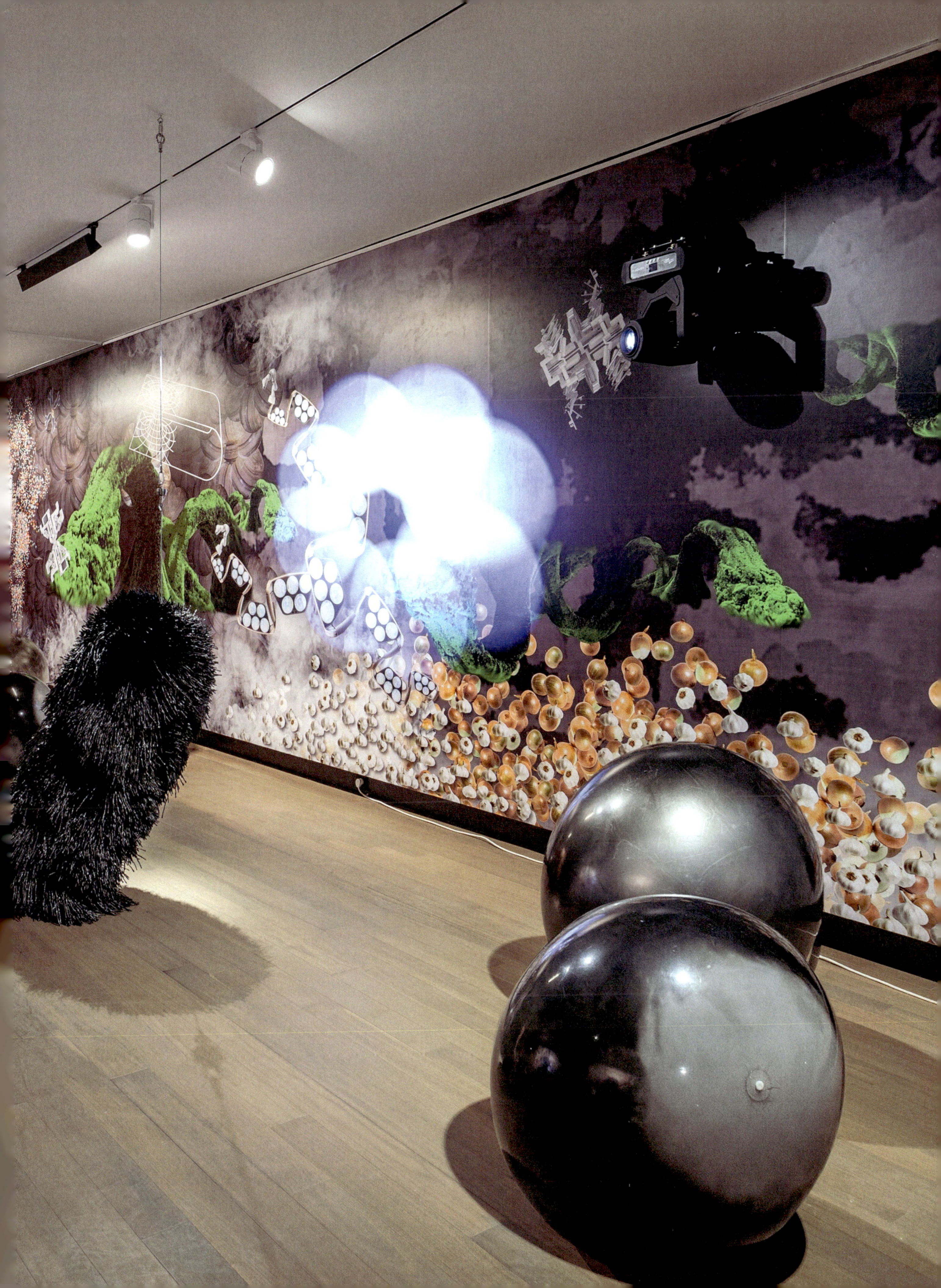

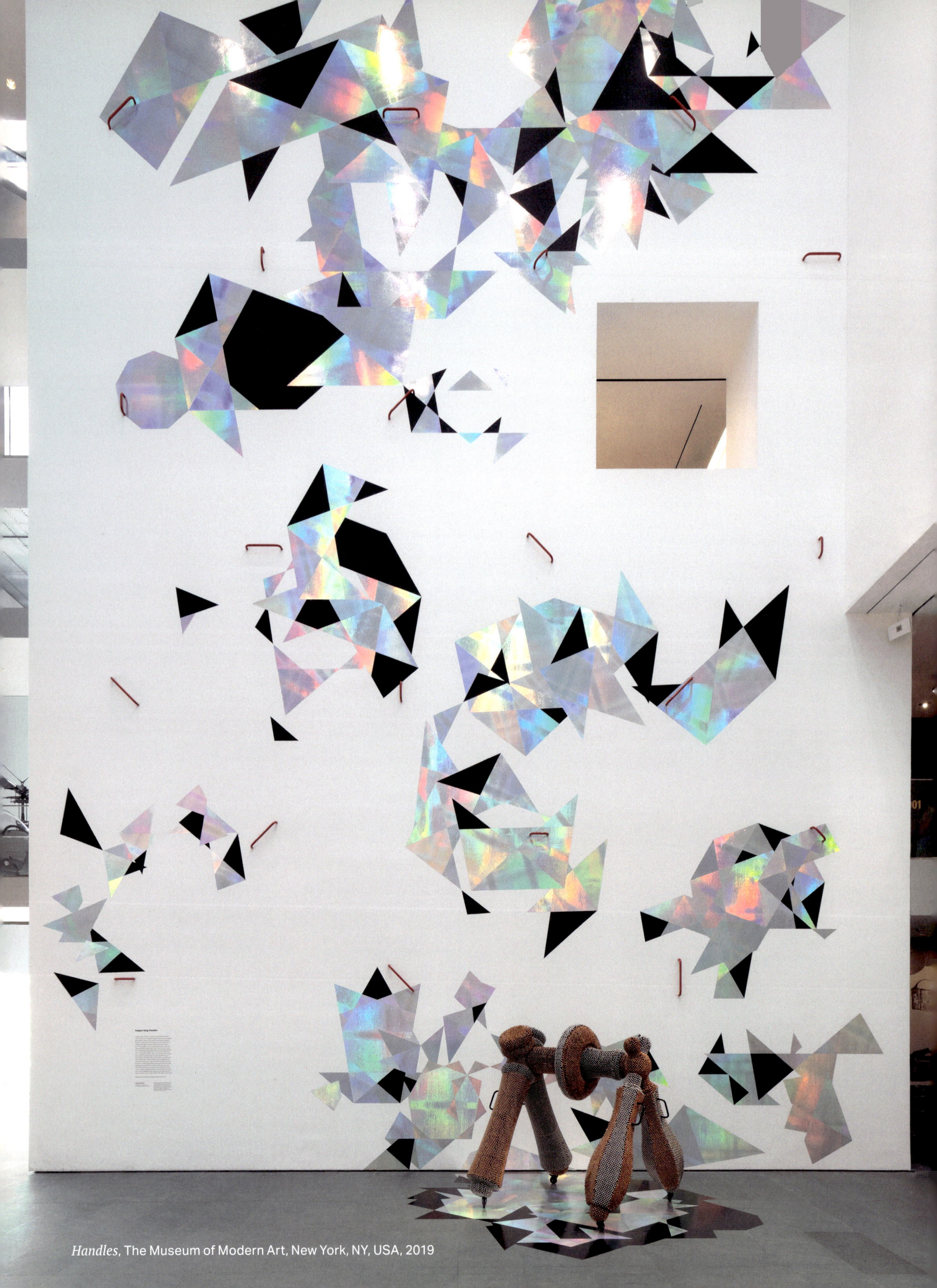

Handles, The Museum of Modern Art, New York, NY, USA, 2019

Handles, 2019

Self-adhesive holographic, black, and transparent vinyl film, powder-coated steel handles
Dimensions variable
Commissioned for the Marron Atrium by The Museum of Modern Art, New York, NY, USA

Commissioned by The Museum of Modern Art in New York for the opening of its newly expanded building in October 2019, Yang conceived a new installation, *Handles*, drawing on her in-depth research into various sources, ranging from everyday objects to the historical avant-garde, esoteric spiritual philosophies to contemporary political events. Handles are points of attachment and material catalysts for movement and change. This most basic implement, a handle, appeals to Yang as a point of contact or connection between individual operators and the material world. The project magnifies this everyday interface between people and things, expanding our horizons of understanding.

On the three walls of the Marron Atrium, a panoramic mural presents a dazzling network of geometries in iridescent vinyls. This mesmerizing composition of shapes, based on the nine-pointed enneagram of the early twentieth-century figure, mystic philosopher G. I. Gurdjieff, is fractured and disrupted by the play of daylight, shining in from various directions. The holographic vinyl is used in four different directions: 0, 25, 50, and 75 degrees. While wallpapers commonly consist of photographic motifs, this mural is an extremely complex and elaborate pure geometric composition consisting of more than 1,500 pieces.

This monumental mural in combination with self-adhesive holographic and black vinyl film continues on the floor, serving as a surface to accommodate six performative Sonic Sculptures, which generate a shimmering sound when activated daily by performers. Steel grab bars are put to functional use in the sculptures whilst also recurring as additional ornamental elements. Mounted on the walls and overlapping the vinyl pattern, red metal grab bars form their own square grid. Heard throughout the atrium, the birdsong recorded at the DMZ in Korea during a meeting between the two nations' leaders creates a ritualized, complex environment with both personal and political resonance.

Handles, The Museum of Modern Art, New York, NY, USA, 2019

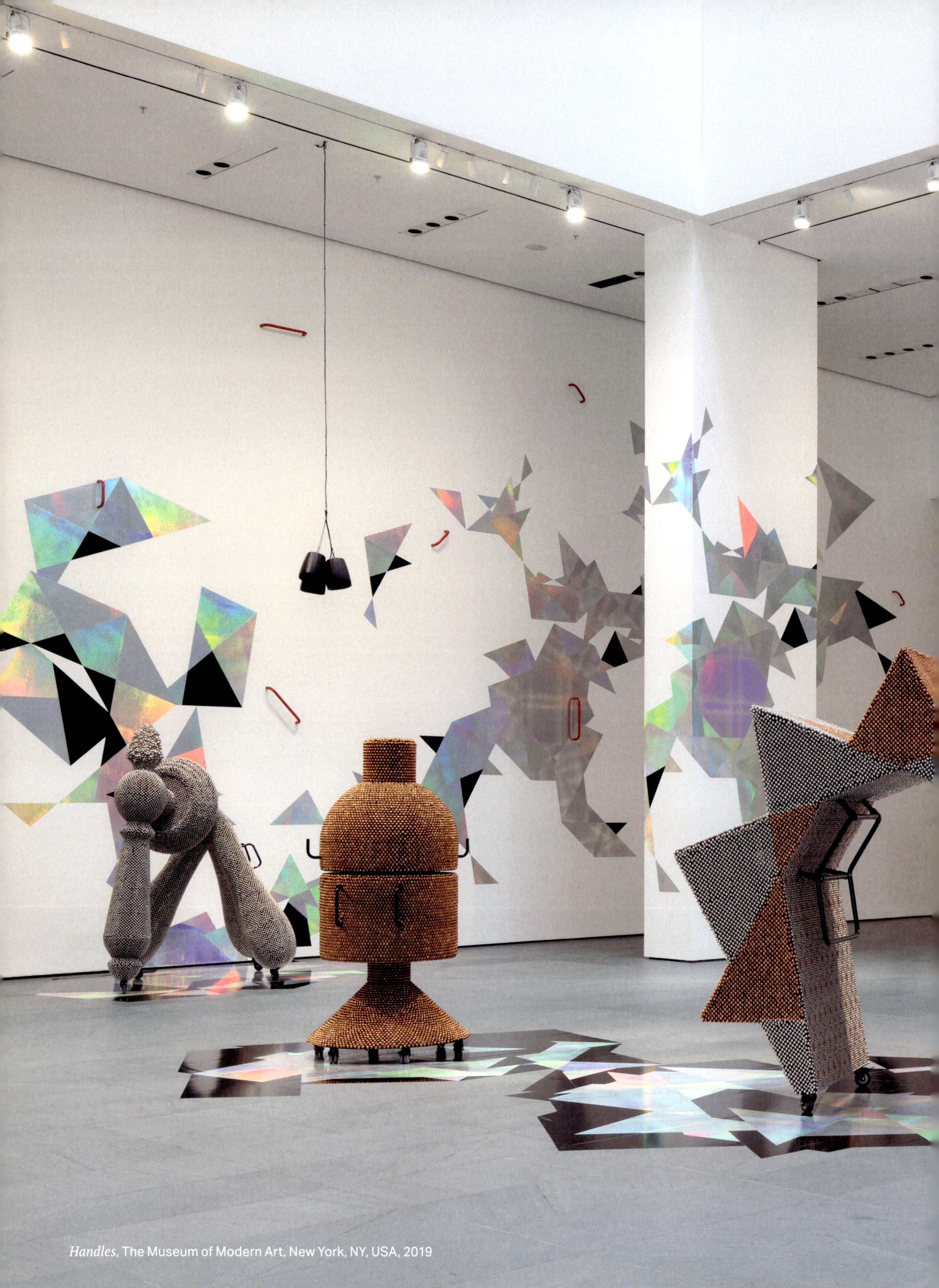

Handles, The Museum of Modern Art, New York, NY, USA, 2019

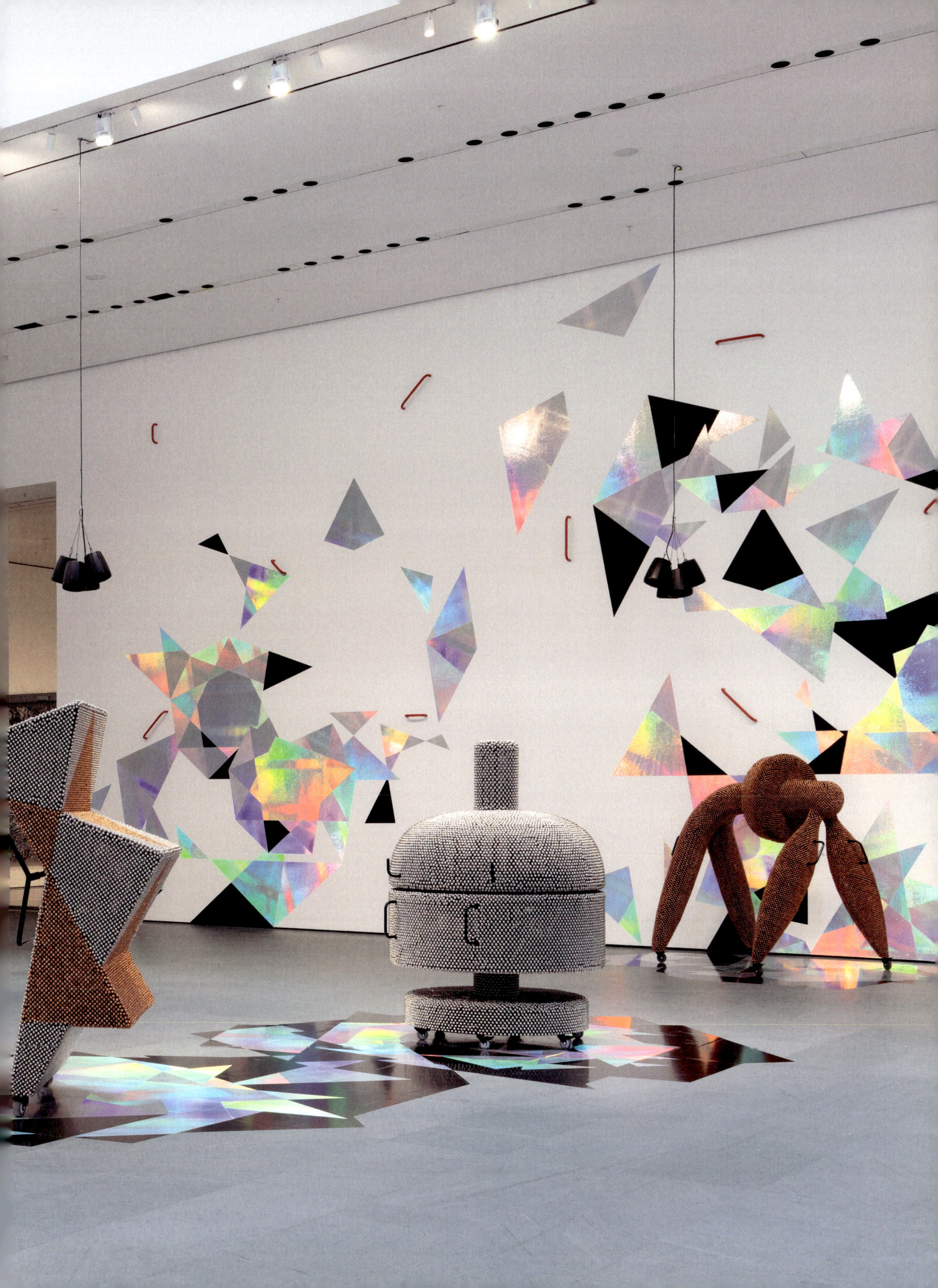

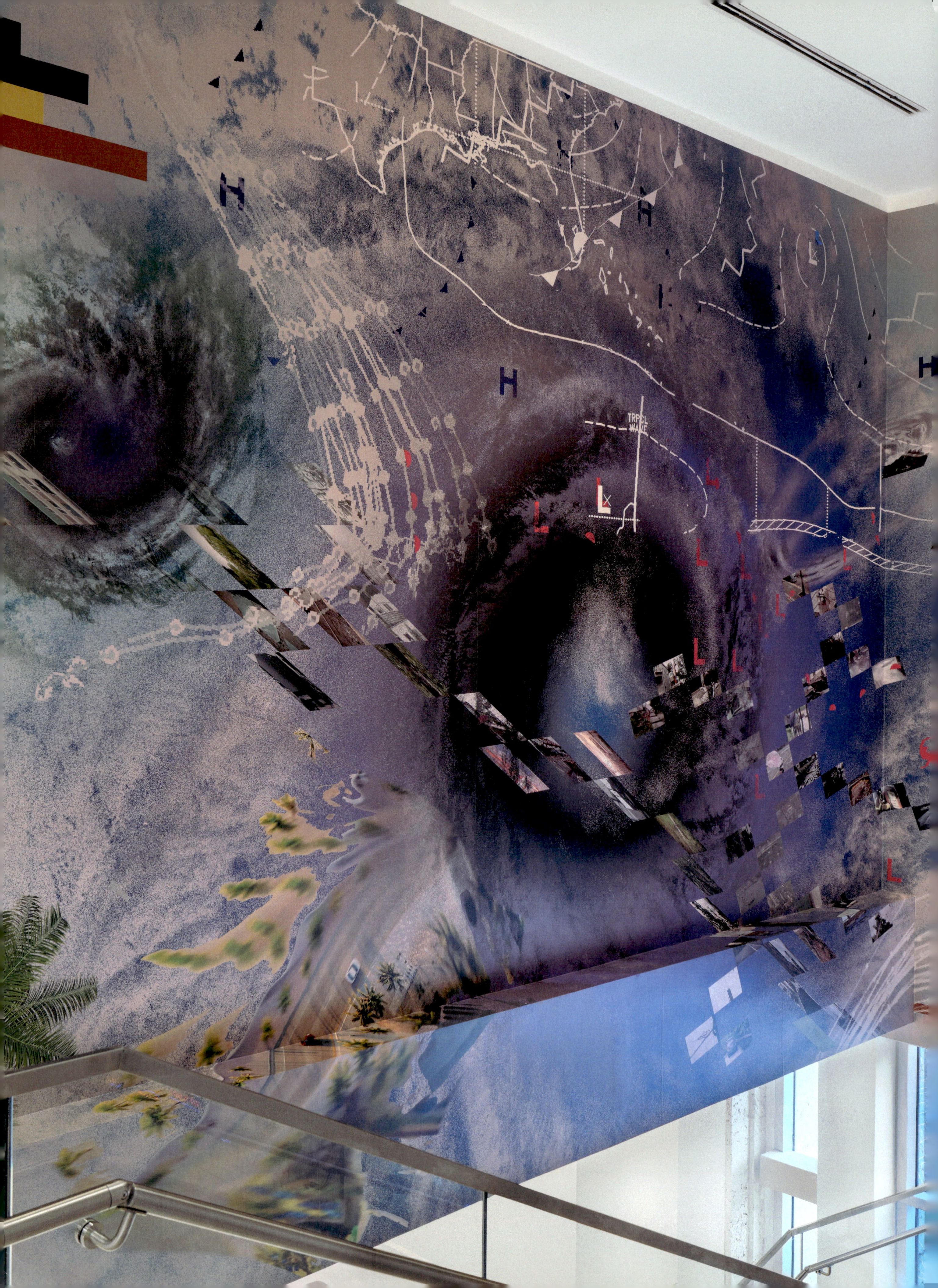

Coordinates of Speculative Solidarity, 2019

Digital color print
Dimensions variable

For this exhibition, Yang conceived a site-specific wallpaper applied to both transparent and opaque surfaces to accompany the path of visitors in the staircase connecting the spaces across the two floors of The Bass. The immersive nature of this wallpaper, placed in a transitory space within the museum and visible from the street, generates profound feelings of alienation on both social and existential levels. Such tensions reflect our current realities and provoke questions about nation-state, diaspora, and metaphorical homelessness. The Bass was a particularly resonant site to present Yang's work, considering that over 50 percent of the population in Miami-Dade County is born outside of the United States.

Informed by research about Miami Beach's climatically precarious setting, the wallpaper's meteorological infographics and diagrams rendered in drastic colors signaling alarm serve as vehicles for abstraction. *In the Cone of Uncertainty* alludes to a future that is largely unstable and ever-changing, but perhaps gradually revealing its path. Referencing statistical models that are used to predict extreme weather trajectories, such as cyclones and hurricanes—ubiquitous to South Florida—it communicates current anxieties related to climate change, overpopulation, resource scarcity, and nation-states, while highlighting thematic tensions in Yang's work by addressing notions of movement, displacement, and domesticity.

Interested in how severe weather creates unusual access to negotiations of belonging and community, as well as the human urge to predict catastrophic circumstances, the wallpaper reflects a geographic commonality that unconsciously binds people together through a determination to react to a challenge in solidarity. Observing hidden structures to reimagine a possible community, Yang re-addresses themes in her works such as migration, diasporas, and history writing. *In the Cone of Uncertainty* offers a substantial view into Yang's rich artistic language, including her use of bodily experience as a means of evoking history and memory.

In the Cone of Uncertainty, The Bass Museum of Art, Miami Beach, FL, USA, 2019

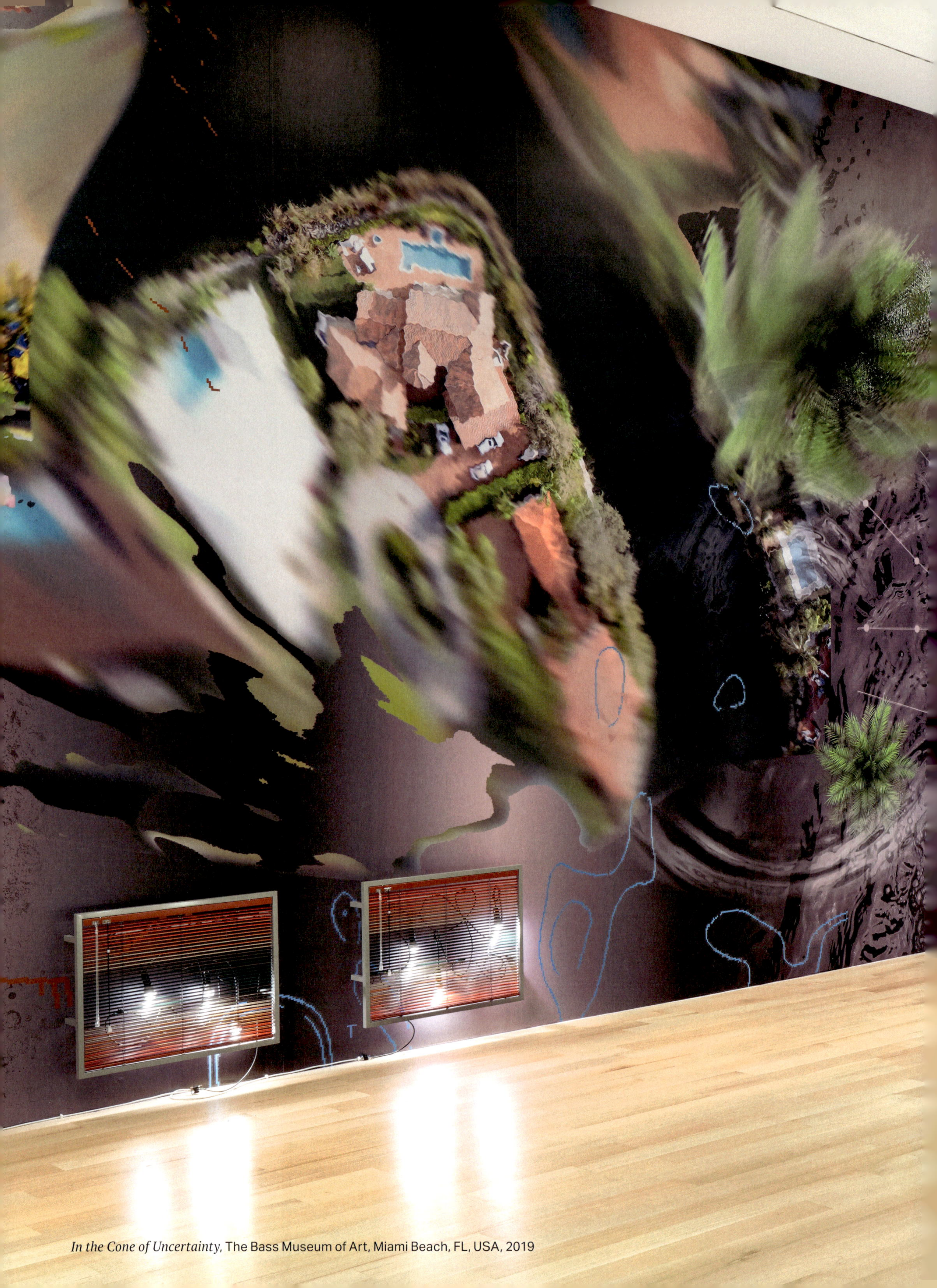

In the Cone of Uncertainty, The Bass Museum of Art, Miami Beach, FL, USA, 2019

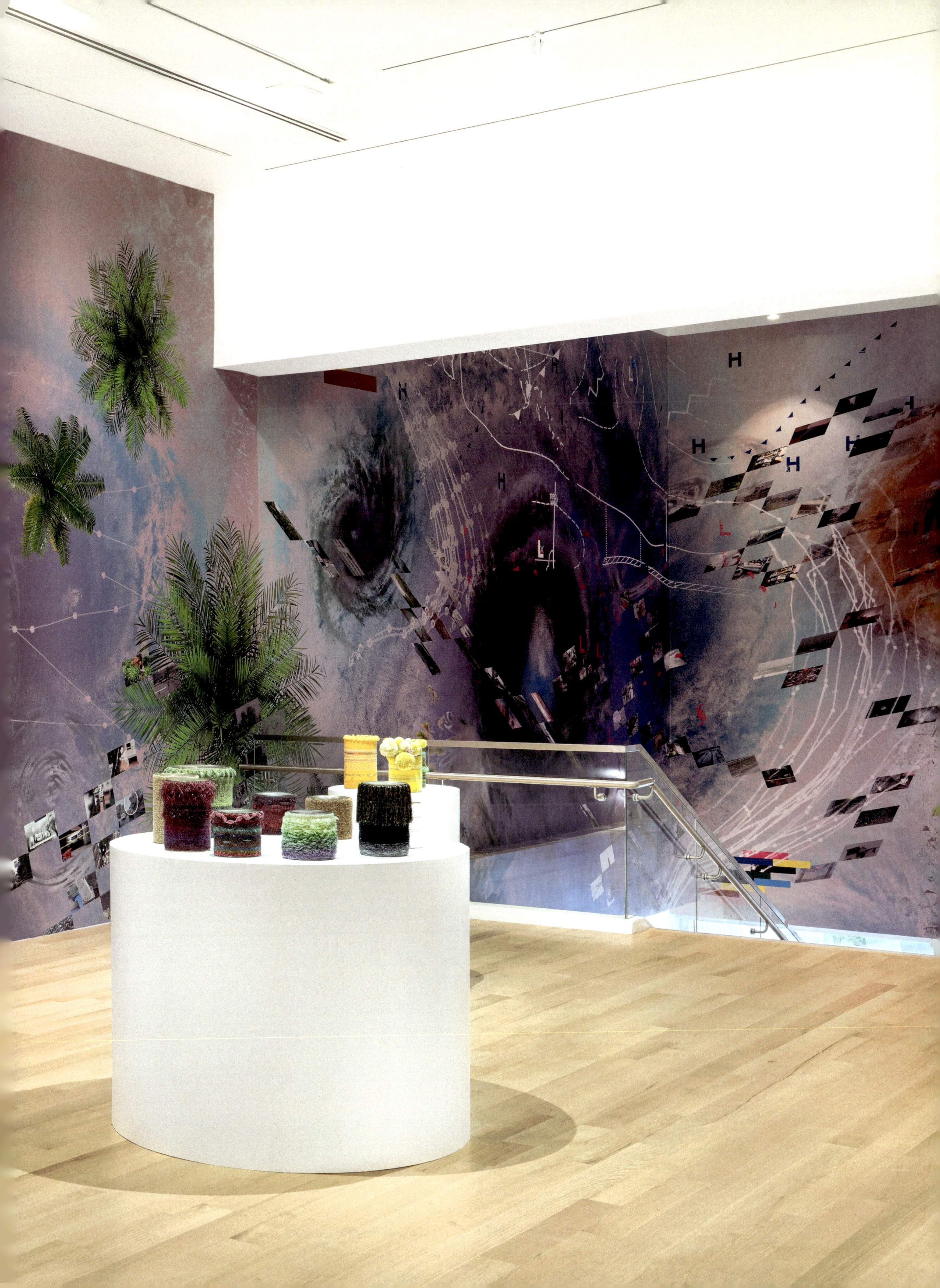

Riccardo and Tatyana Silva Gallery

Rotating Notes – Dispersed Episodes, 2013
Powder-coated steel sheets, ball bearings, notes on paper (laser print), magnets
Rotating Notes – Dispersed Episode I
100 × 80 cm
Rotating Notes – Dispersed Episode II
100 × 60 cm
Rotating Notes – Dispersed Episode III
100 × 70 cm
Rotating Notes – Dispersed Episode IV
100 × 100 cm
Rotating Notes – Dispersed Episode V
100 × 100 cm
Courtesy of Galerie Chantal Crousel, Paris

Sound element
Digital sound file, 29:40 min., loop. Composition of various open-sourced birdsong based on species native to the Korean DMZ (and presumed present on April 27, 2018)

Sound element
Digital sound file, 29:55 min., loop. This live broadcast recording made at the Inter-Korean Summit in the Korean Demilitarized Zone on April 27, 2018, is included by permission of the Presidential Office of the Republic of Korea

Paresky and Gould Family Gallery

Strange Fruit, 2012–13
Clothing racks, casters, light bulbs, cable, zip ties, terminal strips, cord, artificial plants, metal rings, Styrofoam hands, papier-mâché, watercolor, varnish
Strange Fruit – Hanging from the Poplar Trees
180 × 99 × 103 cm
Strange Fruit – Strange and Bitter Crop
206 × 140 × 140 cm
Strange Fruit – Swinging in the Southern Breeze
182 × 97 × 100 cm
Strange Fruit – For the Wind to Suck, For the Sun to Rot
189 × 99 × 96 cm
Strange Fruit – For the Crows to Pluck
190 × 96 × 94 cm
Strange Fruit – The Bulging Eyes and the Twisted Mouth
192 × 105 × 100 cm
Collection of The Museum of Contemporary Art, Los Angeles, purchased with funds provided by the Acquisition and Collection Committee

The Intermediate – Monsoon Mourning Spheres and Disks, 2017
Artificial straw, powder-coated stainless steel frame, casters, artificial plants, turbine vents
170 × 110 × 110 cm
Courtesy of kurimanzutto, Mexico City / New York

The Intermediate – Monsoon Mourning Saekdong Cone, 2017
Artificial straw, powder-coated stainless steel frame, casters, plastic twine, Saekdong fabric, artificial plants, Indian bells, turbine vent
165 × 110 × 110 cm
Courtesy of kurimanzutto, Mexico City / New York

Staircase

Coordinates of Speculative Solidarity, 2019
Digital color print
Dimensions variable
Courtesy of the artist, commissioned by The Bass, Miami Beach

Carsick Drawing – Toward Huu Nghi and Youyiguan #1, 2016
Carsick Drawing – Toward Huu Nghi and Youyiguan #2, 2016
Ink on paper, framed
2 parts, each 28 × 21.5 cm
Courtesy of the artist

Lobby Gallery

Dircksenstraße 37, 2019
Aluminum venetian blinds, powder-coated aluminum frames, light bulbs, cable, zip ties, terminal strips
Living room radiators, left and right: 2 parts, each
96 × 68.5 × 12 cm
Bedroom radiators, left and right: 2 parts, each
96 × 68.5 × 12 cm
Hallway radiator:
57 × 50.5 × 12 cm
Bathroom radiator:
48.5 × 50.5 × 12 cm
Ed. 5 / II A.P.
Courtesy of the artist and Greene Naftali, New York

Jahnstraße 5, 2017
Aluminum venetian blinds, powder-coated aluminum frames and perforated aluminum plates, light bulbs, cable, zip ties, terminal strips
Kitchen boiler:
80 × 44 × 32 cm
Kitchen radiator:
91 × 51 × 12 cm
Living room radiators, left and right: 2 parts, each
60 × 81 × 12 cm
Bathroom radiator:
60 × 81 × 12 cm
Ed. 5 / II A.P.
Courtesy of the artist and Greene Naftali, New York

Can Cosies Triple Jumbo, 2013
3 cans, knitting yarn
Can Cosy – Apfelmus gezuckert 4450g
27.5 × 26 × 26 cm
Can Cosy – Jalapeño Chili Peppers 2063g
18 × 19 × 19 cm
Can Cosy – Peperoni Lombardi 3500g
20 × 26 × 26 cm
Courtesy of the artist

Can Cosies Jumbo, 2011
10 cans, knitting yarn
Can Cosy – Kidney-Bohnen 2500g
15.3 × 15.7 × 15.7 cm
Can Cosy – Deutsche Champignons 4000g
24.5 × 15.6 × 15.6 cm
Can Cosy – Pickled Gherkins 55/60 with Sweetener 9700g
26 × 23.4 × 23.4 cm
Can Cosy – Fagioli Bianchi di Spagna 2500g
15.2 × 15.8 × 15.8 cm
Can Cosy – Sweet Corn 2150g
15 × 15.5 × 15.5 cm
Can Cosy – Milchreis tafelfertig 2500g
15.7 × 15.6 × 15.6 cm
Can Cosy – Schwarze Oliven geschwärzt mit Stein 2450g
24.5 × 15.7 × 15.7 cm
Can Cosy – Pomodori Pelati 2500g
15.2 × 15.8 × 15.8 cm
Can Cosy – Rotkohl tafelfertig 4040g
24.5 × 15.5 × 15.5 cm
Can Cosy – Artischockenherzen geviertelt 2500g
15.5 × 15.7 × 15.7 cm
Courtesy of Greene Naftali, New York

Can Cosies – Dicke Ammerländer Bockwurst 4500g and "40/90 SL" Bockwurst 5300g, 2018
Cans, knitting yarn
2 parts
28 × 19 × 19 cm;
12.7 × 25 × 25 cm
Courtesy of the artist

Roll Cosies – Toilet Tissue Jumbo Rolls, 2011
Rolls of toilet tissue, knitting yarn
6 parts, each
20 × 20.3 × 20.3 cm
Courtesy of Galerie Chantal Crousel, Paris

Can Cosies – Tuna Chunks in Sunflower Oil 1705 g, 2011
Cans, knitting yarn
2 parts, each
10.5 × 15.7 × 15.7 cm
Courtesy of the artist

A Chronology of Conflated Dispersion – Duras and Yun, 2018
Digital print on self-adhesive vinyl
Dimensions variable
Courtesy of the artist

Samples – Wai Hung Weaving Factory Limited, Hong Kong, 2015
Weaving and knot samples, framed
9 parts, each 83 × 91 cm
Courtesy of the artist and Greene Naftali, New York

Alan and Diane Lieberman Gallery

Boxing Ballet, 2013–15
6 Sonic Figures
Powder-coated steel frames and mesh, steel wire rope, casters, brass-plated bells, metal rings
Sonic Figure – Posing Coquette
210 × 130 × 110 cm
Sonic Figure – Fine No-Arm
189 × 100 × 100 cm
Sonic Figure – Vigorous Stretcher
215 × 130 × 160 cm
Sonic Figure – Spiral Woman
186 × 103 × 115 cm
Sonic Figure – Mesmerizing Pirouette
175 × 100 × 100 cm
Sonic Figure – Flat Walker
200 × 120 × 110 cm
11 *Trustworthies*
Various security envelopes, graph paper, sandpaper and spray paint on cardboard, framed, wall paint, vinyl tape
Slowly Unrolling Geometries – Trustworthy #211
5 parts, 72.2 × 72.2; 33.2 × 33.2 cm
Three Thighs Unattached – Trustworthy #212
2 parts, each 142.2 × 102.2 cm
Pivoting Arm beneath Animalesque Shadow – Trustworthy #213
2 parts, 102.2 × 102.2; 100 × 72 cm
Black and White Texture Study in Stacks – Trustworthy #214
3 parts, each 33.2 × 33.2 cm
Acrobatic Prismatic – Trustworthy #215
2 parts, each 72.2 × 72.2 cm
Descending Prismatic – Trustworthy #216
72.2 × 72.2 cm
Extensive Black and White Texture Study in a Grid Space – Trustworthy #217
8 parts, each 41.2 × 41.2 cm
Solar and Lunar Roughening – Trustworthy #218
2 parts, 102.2 × 102.2 cm; 33.2 × 33.2 cm
Principal Alignments – Trustworthy #219
8 parts, 102.2 × 102.2 cm; 72.2 × 72.2 cm
En Pointe – Trustworthy #220
7 parts, 102.2 × 102.2 cm; 72.2 × 72.2 cm
Prismatic Head – Trustworthy #221
102.2 × 102.2 cm
Collection of Leeum, Samsung Museum of Art, Seoul, South Korea

Windy Orbit – Brass Plated Second Cycle, 2015
Powder-coated steel frame and mesh, casters, turntable, fans, speed controller, switches, cable, zip ties, brass-plated bells, metal rings, timer
238 × 90 × 90 cm
Collection of Leeum, Samsung Museum of Art, Seoul, South Korea

Gertrude Silverstone Muss Gallery

Red Broken Mountainous Labyrinth, 2008
Aluminum venetian blinds, powder-coated aluminum hanging structure, steel wire rope, moving spotlights, DMX controller, spotlights
Dimensions variable
Courtesy of the artist and Greene Naftali, New York

Yearning Melancholy Red, 2008
Aluminum venetian blinds, powder-coated aluminum hanging structure, steel wire rope, mirrors, infrared heaters, infrared heat lamps, casters, timer, fans, moving spotlights, DMX controller, drum kit, drum stool, drum trigger module, acoustic trigger, MIDI converter, cable
Dimensions variable
San Francisco Museum of Modern Art
Acquired through the generosity of Helen and Charles Schwab and purchased, by exchange, through a gift of Peggy Guggenheim

PHOTO CREDITS

Pages 2, 8 (bottom), 12–55, 104, 106–107, 110
Zachary Balber, The Bass Museum of Art

Page 7
Scott Groller

Page 8 (top)
Aflo Co. Ltd.
Alamy Stock Photo

Pages 9 (top), 60 (top), 64, 66–67
Florian Kleinefenn

Pages 9 (middle, bottom), 10 (bottom), 62 (bottom left), 78 (bottom)
Studio Haegue Yang

Page 10 (top)
Anna Schwartz Gallery, Sydney

Page 57 (top)
Juan Guerra, Fundação Bienal de São Paulo

Page 57 (bottom)
© Michelangelo Pistoletto; Courtesy of the artist, Luhring Augustine, New York, and Galleria Christian Stein, Milan

Page 58
Kyoungtae Kim (top), Sang Tae Kim (bottom)

Pages 59 (top), 76–77
Mathieu Bertola, Musées de la Ville de Strasbourg

Page 59 (bottom)
Peter Horree
Alamy Stock Photo

Page 60
Alamy Stock Photo (bottom), Masiar Pasquali (middle)

Pages 61, 95, 98–99
Sahir Uğur Eren

Pages 62–63
S1 Artspace, Sheffield (top right), Markus Tretter (top left), Leeum, Samsung Museum of Art (bottom right)

Page 68
Guy L'Heureux, La Biennale de Montréal

Pages 70–71
Charles Mayer Photography

Pages 72, 74–75, 84–85
Tang Xuan

Pages 78 (top), 80–81
Simon Vogel

Page 82
Leeum, Samsung Museum of Art, Seoul

Page 83
Shutterstock Photo

Page 86 (top)
Andy Stagg

Pages 86 (bottom), 88–89
Omar Luis Olguín

Pages 90, 92–93
Roger Sinek, Tate Liverpool

Pages 94, 96–97
Marc Domage, La Panacée-MO.CO.

Pages 100, 102–103
Denis Doorly. Commissioned for the Marron Atrium by The Museum of Modern Art, New York.

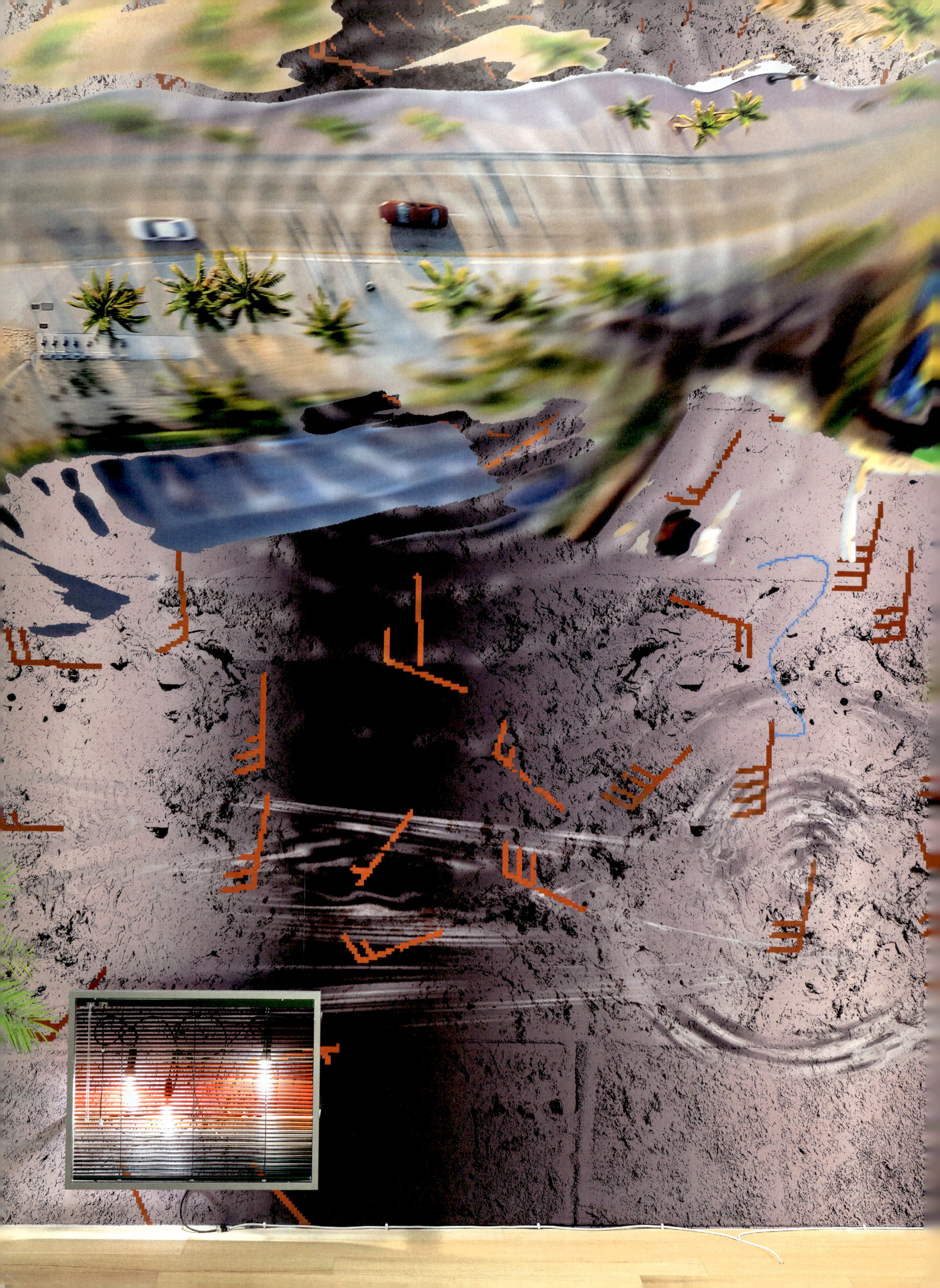

Silvia Karman Cubiñá

Silvia Karman Cubiñá began her tenure as Executive Director and Chief Curator of The Bass, Miami Beach, in 2008. Previously, she was the Director of The Moore Space, Miami, from 2002 to 2008. Cubiñá has curated numerous exhibitions, lectured extensively, and participated in grant panels and award selection committees, including serving as a juror for both the Guggenheim's Hugo Boss Award (2006) and the Biennale de Lyon (2008). She was awarded the Chevalier de l'Ordre des Arts et des Lettres by the French Ministry of Culture (2012). In October 2017, Cubiñá presided over the reopening of The Bass after a major two-year renovation, which has expanded the museum's programmable space by nearly 50 percent, all within the existing architectural footprint.

Philippe Vergne

Currently Director of Serralves Museum of Contemporary Art, Philippe Vergne previously headed some of the most prestigious art institutions in the United States and Europe. He was the Director of the Museum of Contemporary Art, LA (MOCA) (2014–18), and Director of the Dia Art Foundation, New York (2008–14). Vergne was Deputy Director and Chief Curator of the Walker Art Center, Minneapolis (2005–08), promoting more than twenty-five international exhibitions and artists-in-residence programs. He was part of the team that led the museum's expansion. He also co-curated the 2006 Whitney Biennial. Vergne left his mark in Europe as the first director of the Museum of Contemporary Art (MAC), Marseille (1994–97).

Leilani Lynch

Leilani Lynch is Curator at The Bass, Miami Beach. She has curated solo exhibitions with Mika Rottenberg, Karen Rifas, and Aaron Curry, in addition to co-organizing exhibitions with Haegue Yang, Pascale Marthine Tayou, Laure Prouvost, and Paola Pivi. Originally from San Francisco, Lynch relocated to Miami for an Art Table Summer Mentored Internship at The Bass, eventually joining the staff. Before rejoining in 2015, she produced site-specific experimental exhibitions with international artists at Locust Projects, Miami. Lynch has participated on panels and lectures for STPI – Creative Workshop, Singapore, ArtTable, and ICOM, and served on juries for Oolite Arts, FL, The Hopper Prize, and Apexart, NY.

Haegue Yang

Haegue Yang (b. 1971, Seoul) lives and works in Berlin and Seoul and has been a Professor at the Städelschule in Frankfurt am Main since 2017. Yang has participated in major international exhibitions including the 16th Istanbul Biennial (2019), the 21st Biennale of Sydney (2018), dOCUMENTA (13) in Kassel (2012), and the 53rd Venice Biennale (2009). In 2018, she was awarded the Wolfgang Hahn Prize and the Republic of Korea Culture and Arts Award. Her recent solo exhibitions include *Handles*, The Museum of Modern Art, New York (2019); *Tracing Movement*, South London Gallery (2019); *ETA 1994–2018*, Museum Ludwig, Cologne (2018); *Tightrope Walking and Its Wordless Shadow*, La Triennale di Milano (2018); *VIP's Union*, Kunsthaus Graz (2017); and *Lingering Nous*, Centre Pompidou, Paris (2016).

This book is published in conjunction with the exhibition *Haegue Yang: In the Cone of Uncertainty*

The Bass Museum of Art, Miami Beach
November 2, 2019 to April 5, 2020

Exhibition Credits

Exhibition curators
Silvia Karman Cubiñá
Leilani Lynch

Exhibition team
Jan Galliardt
Jesus Petroccini
Sherry Zambrano

The Bass staff
Patrice Carter
Grace Castro
Kylee Crook
Jose Hernandez
Koren Illa
Doralee Mendez
Jean Ortega
Gabrielle Peters
Lisa Quinn
Megan Riley
Julia Rudo
Rebecca Sell
Daphna Starr

Exhibition lenders
Galerie Chantal Crousel, Paris
Greene Naftali, New York
kurimanzutto, Mexico City
Leeum, Samsung Museum of Art, Seoul
San Francisco Museum of Modern Art
The Museum of Contemporary Art, Los Angeles
Haegue Yang

Exhibition sponsors
CHANEL
The City of Miami Beach, Miami-Dade County, State of Florida

Special thanks to
Galerie Barbara Wien
Galerie Chantal Crousel
Greene Naftali
Kukje Gallery
kurimanzutto

Magdalen Chua
interzone, Berlin
Andreas Sachsenmaier

Studio Haegue Yang, Berlin
Sofia Duchovny
Atsushi Fukunaga
Liene Harms
John Matthew Heard
Atsuko Ichikawa
Chieko Idetsuki
Cheongjin Keem
Bokyung Kim
Yoonha Kim
Zarah Landes
Sofia Leiby
Kuo-Wei Lin
Nicolas Pelzer
Christina Pethick
Katharina Schwerendt
Emmy Skensved
Christopher Wierling

Studio Haegue Yang, Seoul
Hanna Hong
U-jung Jang
Hyesook Jung
Myoungjung Kim
Jeesu Lee
Sihyun Ryu
Solkyu Yang
Heejung Ye

Publication Credits

Project management
Claire Cichy, Hatje Cantz

Editors/Essayists
Silvia Karman Cubiñá
Leilani Lynch
Philippe Vergne

Copyeditor
Dawn Michelle d'Atri

Design
Studio Hik

Production
Vinzenz Geppert, Hatje Cantz

Typeface
Aktiv Grotesk
PT Serif

Paper
Magno Volume, 150 g/m²

Printing and binding
Livonia Print, Riga

Lithography
Repromayer GmbH, Reutlingen

The Bass Museum of Art
2100 Collins Avenue
Miami Beach, FL 33139
Tel. +1 305 673 7530
www.thebass.org

The Bass Museum of Art is a nonprofit, tax-exempt organization accredited by the American Alliance of Museums. The Bass is generously funded by the City of Miami Beach, Cultural Affairs Program and Cultural Arts Council, the Miami-Dade County Department of Cultural Affairs and the Cultural Affairs Council, the Miami-Dade County Mayor and Board of County Commissioners, and sponsored in part by the State of Florida, Department of State, Division of Cultural Affairs, the Florida Council on Arts and Culture, and The Bass membership.

Published by
Hatje Cantz Verlag GmbH
Mommsenstraße 27
10629 Berlin
www.hatjecantz.de
A Ganske Publishing Group Company

ISBN 978-3-7757-4629-8

Printed in Latvia

Cover illustration
Studio Hik and Haegue Yang, *Coordinates of Speculative Solidarity*, 2019